Toge

Preparing Christian Educators for the Future

DEAN R. HANSEN, COORDINATING EDITOR

BRENT ALAN MAI, GENERAL EDITOR

CONTRIBUTING AUTHORS

Debra Arfsten	Julie Johnston Hermann	Tim Rippstein
Mark Blanke	William O. Karpenko II	Christine M. Ross
Kevin Borchers	Lisa K. Keyne	Jonathan Ruehs
Richard Carter	Ken Krause	Paul Schoepp
Bill Cullen	James H. McConnell	Gary Schultz
Audrey Duensing	Russ Moulds	Rick Stengl
Bruce M. Hartung		Thaddeus Warren

CONCORDIA
UNIVERSITY

Concordia University
Portland, Oregon

Cover photo by Tim Elliott.

Cover design by Lori A. McKee.

Typography by Lori A. McKee.

FIRST EDITION.

Hansen, Dean R.
　　Together : preparing Christian educators for the future / Dean Hansen, ed.
　　　p. cm.
　　Includes bibliographical references.

Summary: Since 1959, the Lutheran Church–Missouri Synod (LC-MS) has been training Christian educators entering the profession that eventually came to be called the Director of Christian Education (DCE). The chapters of this book compile topics of interest to both practicing Christian educators and those studying to become Christian educators. Some chapters summarize research about DCEs and the DCE experience while others share years of personal experience as a DCE within a congregation.

1. Directors of religious education. 2. Lutheran Church–Missouri Synod. I. Title. II. Mai, Brent Alan (1964-).

BV1531 .H36 2011　　268' – dc21

Library of Congress Control Number: 2010942807

ISBN(10): 1-934961-04-3
ISBN(13): 978-1-934961-04-9

Concordia University – Portland
2811 N.E. Holman Street
Portland, Oregon 97211
www.cu-portland.edu

Printed in the United States of America.

As we celebrate the 50th anniversary of DCE Ministry, TOGETHER is dedicated to all the Directors of Christian Education who have served their Lord and Savior Jesus Christ and the Lutheran Church Missouri Synod faithfully, some for a few years, some for many years.

Secondly, this book is dedicated, with love, to my wife Carolyn and daughters Emily and Chrisanna. Their love, support, and understanding give me daily strength and inspiration.

D.R.H.

Acknowledgements

Thoughts and dreams about this book have reared up over many years. Coalescing those thoughts and bringing those dreams to reality has taken the effort of many people. Putting together a book like this required the efforts of a number of individuals.

To my wife, Carolyn, and daughters Emily and Chrisanna, who continue to support my ministry even when that means being away from home or working additional hours;

To Dr. Jan Albrecht, who graciously edited each chapter;

To Brent Mai, who served as General Editor;

To Concordia University librarians Judy Anderson and Krista Reynolds, who checked facts and references; and

To my Partners in Ministry at Concordia Universities that prepare students for DCE ministry:

> Concordia University Chicago
> Concordia University College of Alberta
> Concordia University, Irvine
> Concordia University, Nebraska
> Concordia University - Portland
> Concordia University, St. Paul
> Concordia University Texas

I give you all my prayerful thanks!

D.R.H.

In Appreciation

Together is made possible by a grant from the Endowment Fund of Zion Lutheran Church, Portland, Oregon.

Northwest District of the Lutheran Church Missouri Synod

www.nowlcms.org

Our thanks to the Northwest District of the Lutheran Church–Missouri Synod for their financial support of *Together* and their ongoing support of DCE ministries.

Contents

Foreward

Perhaps the most difficult challenge in preparing a book with many authors is choosing an appropriate title. Several possibilities came to mind. *Chaos* was certainly under consideration from the beginning. How does one get more than twenty authors to submit articles on time, in the same format, and with limited overlap in material? Answer: it is impossible. That reality led to the second choice: *Frustration*. As deadlines approached, the popular selection for a title might have been *Scramble*. Finally, *What Was I Thinking?*, seemed a natural pick.

The final title, *Together*, was inspired by a photograph taken by Tim Elliott – the photo that became the cover of this publication. It was taken at an annual retreat of Concordia students preparing for church work. In the photo you find many hands united *Together*. The first time I saw this picture, I was reminded of the children's simple hand game: "Here is the church and here is the steeple, open the doors and here are all the people." The ministry of the Director of Christian Education (DCE) in the Lutheran Church–Missouri Synod (LC–MS) is very much like this photo. A person surrounded by God's people, the church, supporting each other, and working *Together*.

Directors of Christian Education have served in the LC-MS for over fifty years. Today, approximately one thousand DCEs are called to this educational ministry of the Church. They are called as individuals but also called to serve *Together*.

> *Together*, with congregational members, DCEs serve those who need prayer, love, and support.
>
> *Together*, in DCE clusters and with the National Association of Directors of Christian Education, DCEs lend support to each other.

Together, with the congregation, DCEs carry out the Great Commission to make disciples.

Together, with pastors and fellow church professionals, the Gospel of Jesus Christ is proclaimed.

Together, with fellow Christians, DCEs make a difference in our world.

None of this would be possible without the most important *Together*, the togetherness we have with our loving Heavenly Father, made possible through the redemptive work of His Son, Jesus Christ, and the power of the Holy Spirit. This is truly humbling, Almighty God working through sinful man. While our role is to merely be a tool in His hands, it is this *Together* that gives purpose and meaning to our lives.

Chapters on a variety of subjects have been compiled *Together* in this book. Some summarize research about DCEs and the DCE experience; others share years of personal experience as a DCE within a congregation. Some are objective; some are opinionated. One might agree with some conclusions and disagree with others, yet *Together* they have great value for both practicing Christian educators and those studying to become Christian educators. Your heart for ministry has led you to serve! Whether you are a student or already serving in a position bearing the title of DCE or Christian Educator or Children's Minister or Family Minister or Youth Minister, whether you are serving in an LC–MS congregation or a congregation of another denomination or in a non-denominational setting, whether you are a lay person or a volunteer, my prayer is that you will find inspiration and guidance in *Together*.

Dean R. Hansen
Director of Christian Ministries
Concordia University - Portland

CHAPTER 1

Critical Competencies in the Formation of a DCE

THADDEUS WARREN

Critical to any profession is its ability to clearly define itself and establish a distinctive discipline as it trains and prepares people for service in its unique field. "A prerequisite for developing the appropriate theory base from which future practitioners are to be equipped is clarity regarding the function and mission of the profession" (Keyne, 1995, p. 189). The following chapter briefly explores the formation and foundation of the unique functional roles and sub-roles, critical ministry abilities, and the definition of the Lutheran Church–Missouri Synod Director of Christian Education.

As the DCE profession in the Lutheran church has developed over the past fifty years, the program directors at the training schools have become very aware of the need to identify critical competencies for the training of students. Probably the most notable of the directors is Dr. William Karpenko who served as director at two of the training institutions through most of the formative years

Thaddeus Warren, Ph.D, serves as Associate Professor of Education on the DCE Faculty at Concordia University, Nebraska.

of the profession. He was very instrumental in drawing research from the field that could be used in the formation of educational outcomes in the preparation of DCEs. While much of his leadership and work is unpublished, it has and continues to serve as a foundational framework utilized for the training institutions and for national leadership in defining and guiding the DCE profession.

FUNCTIONAL ROLES

The most formative research was conducted by Karpenko along with the other DCE program directors throughout the 1980s and 1990s in a multi-phased study which determined the ten major roles and the complimenting sub-roles of this position. These roles are outlined in Table 1.1.

Paul Schoepp (2003) in his dissertation work on the study of lay practitioners in the Lutheran Church–Missouri Synod reviewed the literature related to the identification of roles served by DCEs. His work serves as a fairly comprehensive review of the differing roles that have been identified throughout the profession–including those in other protestant denominations. While Schoepp's work is not exhaustive, it clearly covers the significant contributions to the literature base. In Table 1.2, Schoepp (2003) provides a comparison of the major contributors and the roles they have identified for DCEs in comparison to work done by Dr. William Karpenko (1986, 1990, 1997). Schoepp notes that the table does not give a comprehensive list of all "roles historically assigned to DCEs" (p. 27), but the table does include the major contributors to the literature on the DCE profession. Other noteworthy contributors to the literature concerning roles not identified in Table 1.2 are Kraft (1957), Harris (1976), Griffin (1981), Giles (1983), and Lines (1992).

The functional role identification of those serving in the field is critically important to training institutions as they seek to develop curriculum that will best prepare students for their service as DCEs. Warren (2008) in his dissertation on critical outcomes in DCE ministry confirms the use of roles and sub roles in DCE preparation at all six of the DCE training schools. The implementation

TABLE 1.1

Karpenko's Roles and Sub-Roles for DCE Program Directors

Role	Sub-Role
Leader	visionary; change agent/initiator; planner/organizer; group process facilitator; and networker
Administrator	coordinator/director; promoter/PR writer; evaluator/researcher; institutional problem-solver; conflict management resource; budget develop/monitor; and facility/office manager
Age Group Resource	early childhood specialist; elementary age specialist; middle school specialist; senior high specialist; young adult specialist; middle-age adult specialist; older adult specialist; and intergenerational specialist
Care Action Minister	visitor; one-to-one listener; community resource giver; and support group leader/participant
Church Professional	church worker role model; teammate; personal office manager; lay practitioner peer support, and church professions encourager; life-long learner; and church-at-large resource
Educational Program Resource	resource identifier/developer; curriculum specialist; drama/visual arts resource; teaching/learning resource; educational technologist; topic/devotional leader; and board/committee member
Music Facilitator	choir/ensemble director, organist; instrumentalist; cantor; song leader; and accompanist on guitar, etc.
Pastoral and Staff Support	evangelist; parish worship assistant; and chapel leader
Parish Teacher	day school teacher; theological resource; small group facilitator; and faith mentor
Volunteer Specialist	volunteer coordinator; recruiter; trainer; supervisor/sustainer

TABLE 1.2

A Comparison of the Identified Roles of Christian Educators

Karpenko (1997)	Furnish (1976)	Emler (1989)	Lawson & Choun (1992)	Stubblefield (1993)
Leader	Leadership	Diagnostician	Control & Leadership	Planner
Administrator	Coordinating	Administrator & Evaluator	Administration & Management	Administrator & Evaluator & Communicator and Promoter
Age Group Resource	Improve Teaching	Learning Specialist		Growth Agent
Care Action Minister		Faith Interpreter	Relate to Church and Community	
Church Professional	Team Relationships	Faith Interpreter	Relate to Staff	
Educational Program Resource	Improve Teaching	Program Developer & Educational Consultant & Researcher	Supervision & Training of Leaders and Teachers	Growth Agent & Educator
Music Facilitator				
Pastoral and Staff Support				
Parish Teacher	Improve Teaching	Learning Specialist		Educator & Theologian
Volunteer Specialist	Coordinating Ministry		Recruit Teaching Staff & Relate to Volunteers	Equipper and Enabler & Delegator

and emphasis on each role does vary by institution, and often is articulated in differing formats but does indicate there is curricular alignment among the schools teaching to these functional roles. Warren also indicates that all ten roles continually are being filled by DCEs in the field to some degree. The role of music facilitator, however, is minimally utilized in the field and is rarely emphasized at the training schools. In his summary of findings, he recommends a de-emphasis of this role in DCE preparation. The role music facilitator is significantly rated lower in both training and function for DCEs at this point in the profession. With the development of the role of Directors of Parish Music this will only continue to decline. With the exception of the role of Music facilitator Karpenko's roles and sub roles are found to be valid as the profession moves into the future. While there has been stability in the functional roles over the past thirty years, ministry is always shifting and as roles are assumed by others in the ministry, ongoing research will be needed to assure proper preparation for the functional roles in the DCE profession.

MINISTRY CHARACTERISTICS

Closely related to functional roles are ministry characteristics or what sometimes are referred to as critical ministry abilities. These are the more personal attributes of the individual serving in the role of DCE. Karpenko's studies (1986, 1990) also determined ten critical ministry abilities as identified by field DCEs. They model a deep and expressive spirituality, based upon a devotional life that encourages daily prayer, bible study and willingness to share the Gospel; maintain a balanced perspective of themselves, their family and their work life; manage their time realistically; respond to an individuals concern in an open, caring, non-threatening way; listen empathetically within a Christian approach that respects people and maintains confidences; convey a respect for and trust of the Holy Scriptures; teach in a manner that is genuine, organized, knowledgeable, spirit inspired, scripture-based, and full of enthusiasm for the subject being taught; lead and involve others whether in planning, organizing or carrying out a program service class, activity, or event; recruit, train and sustain ministry volunteers with a gospel motivation, and publicly affirm and privately encourage staff and laity (p. 20).

The related research in other denominations tends to mirror that of Karpenko (1990). Two significant works are listed: Stubblefield (1993) and Majovski (1982).

Stubblefield identifies personal characteristics important for the DCE. These include; integrity, good people skills, Christian growth, love for people, a healthy self-image, ability to teach, intellect, enthusiasm, being a Christian model, and steadfastness of purpose. Stubblefield would also add the characteristic of being a professional. Laura Majovski (1982, p. 13) determined that there are eight behavioral characteristics of effective ministers:

1. Having an open mind and an affirming style
2. Caring for persons under stress
3. Evidencing congregational leadership
4. Being a theologian in thought and life
5. Undertaking ministry from a personal commitment of faith
6. Developing fellowship and worship
7. Having denominational awareness
8. Not having disqualifying personal and behavior characteristics.

Once again like the functional roles the ministry characteristics do not completely align across all three researchers, but the core issues are very similar. Warren's research also confirmed the relevance of Karpenko's stated ministry characteristic or "critical abilities."

DCE DEFINITION

The critical ministry abilities identified by Karpenko (1990) along with a compilation of work developed over the formative years served as foundational research for the 1999 DCE Summit. The 1999 DCE Summit (a meeting of DCE national leadership including DCE directors, officers of NADCE,

LC–MS representation and other invited field representatives) sought to provide direction to the DCE profession by establishing a clear picture of what DCE ministry is, determining what values should be represented, and shaping the direction to which they hope the DCEs will aspire. The resulting effort of the 1999 Summit is the current definition, mission, and values of a DCE.

DCE Definition

"A Director of Christian Education is a synodically certified, called, and commissioned lifespan educational leader prepared for team ministry in a congregational setting" (LEA, 2000, p. 1).

Mission statement

"Empowered by the Holy Spirit, the Director of Christian Education plans, administers, and assesses ministry that nurtures and equips people as the body of Christ for spiritual maturity, service, and witness in home, job, congregation, community, and the world" (p. 1).

Important Values for DCEs

"...exhibit Christian character; display a spiritually maturing faith; relate well with people of all ages; express a passion for teaching and learning; possess a servant heart; manage personal and professional life effectively; seek to work in team relationships; strive for excellence; operate in a self-directed manner" (p.1).

The development of the definition mission statement and values is a reflection of the work done by those individuals who shape the profession by the work they do every day. A number of hard working people have contributed to the formation of the DCE ministry in the LC–MS throughout the past fifty years. Some have been recognized here but most have been silent heroes of faithful service in serving God by delivering quality Christian Education in parishes, camps, the mission field, and beyond. These silent heroes have led the way in forming the profession and in shaping the training by spending their time in the trenches, loving people, and pointing to Christ. Critical competencies in DCE ministry have and always will be derived from the work which is accomplished on the front lines.

CHAPTER 2

Leviticus, Lepers, and Lutherans

Directions for the Priesthood of All Believers

RUSS MOULDS

Here is a practical question. How may the director of Christian education direct fellow Christians in their understanding and practice of the priesthood of all believers (PoaB)? The question is simple. The answer, however, is thick and chunky and also a bit spicy and complex.

A "priest" is a go-between or intercessor. The role and need for a priest imply two alienated parties who cannot otherwise get together. (In Latin, a word used for priest is *pons* or "bridge.") In the Old Testament, God designated Aaron and his sons as the priests for Israel (Ex. 28). Their role at the tabernacle in the sacrifice activities is described in Leviticus.[1] In the New Testament, the Letter to the Hebrews presents an extended argument that Jesus is the true High Priest who intercedes between humankind, who are all sinners (including Israel), and God who, because He is holy, cannot abide sinners and their sins. Christ is the Priest who gets God and sinners together.

---

[1] In addition to sin offerings for reconciliation, the tabernacle priests also assisted with thank offerings, fellowship offerings, and general worship offerings. Priestly activity can include more than intervention for sin. See Lev. 1 – 7. Note also that the role of priest is already active in Genesis (Noah, Gen. 8:20ff, and Melchizedek, Gen, 14:17ff).

Russ Moulds, Ph.D., teaches psychology, education, and theology at Concordia University, Nebraska.

But the biblical concept of priest includes more than Israel's tabernacle (and, later, temple) priests, and Jesus as our one high priest. Before we take note of definitions and doctrinal summaries of the PoaB, let's begin with this concept's seminal theme at Mt. Sinai and a curious illustration from Leviticus. This theme and illustration will help us consider later in this chapter how Christians can be active in their priesthood.

> Moses went up to God, and the LORD called to him from the mountain and said, "This is what you are to say to the house of Jacob and what you are to tell the people of Israel: 'You yourselves have seen what I did to Egypt, and how I carried you on eagles' wings and brought you to myself. Now if you obey me fully and keep my covenant, then out of all nations you will be my treasured possession. Although the whole earth is mine, you will be for me a kingdom of priests and a holy nation.' These are the words you are to speak to the Israelites" (Ex. 19:3-6).

Thus, before commissioning Aaron and his sons in Ex. 28 as the tabernacle priests, God had already covenanted with all the tribes and people of Israel in Ex. 19 to be for him a kingdom of priests and a holy ("set apart," "selected") nation. All the Israelites are in on the act of being a kingdom of priests.[2] Bible commentators remark that the "kingdom-of-priests" theme established at this pivotal and dramatic covenant event is rarely mentioned again in the Old Testament in an explicit way.[3] However, Leviticus expands on Exodus and describes actively (rather than explains conceptually) this priestly role of all the Israelites, a role which dovetails with the activity of the tabernacle priests. To see an example of these complementary roles, we turn to Lev. 13-14, God's detailed instructions to Israel regarding Israel's lepers.

---

[2] Two points: First, nothing in the text here or elsewhere excludes the women of Israel from an identity with this kingdom of priests. Second, the priesthood of all Israel's people, not just Aaron's sons, is demonstrated in their conduct prescribed by Leviticus that is coextensive with the sacrifices made by the tabernacle priests. The scholarly literature sometimes discusses whether these biblical concepts refer to individuals as priests in the "kingdom of priests" and "priesthood of all believers" or if these expressions refer only to the collective identity of all members of the kingdom or priesthood as a priestly identity. My subsequent illustration from Leviticus about lepers suggests both that members are to conduct their individual lives in a priestly go-between fashion and their collective identity as a priestly community.

[3] Isa. 61:6, "but you shall be called the priests of the Lord," is the only other direct reference to priesthood of all Israel. Their priesthood may be implied in other texts such as Isa. 1:11, Hos. 6:6, Mic. 6:6-8, and Pss. 50:13-23, 51:17, and 141:2. See Best, 1960, p. 276.

Leviticus is a compendium of "instruction to the *congregation* in matters pertaining to the cult [cultivating their whole life as worship], i.e., the correct procedures for making sacrifices, for observing the high times in the calendar, and for living as a holy people" (LaSor, Hubbard, & Bush, 1996, p. 82.) These practices and conditions are not comprehensive but are selected from the everyday life of Israel.[4] God seems to have specified them in the context of his covenant with Israel—his kingdom of priests—as ways to constantly exhibit the sinner's fallen and sinful condition and God's intercession to forgive sin. To do this Leviticus uses, for example, the circumstances of child birth (Lev. 12), blood in meat (Lev. 17), and money-lending (Lev. 25). In several ordinary yet conspicuous ways, God makes it clear that we live in separation from him unless we are made to be at one (atonement) with him through some vicarious intervention which he has enacted. These "slices of life" are necessarily immoral or "sinful" in that sense. Rather, Leviticus uses them to show that God is holy and fallen humanity is unholy. The tabernacle rites portray the sinner's need of expiation for sin effectual through the sacrifice system prescribed for Israel in Leviticus. Today we might call these object lessons. Hebrews calls them "shadows" of Christ's all-sufficient sacrifice (Heb. 8:5 and 10:1).

PRIESTS AND LEPERS

One of these selected slices of life is leprosy. The Hebrew word for illness or disease as we think of them is *madveh* (cf. Deut. 7:15) or sometimes *choliy* which means malady or anxiety (cf. 2 Kings 8:8). And the word used to describe leprosy in Lev 13:2, 45, 47, etc., is translated as "disease" (NIV, RSV) or "plague" (KJV). However, the Hebrew noun in these texts actually is *nega*, derived from the verb, *naga*, which means to smite, strike, or punish. Thus, *nega* refers not to

---

[4] "Holy" is a multi-faceted word that can include the ideas of piety and moral rightness. However, in Leviticus, its connotation seems to be on Israel being set apart and different from the other nations so that other nations could notice this difference. This difference enables them to function in a priestly "go-between" manner that draws others' attention to God's mercy toward sinners. To accomplish this priestly difference, God arranges Israel's civil, moral, and religious practices (all nations had such practices) in ways curiously different from the other nations.

a sickness but to a blow, strike, or affliction, (which could, among other things, be an illness—cf. Job 1-2) perhaps from God or from the devil, the world, or our sinful self. The word in Leviticus for leprosy, *nega*, carries spiritual rather than merely medical meaning.

To employ this *nega* or leprosy as a conspicuous example of humanity's fallen condition and God's intervention, Leviticus includes two detailed chapters assigning certain activities to the leper and the tabernacle priest.[5] For instance, the priest was to examine the leper carefully yet modestly (Lev. 13:12) for specific skin conditions, then designate the appropriate location of the person afflicted in relation to the community and tabernacle.[6] The afflicted might be assigned no change in day-to-day activity, or be shut away for seven days, or be declared ritually unclean and relocated outside the camp until further examination found the leper to be clean of the affliction.[7]

---

[5] The prescribed ritual in Lev. 14 is somewhat complicated and seems to imply different kinds of offerings including a sin offering. But we should not assume some simple "immorality-punishment-forgiveness" formula here. The leprous person did not do something wrong for which he was being punished. Similarly, the man or woman with a bodily discharge described in Lev. 15 did not do something immoral. Rather, Leviticus uses such condition to signify fallen creation and our condition and how God draws us back into his own holiness and "otherness" from this fallen condition. Consider parallel instances from Jesus' "restorative" ministry such as Mk. 2:1-12, forgiving the paralytic, and Jn. 4:7-42, giving "living water" to the woman at the well.

[6] In the Bible, "leprosy" refers to a variety of skin conditions perhaps including psoriasis, lupus, and ringworm, and may or may not have included Hansen's disease. And even clothing and houses could be leprous (Lev. 14, likely referring to mold, mildew, fungus, etc.). Note that other diseases known to Israel and ancient peoples are not selectively addressed in Leviticus—only skin diseases, though God does not explain his selection in the text. Perhaps the visibility of a skin disorder made it the obvious object lesson for the sake of Israel. Note also that many of Leviticus' selected issues of clean and unclean have to do with common idolatrous practices of other nations at that time. Israel's different practices would help set them conspicuously apart as a priestly nation.

[7] The word "quarantine" is not appropriate here. The tabernacle priest did not work for the U.S. Department of Health and its Centers for Disease Control. He was a go-between for God and God's people, Israel. And Israel was a go-between nation (a "kingdom of priests") for God and all the other nations. The tabernacle priest did not "diagnose and treat" all manner of illnesses among Israel as a shaman or medicine man. However, for a medical-clinical view of this text, see Harrison, 1980, p. 136-148 and an experimental clinical translation on p. 241-247.

Casting lepers out of their community has a miserable and ironic history since most of it sadly has nothing to do with Lev. 13-14.[8] Rather, Leviticus tells us that lepers were not cast out and isolated in a separate, distant leper colony. Instead, they were stationed outside the camp of Israel with access for inspection by a tabernacle priest. The leper was positioned in close proximity to Israel's encampment and given these instructions:

> The leper who has the *nega* shall wear torn clothing, let his hair hang unkempt, and he shall cup his hand above his upper lip and cry, "Unclean, unclean." He shall remain unclean as long as he has the *nega*. He is unclean. He must live alone. He must live outside the camp (Lev. 13:45-46).[9]

In this way the leper, in conjunction with the tabernacle priest, conducted a significant intercessory function as prescribed by God to his kingdom of priests (Ex. 19:6). As instructed, he (or she) presented himself publicly as one in mourning (torn clothing, not groomed, and wailing were the common funeral practices) and bereft so that all passing into and out of the camp would be confronted by this vivid, immediate image of death and separation. The leper served the critical function as a public go-between for portraying sin and death to the rest of the congregation (remember: the leper did not *do* something "wrong"), while the tabernacle priest publicly portrayed God's intervention for sin and death in the substitution sacrifices at the altar as described in Lev. 14.[10] In terms of Law and Gospel, the leper's separation by the priest served vividly to portray the Law and its condemnation of sin. The leper's restoration to the congregation of Israel through the tabernacle's priest-and-sacrificial system served to portray the Gospel and its substituting atonement for sin. No doubt, these priest-and-person depictions made

---

[8] By New Testament times, much religious sentiment (especially among some rabbis) had equated leprosy with individual, personal sin and treated lepers in this way. In some Mishnah documents, the writers boast of screaming at lepers and throwing rocks at them to keep them away.

[9] The important concepts of holy and common and of clean and unclean cannot be addressed here. See Kleinig, 2003, p. 1-12 and Noordtzy, 1982, p. 16-24.

[10] Substitution is one of Scripture's powerful themes for atonement. Two other atonement themes include Christ the victor, e.g., 1 Cor. 15:57, and Christ who loves us and draws us to himself, e.g., Jn. 12:32 (sometimes called the magnet theme).

an impressive and provocative combination for the congregation to contemplate and discuss in their life as God's priestly nation among the other nations—and for other nations to notice.[11] What's more, this combination served as one among a small set of other prescribed person-and-priest actions in Leviticus (see Lev. 11-19) that foreshadowed the high priestly work of Christ who on the cross became both sin and High Priest for us (1 Cor. 5:21, Heb. 4:14).[12]

Now, would you want to be the leper and serve this important kingdom-of-priests function in the worship life of Israel, interceding to remind them that we are all "unclean, unclean" and in need of a substitute sacrifice? Should our congregation members today be willing to take on similar intercessory roles? Would they? If so, in what ways might they do this? And must all roles be as morbid as the leper's function in God's kingdom of priests?

---

[11] This priest-and-person combination was a central feature that distinguished Israel as a kingdom of priests, different from the other nations. "Here the priest was nothing more than a member of the family group [Aaron's family in the tribe of Levi] which the Lord had called to serve as mediator between himself and his people and to 'minister in the Holy Place' (Ex. 28:43). He was not in possession of a secret ritual, nor was he, as elsewhere [in other nations] a sorcerer or healer, for he was called solely 'to stand before the Lord to minister and to pronounce blessings in his name' (Dt. 10:8). The sacrifices in Israel were brought by the people themselves, the 'holy people' who knew the Lord's decrees and laws, since the latter [these decrees and laws] were directed not to a separate caste, but to the people themselves (Lev. 1:1-2, 11:2, etc.). The people thus took an active role in the presentation of offerings rather than being mere observers. He who brought the offering laid his hand on its head, slaughtered it, skinned it, and cut it into pieces (Lev. 1:3-6, etc.)" (Noordtzy, 1982, p. 22). Kleinig (2003, p. 12) similarly comments, "While it is true that some of the material in Leviticus concerns the ministry of the priests and their participation in God's holiness, the book as a whole and many of its speeches are addressed to the people of Israel, for they are the main beneficiaries of all the services performed by the priests. *The whole of their life in the camp and later in the land was regarded as priestly service to God* (Knohl, 1995, p. 190). Joosten (1996, p. 135) rightly maintains that they were envisaged as temple servants who were called to offer holy service to God. They were therefore bound to observe a basic level of ritual purity in their common life apart from the sanctuary" [Kleinig's italics].

[12] Jesus was not a descendant of Aaron or even a Levite. Though he is our true High Priest, Jesus was a member of the tribe of Judah, among the tribes who were a nation of priests, and not eligible to be a tabernacle or temple priest. Perhaps the author of Hebrews has this ineligibility in mind when he encourages all of us who are not tabernacle priests to, nevertheless, "with confidence draw near to the throne of grace [as only the priests could do in the holy place and the holy of holies] that we may receive mercy and find grace to help in times of need" (Hebr. 4:16).

"NOW YOU ARE THE PEOPLE OF GOD" – SAYS WHO?

The Old Testament elaborates behaviorally rather than doctrinally on the Exodus 19 "kingdom of priests and a holy nation" language. Significantly, Peter chose that text as the church's proper behavioral response to God's intervention for sin through the sacrifice of "the precious blood of Christ, like that of a lamb without blemish or spot" (1 Pet. 1:19):

> As you come to him, the living Stone—rejected by men but chosen by God and precious to him—you also, like living stones, are being built into a spiritual house to be a holy priesthood, offering spiritual sacrifices acceptable to God through Jesus Christ.... But you are a chosen people, a royal priesthood, a holy nation, a people belonging to God, that you may declare the wonderful deeds of him who called you out of darkness into his wonderful light. Once you were not a people, but now you are the people of God; once you had not received mercy, but now you have received mercy (1 Pet. 2:4, 9-10).[13]

And as one who helps direct the learning and activities of this royal priesthood, the Director of Christian Education (DCE) needs to be aware of some background and several views in circulation about the doctrine of the priesthood of all believers. The literature is available, and this chapter includes a reading list, so we will simply introduce some of those themes here. Keep in mind that the larger discussion is "spicy and complex," not to be oversimplified at the risk of ones being dismissed as uninformed. Here are some ingredients to keep in mind.

The theological literature identifies the priesthood of all believers by various expressions which sometimes indicate how its writer views this doctrine. The list includes: the priesthood of all believers; the priesthood of believers; the priesthood of the believers; the priesthood of some believers; the priesthood of the believer; the priesthood of the baptized; the priesthood of the church; the universal priesthood; the royal priesthood; the common priesthood; the priestly kingdom, as well as other expressions. The writer of a book or article

---

[13] The usually cited biblical texts for the PoAB are 1 Pet. 2:1-9, Ex. 19:5-6, Rev. 1:4-6, Heb. 13:10-16, and Deut. 6:7.

may want to emphasize a particular topic such as outreach and evangelism, or the role of the clergy in the church, or the Reformation concern about Roman Catholic priests, or the ministry (some prefer the word "service") of every Christian, or the doctrine of vocation, or the office of the keys, or decision making and organization—this is called "polity"—in the church. Depending on the writer or the speaker's concern and goal, she or he may prefer one of these terms for what Peter calls "a chosen people, a royal priesthood, a holy nation, a people belonging to God" (1 Pet. 2:9).

The theological literature includes assorted "job descriptions" or "assigned characteristics and tasks" for the priesthood of all believers—and not all writers agree on the description. Scripture does not itemize a list of duties and characteristics for the PoaB such as we find in 1 Tim. 2 for bishop and deacon and Titus 1 for elders.[14] We Lutherans, therefore, look next to the Book of Concord for explanation—with limited though helpful results. The Lutheran confessions include only one reference to Peter's words, "You are a royal priesthood," found in the Section 69 of the Treatise on the Power and Primacy of the Pope written by Philip Melanchthon (McCain, 2005, p. 289). Melanchthon cites 1 Pet. 2:9 to challenge the ecclesiastical power that the Church of Rome has vested in its hierarchical system of bishops and the pope. He insists that the local congregation—the royal priesthood—alone retains "the right of calling, electing, and ordaining ministers" (Section 67). We see here an example of an important document invoking the PoaB to clarify and define an area of variant teachings and practice in the church. (Read in its entirety, the Book of Concord has much to say about the priesthood of all believers without explicitly using that term. Each of its documents contributes to our understanding of what, who, and whose the church is.)

---

[14] In this absence, some readily connect the PoaB to such themes as the Great Commission in Mt. 28:19-20 or to Jesus' own priesthood as described in Hebrews (consider Heb. 13:10-13). Since Peter selected Ex. 19:6 as his anchor text for his message, perhaps we can read the rest of his letter as a description of the PoaB.

Some detailed descriptions of the PoaB are available, then, not from the Book of Concord but from other sources. We start with some standard excerpts from Luther:

> After we have become Christians by this Priest [Christ] and his priesthood, and have been incorporated into him through baptism by faith, then we also receive the right and authority to teach and confess publicly [*vor jedermann*] the Word that we received from him, everyone according to his calling and state. Though we are not all called into the public ministry, yet every Christian may and should teach, instruct, admonish, comfort, and reprove his neighbor from God's Word at every opportunity and whenever necessary (Luther, 1955, p. 5:1036).[15]

> A shoemaker, smith, and farmer all have their office and the work of their occupation, and yet all are equally priests and bishops. Each should benefit and serve the others by his office and work, so that all these manifold works in a community aim to benefit body and soul, just as the members of the body serve one another (Luther, 1955, p. 10:270).

> We firmly maintain that there is no other Word of God than the one all Christians are told to preach; there is no other baptism than the one all Christians may administer; there is no other remembrance of the Lord's Supper than the one any Christian may celebrate; also there is no other sin than the one every Christian may bind or loose; again, there is no other sacrifice than the body of every Christian; also, no one should judge of the doctrine than but the Christian. These, however, are certainly the priestly and kingly functions (Luther, 1955, p. 10:1590).

> Now Christ is the High and Chief Priest anointed by God himself. He sacrificed his own body for us, which is the highest function of the priestly office. Then he prayed for us on the cross. In the third place, he also proclaimed the Gospel and taught all men to know God and him himself.... These three offices he also gave to all of us.

---

[15] Note that this and the following citations are not extraordinary rarities cherry-picked to support a particular view. They are the usual references in the literature. For example, Walther (1987) includes this and several such citations in his book, *Church and Ministry*.

Consequently, since he is the priest and we are his brothers, all Christians have the authority, the command, and the obligation to preach, to come before God, to pray for one another, and to offer themselves as a sacrifice to God (Luther, 1955, p. 30:53; Preus, 1979, p. 57).

Another standard reference is David Chytraeus (1531-1600), Luther's student and one of the authors of the *Formula of Concord*. James Pragman (1983, p. 59-60) summarizes the commentary of Chytraeus on 1 Pet. 2:1-9:

Chytraeus asserted that "priesthood" is not the prerogative of a special class of men, but rather belongs to all Christians: all Christians have equal priestly dignity and worth in the sight of God and man…. All Christians are obligated and privileged to make sacrifices to Almighty God. Second, each Christian can approach God in prayer on his own behalf and for the sake of the neighbor. In the third place, all Christians have the right to teach others and to proclaim the Gospel for the welfare of others. Fourth, Christian priests are also commanded to pass judgment on doctrines taught in the church and on spirits [1 Jn. 4:1-6]: they have the right to accept or reject doctrines and their teachers. Fifth, all Christian priests have the power of the keys, the power to bind and loose sins. Finally, all Christians have the privilege of receiving and administering the church's sacraments of Baptism and the Lord's Supper; this is not a privilege reserved only for the ordained clergy of the church.

In these ways, the PoaB is employed by Christ, the High Priest, to minster his intervention between God and sinners. The play-by-play action for priestly going-between goes like this: first, the PoaB is drawn by the Holy Spirit to God to receive from him what he wants delivered to sinners—mercy and forgiveness in Christ. The PoaB then, on God's behalf, turns to the sinner to share this mercy and forgiveness through the means which God has also provided for this grace. Luther lists these means as five: the spoken word, baptism, the Lord's Supper, the office of the keys, and mutual conversation and consolation with the sinner.[16] Next, the

---

[16] Smalcald Articles, Part III, section IV. By including all five and not just listing the typical pastoral functions of preaching and the sacraments, Luther conspicuously locates the means of grace with the PoaB.

PoaB, on behalf of the sinner, turns back toward God and pleads for the sinner through intercessory prayer, begging God to give that sinner faith and trust that God does what God promises to do in those means of grace. Additionally, the PoaB demonstrates the reality of God's goodness and promises in persuasive, concrete ways through sacrifices of care, assistance, and every variety of good works, and also by making sure God's promises are presented clearly and accurately ("passing judgment on doctrines").[17]

ISSUES: THE USUAL SUSPECTS

Such strong, clear statements about the PoaB from Luther, Chytraeus, and others in the church's history were generated because of abuse and confusion about nature of the church and its members' ministry. Abuse and confusion also generate controversy, and the DCE should be aware and reasonably well-read in these controversies so as not to be blind-sided by variant views. Yet clarity can come from controversy, provided we include good instruction. A key feature of Lutheran theology for seeking understanding about God's Word and our human controversies is "tension"—a creative tension as God's two Words of Law and Gospel do their creative work. The above descriptions of the PoaB suggest some of those tension points. We will consider four of them.[18]

One is the relationship between all Christians in the PoaB and the public ministers of the church. Luther and his fellow reformers were correcting errors and abuses of the Church of Rome which had for hundreds of years institutionalized sacerdotalism, a hierarchy in which clergy are the first-class Christians and all others in the church are subordinate second-class Christians who are to "pay, pray, and obey." These reformers carefully reexamined the Biblical texts on the PoaB (as well as many other texts particularly about the Gospel itself)

---

[17] A study of the PoaB should be accompanied by a thorough reading of the theme and doctrine of Christian vocation. Several good sources are available. *Luther on Vocation* by Gustaf Wingren remains the standard reference.

[18] Each of these tension topics is more complex than presented in this chapter. The reading list at the end of this chapter will help the reader explore implications and concerns we cannot address here.

and concluded that this teaching had been lost and needed to be restored to the church. One of its key applications is that the church's public ministers cannot be appointed by a church hierarchy but must be elected by the very Christians these public ministers serve. Lutheran and other churches today employ different practices regarding whether and how the PoaB calls its own public ministers into service.

A second tension revolves around whether the nature of the public ministry of the church derives from and is an extension of the PoaB or is, rather, established directly by the authority of God's word. During the Reformation, the Anabaptist radical reformers and later the Baptist movement in England generally subordinated the public ministry to the PoaB, emphasizing the individual Christian's standing and "soul competency" before God without need of any church authority such as a parish priest or pope. In contrast, Luther and the Lutheran tradition have sustained both the PoaB and the office of the public ministry, each confirmed and established by clear texts in Scripture (for example, Eph. 4:11 and 1 Cor. 12:28) and designed by God to work together to sustain the Gospel in His church in order to share it with the world.[19]

A third tension point oscillates around which acts of ministry the PoaB conducts. Notice the statements from Luther and Chytraeus include praying, comforting, admonishing, acts of service through our vocations (cf. 1 Cor. 7:17-24), and sacrificial service beyond our daily callings (cf. Rom. 12:1-2 and 1 Pet. 2:21). But notice the statements also include preaching, teaching, forgiving and retaining sin, baptizing, and administering the Lord's Supper as activities of the PoaB. Much of the Lutheran literature past and present concerns which of these activities individual members of the PoaB should customarily enact and which activities the PoaB assigns to the church's public ministers. A related issue is whether the PoaB assigns or delegates certain of its

---

[19] Luther's own writings about the public ministry seem to make use of both a delegation-from-the-PoaB view and a Biblical-institution view, depending on the problem in the church he was addressing. See Gerrish, 1965, p. 404-422.

activities to the public ministry or whether God in his word already associates certain activities to the public ministry.[20]

The conventional understanding in the Lutheran tradition about this tension is that God in his word has established both the PoaB and the office or offices (including teachers, pastors, and DCEs—this is another point of tension we will not pursue here) of the public ministry and keeps them in mutual relationship with each other, with neither subordinate to the other. The PoaB does not create the public ministry (God has done that in his word) but does call from among itself those who will occupy an office of public ministry. In doing so, the PoaB delegates to its congregation's public ministry certain of its own ministry activities—specifically, those usually located and enacted in corporate worship such as pulpit preaching, corporate absolution, and public administration of the Lord's Supper.

This delegation is called the "transfer theory." A related issue that recycles in the PoaB discussions is whether and to what extent the PoaB forfeits or still retains those "transferred activities." One view says that the appropriately transferred ministries were not given by God to the individual members of the PoaB but were given to the entire congregation which then, while remaining collectively responsible for them to God, practices them through God's additional gift of the public ministry. This view has the important virtue of simplicity, locating the sacraments, for example, in the pastoral office so that our worship practices may be done "decently and in order" (1 Cor. 14:14).[21] However, other views note that

---

[20] A useful exercise while reading this and other writings is to substitute different nouns and verbs in key sentences that describe points of tension, then consider the implications of each noun or verb. For example, in this sentence about the PoaB's activities and the public ministry, should we say that the PoaB assigns, delegates, shares, recognizes, cooperates mutually; or should we choose yet some other predicate? Each carries certain implications about the nature of the church's ministry. Be thoughtful and critical about the author's choice of words as you read.

[21] Paul's concern here is not decency and order for its own sake. That would be a bit too Pharisaical. His concern is that sinners, and especially weak or confused sinners, be able to hear the Gospel. See 1 Cor. 14:20-25. Therefore, the congregation organizes its use of the means of grace, whether publicly or personally, not according to some supposed ecclesiastical order (the sort of thing the Reformation was seeking to reform) but as the practice of the PoaB and the public ministry which may best intervene between God and sinners. And what is best may change with needs and circumstances, as Paul describes earlier in 1 Cor. 9:19.

while it is good practice to locate baptism and corporate and home communion for shut-ins in the pastoral office, any Christian can and should baptize when the circumstances warrant it, and God's forgiveness is present in communion no matter who administers it. Thus, the PoaB does not transfer any ministries unilaterally to the public ministry. Instead, each congregation must consider and decide how it will exercise good stewardship over the entire ministry God has entrusted to us.[22]

A fourth tension has to do with church polity. The Lutheran Church–Missouri Synod has a distinct history that influences its own particular slant on the PoaB. Its original members immigrated to Missouri from Germany in 1838 under the leadership of Martin Stephan, an older pietistic pastor in Saxony who had garnered for himself a strong influence over a group of younger pastors and their congregations. He convinced these Christians to appoint him as their bishop as he led them to start a new church and life in the United States. Stephan, while charismatic in certain ways, proved to be a person of flawed character who insisted on his own unquestionable authority, then squandered the immigrants' funds on personal extravagances. On May 30, 1839, in Perry County, Missouri, Stephan was excommunicated and sent away by these disillusioned Christians when three young women came forward to confess their involvement in his sexual improprieties.

We review the sordid beginning of the LC–MS not as voyeurism but to understand why this new church body took deliberate steps to define and limit the role of the clergy and establish clear roles for the PoaB. Among these forlorn "strangers in a strange land," it was the laymen who first turned to Scripture and to Luther's writings to begin their own re-discovery of the church and the ministry. The pastors refused to join that effort for a full year, and then only reluctantly. However, when they eventually did agree to study and dialogue with their fellow

---

[22] From Luther: "All Christians are priests, but they are not all pastors, for they [pastors] must not only be Christians and priests but also be in charge of the office [of public ministry] and a parish" ("Exposition of Ps. 82," StL 5:721). As a matter of good form and practice, then, non-clergy refrain from conducting any ministry of Word and sacrament normally delegated to the public ministry except in an emergency, that is, a situation where someone in an office of public ministry is not available and the Christian(s) present exercise sound Biblical judgment for the sake of the sinner in need of God's grace. Emergency baptism is the usual example.

Christians, C.F.W. Walther, one of the pastors, was instrumental in developing and documenting the theology which would guide the church that almost failed.

Some chief features of this theology and its practice of ministry in the PoaB and the public ministry are: congregation decisions are made by a voters' assembly, not by those in the public ministry; the congregation, not those in the public ministry, manages the funds; and the congregation is directly responsible for monitoring, encouraging, and correcting the teaching, preaching, doctrine, and ministry practice in its midst. This division of labor and system of checks and balances allows those in the congregation's public ministry the needed freedom to focus on the spiritual welfare of the congregation as they use the power of the Word and sacraments in our "public" or "at-large" ways.[23]

Among all Christians, including Lutherans, various views and their tensions continue to circulate regarding the PoaB and the office of the keys, teaching and proclaiming the Gospel in personal, small group, large group, and public settings, and judging doctrine. Our aim in this chapter is not to resolve such questions and tensions—perhaps keeping them lively keeps all of us lively about our faith and life together—but to alert the DCE to matters of importance, instruction, and direction about the PoaB. Much good reading is available. Whatever one's view may be on these issues, Scripture and the Lutheran tradition plainly acknowledge both the collective priesthood of the church and the priestly role of the individual Christian. For Luther's part, he sought to keep both together, neither eclipsing the other, given Paul's dictum, "Now you are the body of Christ and individually members of it" (1 Cor. 12:27). Paul Althaus summarizes Luther's view this way:

> Luther never understands the priesthood of all believers merely in the "Protestant" sense of the Christian's freedom to stand in a direct relationship to God without a human mediator. Rather he constantly emphasizes the Christian's evangelical authority to come before God

---

[23] For further background, see Mundinger (1947) and Walther (1987). Walther articulated what is called a "mediate" view of the PoaB and the public ministry which avoids the excesses of hierarchy and of a church under every man's own hat. See for example his Thesis IV in Part Two, Concerning the Holy Pastoral Minstry.

on behalf of the brethren and also the world. The universal priest-hood expresses not religious individualism but its exact opposite, the reality of the congregation as a community (Althaus, 1966, p. 314).[24]

LUTHERAN "LEPERS"

We began by considering the Levitical instruction to lepers as part of Israel's calling to be a kingdom of priests. Sounds a little strange: "Congratulations! You've developed a persistent skin condition, so now you get to use this condition as one of our community object lessons. You get to portray to us and to the other nations that all our lives are sinful and unclean, that we sin against God in thought, word, and deed, but that God has intervened and put in place a system of altar priests and sacrifices to cover our sin and keep us at one with him. Now, to point us toward this at-one-ment, station yourself out there—that's it, just right outside there—and look haggard. Oh, and yell, 'unclean' at us from time to time." (Imagine the teenagers' anxiety when they got acne.)

What is it like to be a kingdom of priests? It means you have to be enough like the other kingdoms and people that they can identify with you. And it means you have to be different enough from them that they can notice the difference and ask about it. You have to be peculiar—but not weird. Peter explains this to his readers whom he addresses as "exiles of the dispersion" (1 Pet. 1:1, alluding to Israel's exile, diaspora, and taking their priestly presence as a messianic people out to the nations). He tells these Christians they are to conduct themselves honorably toward non-Christians as well as one another, but they are to live as aliens and exiles (1 Pet. 2:11-17). When others notice and ask about this peculiarity, Christians can then "give an answer to everyone who asks you to give the reason for the hope that you have. But do this with gentleness and respect" (1 Pet. 3:15). Peter also gives specific examples to demonstrate that the

---

[24] Similarly, B.A. Gerrish encapsulates Luther's perspective this way: "The notion that every Christian is a priest, and that no Christian needs a [fellow Christian] priest comes perilously close to being nonsensical" (1965, p. 411).

ministry of the holy, royal priesthood is not merely corporate or delegated to its public representatives but is lived out in the lives of its individual members as the Christian interacts with the government (1 Pet. 2:13-17), masters and employers (1 Pet. 2:14-25), the family (1 Pet. 3:1-7), and all of life (1 Pet. 3:8-12).

Today, employing those among us with skin conditions as priestly intercessors is probably a little too weird, and not an effective strategy. Instead, we can consider what priestly strategies would be effective in our congregation and community. Paul may have had this in mind when, in 1 Tim. 5:3-16, he gives Timothy detailed instructions to enlist the widows as a distinct group to do ministry at the congregation in Ephesus. "She who is a real widow, and is left all alone, has set her hope on God and continues in supplication and prayer night and day" (5:5). A squadron of such widows could present an impressive priestly portrayal of trust in God to any community, not to mention their constant intercessory prayer. This plan also may seem a little unusual to readers today, and we don't seem to practice this New Testament instruction much. Perhaps we could, but that decision must be made by the local PoaB (and the widows).

Or we could identify other clusters of sinner-saints among us who might formally or informally share in a variety of formats (worship, small groups, Bible classes, potlucks, etc.) how sin has afflicted them and how God's rich grace in Christ has restored and renewed them. For example, those successful in business know well the temptations of not helping our neighbor to "improve and protect his property and means of making a living" (8th Commandment) and of coveting (9th and 10th Commandments). They may be particularly effective as our local go-betweens, alerting us to our own similar temptations, and then directing us to God's forgiveness and the Holy Spirit's help.

Perhaps those among us who have experienced the hurt and grief of divorce might by their teaching and testimony remind us sinners of both the blessings and difficulties of marriage, yet also remind us that "if anyone is in Christ, he is a new creation" (2 Cor. 5:17) and that God can make all things new again.

We sinner-saints have plenty of sin to go around, so other ideas should not be hard to imagine (though not every human or congregational condition will have priestly suitability). What's more, God's grace is always more plentiful than our sin, and he has given us the means to share that grace. (Consider the earlier quotations from Luther and Chytraeus.) This then, is a potentially strong ministry for the DCE with the PoaB: help them practice their priesthood by identifying real-life conditions among us that clearly yet gently exhibit God's goodness to us in Jesus, for He who calls us his sisters and brothers is the great High Priest who gets God and sinners together.

CHAPTER 3

"Working 9 to 5?"

The Doctrine of Vocation
and its Application to DCE Ministry

JONATHAN RUEHS

INTRODUCTION

My first call into DCE ministry was in a parish in Burbank, California. Down the street, about a half a mile away, was Ralph's Grocery Store. It was here that I stumbled upon a great revelation concerning vocation. One day, after work, I stopped into the store to pick something up for dinner. While my groceries were being scanned and bagged I happened to glance upon the nametag of the grocery clerk who was placing my goods into the requested plastic bags. The name on the nametag read "Jesus." A smile came upon my face as I said to myself, "Jesus is bagging my groceries." Now the young Hispanic man bagging my groceries with that nametag on most likely pronounced his name "Hay-sus." But for me this encounter was the impetus to begin to dig deeper into the Lutheran doctrine of vocation. For it is within this particular doctrine that we can say that not only does *Hay-sus* bag my groceries, but Jesus, the Son of God, does so as well.

Jonathan Ruehs serves as Associate Director of the DCE programs at Concordia University Texas.

VOCATIO

When you hear the word "call" what pictures come to mind? Do you think of pews, robes, pulpits, and altars? Do you think of people preaching and teaching God's word? How about the guy who bags your groceries, or the maid in the hotel room who makes the bed each day? What about the stay-at-home mom? Does your conception of the word "call" limit you to think only of churchly things, or does it include a broader understanding of how God works in the world? The word "call" is from the Latin term voce, which is transliterated into English as voice. *Voce* is the root word for another Latin term *vocatio* (Wingren, 1957). Once again when vocatio is transliterated into English it becomes vocation. Since *voce* means "call," *vocation*, therefore, means "calling."

In the Middle-Ages, the Catholic Church specifically applied the term vocation to those who were engaged in full-time church careers (Veith, 2002, p. 18). Only priests, monks, nuns, bishops, the Pope, etc. could claim to have a calling from God. Then along came Martin Luther and through his passionate study of God's word he came to the conclusion that all of God's people are called to be priests (1 Pet. 2:9). If the concept of the priesthood extends to all of God's people then it means that no particular class of people can claim a special status of being called by God to their position. Although the doctrine concerning the "priesthood of all believers" does not make every Christian into a church-worker it does, however, endow every Christian with the title of "priest," and turns every vocation into a sacred calling (Veith, 2002, p. 19).

Already you are probably seeing ways in which the doctrine of vocation connects to your future calling as a DCE. Most likely the call to become a minister did not happen through a "burning bush" or a thundering voice from the heavens; rather it was probably God's still small voice, through family and friends, which confirmed your call to enter into church work. Your desire to enter into ministry may also have come through the experiences that you have had in life. A servant event, a Bible study, a youth gathering experience, or time spent counseling a friend may have been the important event that God placed in your life confirming His call for you to enter into full-time ministry (Veith, 2002, p. 54-55).

VARIOUS VOCATIONS

Luther described the term vocation as a type of "station" in life, which not only included occupations, but also included what Luther referred to as "biological orders" (Wingren, 1957, p. 4). Biological orders are those orders which deal with familial relationships. Therefore family roles are equally important stations in life as are occupations. In Genesis we read how God brought about the vocation of husband and wife (Gen. 2:18ff). In naming the animals Adam came to realize that every animal had a corresponding mate with one exception, himself. The text states that it was not good for man to be alone so God created Eve out of Adam's rib. Also in the Ten Commandments we read about the importance of the vocation of parenting and the honor there in that is due (Ex. 20:12). Other biological orders such as son or daughter, nephew or niece, uncle or aunt, or even a second-cousin twice removed are also important vocations that God has placed people into.

The doctrine of vocation helps us to realize that we don't just serve in one vocation; rather we serve in multiple vocations at once (Wingren, 1957, p. 5). For instance you are probably a college student, who is someone's son or daughter, and simultaneously you might be serving in the role as a sales clerk, gate security guard, or waitress. You may not like having to work a part-time (or maybe full-time job) while going to school, but the whole reason why you are in school is because you are trying to receive an education to prepare you for your future calling into DCE ministry. Your parents may also be helping to support you as you go through college. As you can see your vocation as a son or daughter and your vocation as a paid worker come together to help support you in your vocation as student, which helps you to reach your goal of one day entering into the vocation of DCE ministry.

NEIGHBORLY LOVE AND THE HIDDEN NATURE OF GOD

This brings us to the question of what does one do in vocation. Luther answered this question by stating that love is the main thrust of vocation, and remarked that both works and love belong to the earth (Wingren, 1957, p. 64). In stating this he wanted to get across the idea that loving one's neighbor in vocation is not an act of salvation. Earthly vocation, according to Luther, has nothing to do with our standing before God. Our work is never directed upward; rather it is all directed horizontally in our relationships with others (Wingren, 1957, p. 14). In our vertical relationship with God, we stand alone, but within our horizontal relationship we are always bound to each other (Wingren, 1957, p. 5).

All people are called to serve one another in their various vocations in life (Wingren, 1957, p. 7). "How," you may ask, "is this done?" Here is where Luther puts forth the notion of the hidden nature of God. In his struggle to comprehend God's ways in the world the prophet Isaiah remarked, "Truly you are a God who hides himself" (Isa. 45:15). In other aspects of our theology we note how God accomplishes this act. God was hidden in the incarnation. God is hidden in the bread and wine of communion. God is also hidden, in a sense, behind the ink and paper that makes up the Bible (Veith, 1999, p. 55). God also uses people as a "means" whether or not they believe he exists. For instance God used the pagan king Cyrus as a means whereby the Jews were able to return to Jerusalem (2 Chron. 36:22; Ezra 1:1-4).

Even the petition "Give us this day our daily bread" is answered by God through all kinds of people (Matt. 6:11). God is hidden in the farmer who tills the soil that brings forth the wheat. God is hidden in the factory worker who oversees the process of the wheat being made into flour. God is hidden in the baker who takes the flour to produce bread. God is hidden in the manager of the company that hires the employee, that gives them money to purchase the bread. God is hidden even in the check-out clerk who places the bread into the bag for you (Janzow, 1978, p. 90).

DCEs wish that all of their students were attentive and involved in their Bible studies, but they have to admit that there are times when their Bible studies just seem to fall on, what is perceived to be, deaf ears. They are very shocked when one of those seemingly apathetic teenagers comes back to them a week later and tells them that what was said in youth group made an impact upon them. Jesus told his followers that the Spirit blows where it will and therefore a person cannot track, like a meteorologist, the movements of the Spirit (Jn. 3:8). As stated above God is hidden in the ordinary and seemingly mundane things of life. Even the Bible study that seemed to come across as a "lead balloon" can be used by God to move the indifferent heart of teenagers within a youth group.

When people see tension and factions rising in the church they are sometimes tempted to say, "God is not in this!" Yet, we have to be careful not to become too hasty in saying where God is and is not. For starters when we make these types of declarations we are claiming to have a universal knowledge on how God works. God is present everywhere, as our doctrine of omnipresence states, and God can even be hidden behind the contentious actions of congregation members. Part of the beauty of God's mercy and grace is that he is hidden even in the messiness of life. Remember that even in the darker moments of his saints, God's light can shine through.

THE CALLED BELIEVER

God even calls us into the Christian faith, which is infiltrated throughout all of our other vocations. We may view the other vocations as roles that we may fulfill at differing parts of our day. The believer does not put on the vocation of "Christian" as they get dressed on Sunday morning for church, and then discards that vocation when they come home. It is, once again, something that is part and parcel to all that we are, say, and do.

As Christians we were "called out of darkness and into His marvelous light" (1 Pet. 2:9). We are brought into a saving relationship with Jesus through his painful death upon the cross and triumphant resurrection from the dead. The bonds of sin, Satan, and death are shattered in our life through the victory that Christ won for us through the cross and tomb. God even works through the vocation of his children in order to bring us into His kingdom. For instance it is through the vocation of parents and godparents, whereby many of us were brought to the baptismal font. It is through the vocation of the pastor whereby the Trinitarian formula was spoken over us while water was sprinkled upon our forehead.

Our vocation as a Christian definitely helps us to understand the greater way in which God uses vocations for his good purposes. We may not like waiting tables, bagging groceries, or even working in retail, but this Christian understanding of vocation can help us to see the greater role that our seemingly insignificant job plays in our day-to-day life. What this does mean is that for Christians we can understand that even our scrubbing of toilets is an act of love toward others. As Christians we have a unique understanding of vocation that the non-believer does not have which states that our various roles are imbued with meaning and purpose.

It is important to understand that the vocation of being a Christian is not to be confused with the vocation of being a DCE. Now being a Christian is an obvious pre-requisite for service in the church, but it is part and parcel to that vocation just as much as it is in your other vocations. What this means is that we are not called to just serve our neighbor while on the "clock," but we are called to serve our neighbor through all our vocations. Service to your neighbor, outside of the church, may mean helping to bring the mail in for the lady across the street who has taken ill. You don't do this because you serve in the church; rather you do it because God has called you to do this through your vocation of being a next door neighbor.

Many well-intentioned Christians have found it helpful to take a "tiered" approach in their understanding to how people are to love God first, and neighbor second. One such approach looks like this: "God, family, and work." The tiered approach may at first glance be a good working theory, but in the end it results in confusion, especially when one's work is in the church. If a person's work is in the church are they keeping God first by being extra involved in the day-to-day affairs of the congregation? What happens when they decide to not attend a stewardship meeting in favor of going to their son's soccer game? Are they, in turn, putting God second? There is a strong temptation, amongst church workers, to confuse the vocation of believer with the vocation of church worker. God calls us to love him with all that we have and in all that we do. Keeping God first in life means that we keep God first in all of our vocations. It calls us to ask: "What does it mean to be a godly parent or spouse?" as well as: "What does it mean to be a godly worker?"

SIN AND VOCATION

Every vocation carries its own temptations to fall into sinful behavior (Veith, 2002, p. 135). The student may be tempted to cheat on his test in order to get a good grade. The parent may be tempted to physically abuse their child due to the irritation they face in light of a child's disobedience. The construction company may be tempted to cut corners in a project in order to save on money, time, and resources. Sin, therefore, is contextual in nature.

Vocation also carries a certain right that authorizes specific actions, but does not authorize others. For instance only a married couple is authorized to have sex, since it is within the context of marriage that God established the appropriateness of this act. Although everyone is capable of having sex this does not mean that they should have sex. Fornication is outside of the authority of marriage, and adultery is a violation of that authority. Since sin is contextual to a vocation, a particular action, therefore, may be a sin in one vocation, but not be a sin in another (Veith, 2002, p. 137).

It is also important to note that we don't always have the ability to carry out a certain function, because God has not given us the particular gift or talent to do so. The electrician, for instance, is trained and certified to deal with electrical issues. Persons who attempt to rewire their houses may not have the ability to do so. If they attempt to engage in this activity they may quickly receive the shock of their lives! What this means is that when we seek to engage in an activity that is outside of the parameters of our gifts and talents then we are seeking to act outside of our vocation. Although acting outside of vocation can indeed be related to sinful behavior in many instances these actions can be morally neutral (Veith, 2002, p. 139). Through all of this we need to come to the realization that God has gifted people in different ways and He has created a world in which we are dependent upon one another for our well-being.

As a student you may be anxious about starting your work in the church, but it is important to understand that your calling to be a student is a vital part of the process to bring you to that final goal of ministering in the parish. Professors play an important authority role to help guide you and shape your thinking when it comes to working within the church. Disdaining those in authority is dishonoring the call of being a student. Having a flippant attitude about having to go through the "hoops of classes" is also an attitude of sinfulness. You may not always understand why you have to take algebra or sit in on that sociology class, but these classes can help to round out your education and make you a more informed, better-educated person. Having a broader, liberal arts education also helps in your service in the church since you will be serving others who come from all walks of life and are engaged in various occupations.

Every person needs to find a balance and maintain boundaries in their various vocations. The DCE is no different in this regard. A major temptation for those who work in the church is to spend so much time doing the work of the church that they neglect the vocation of being a spouse, parent, or friend. Spending inordinate amounts of time away from home can result in a person's spouse or children feeling neglected and unloved. Of course these feelings can lead to hostility in the home, which has a direct impact upon the person's work in other vocations. Think of it this way, if a DCE's family is in chaos what chance does that person have of being productive in the church (1 Tim. 3:5)?

The temptation to work outside of a person's vocation is also strong within the parish. Each of the called staff members of a congregation is called for a specific purpose. Within the LC–MS we would say that a female DCE who took up the charge to preach or administer sacraments is doing something that is outside of their vocation. A pastor, on the other hand, who takes charge of a youth group, although he is not gifted in that area could also be considered as someone who is working outside of his vocation. Although we need to remember that working outside of our vocation is not always viewed as a sinful thing. God has gifted and equipped you in unique ways so that you too can use those gifts in service in His kingdom.

BEARING THE CROSS IN VOCATION

Jesus taught his disciples to "pick up their crosses and follow him" (Lk. 14.27). The bearing of the cross happens in all parts of our life. Despite what some televangelists preach Jesus never promised that becoming a Christian meant that we would become healthy, wealthy, and wise! The business man, for instance, may get fired from his job for not following the unethical practices of his superiors. The High School football player may lose friends for his unwillingness to engage in sexual activity outside of marriage. Even marriage itself has its struggles as a husband and wife seek to make a marriage work despite the troubles they face.

Cross bearing will always be a continual action on the part of the Christian as long as they have breath in their lungs. The reason for this is due to the fact that suffering is an ever-present reality. Christians are not called out of the world; rather they are called to live in the world. Living means battling the tripartite forces of sin, the devil, and the world. Although Christ has won the war against these forces we understand that these forces try and continue to wage a losing war against the church. When we pray in the Lord's Prayer "…deliver us from evil" (Janzow, 1978, p. 96-97) we are praying that God will bring protection for us as we bear the cross in vocation. Just as sin is contextual, according to the vocation, so is evil in its pogrom against the Kingdom of God. Yet, despite our sufferings we know that the crosses we bear are not too heavy for us to lift, for it is through Christ—who himself lifted the burden of the cross for us--that we are able to bear the burdens that seek to bring us down (Jn. 3:14). Scripture states that God does not give us a burden too terrible to bear, and with the help of the Holy Spirit we are able to stand upright underneath that load (Matt. 11:30).

The church, like all of life, is also not perfect. One of the reasons why the church is referred to as the church "militant" on this side of Heaven, is because the church fights the devil, the world, and the sinful nature both inside and out-side the community of believers. We all struggle with the internal battle between saint and sinner (Wingren, 1957, p. 26). In one sense we are broken servants called to minister to broken people. It is through all of this brokenness, whereby we bear our cross. Sometimes, for instance, the church does not recognize the importance of a DCE to protect his family time. It may be viewed that the ministers of a congregation should be on call 24/7. A DCE who seeks to set up boundaries, in order to serve in the vocation of spouse and parent, may very well have to contend with congregation members who get upset when the DCE says "no" to being involved in certain activities, boards, or committees.

DCEs serve in a church that is filled with people who bring their Old Adam with them on Sunday mornings (Bachman, 2007, p. 1). Of course you also have to remember that your Old Adam is there as well. With all of these Old Adams clashing together is it any wonder that conflicts are part of every congregation? Yet, we need to remember that the perfection that a person seeks in a church will always be a fleeting myth. No church, no matter how "functional" it appears to be is perfect. We should not seek to focus only on the sinner aspect of the church; we also need to see the saint side of those within. The saints of God are saints that are perfect (Mueller, 2005, p. 3:391). It is a perfection that is not found through works; rather it is Christ's perfection, won for us on the cross, that is given to beautify His bride, the church (Eph. 5:25-27).

CONCLUSION

Hopefully by now you understand how it is that Jesus, the Son of God, worked to serve me through "Hay-sus." You should also begin to see and understand how it is that God is hidden in your vocation as a DCE student and how He will continue to remain hidden in your work as you are a DCE in the parish. The hidden nature of God also means that your mistakes allow opportunities for His grace to shine through. Our vocations allow for God to bring about His will through our lives in various and sundry ways despite our sinfulness. What an amazing thing it is that God chooses us to do His work in the world. To God alone be the glory!

CHAPTER 4

The Office of Public Ministry

BILL CULLEN | KEN KRAUSE

PASTOR KEN

To be called by God is a wonderful surprise. That God, who is all powerful, all wise, all self-sufficient, would call us to serve Him and His people is an awesome, surprising, scary, wonderful, empowering, delightful, and joy-filled experience. Imagine receiving a phone call from the President of the United States. You'd be thrilled, once you assured yourself that it was not a prank call. God contacting us would be way beyond that in wonder and in excitement. He does not just contact us, but He asks us to serve Him. Would you serve on the President's cabinet if asked? Will you serve God no matter what He asks of you, no matter what the personal cost? As we remember all that our dear Lord has done for us, we are honored to serve Him however He desires, even if sacrifices must be made to do so.

God calls His people in various ways. Generally, God does not use a telephone to make contact, though He certainly could. Sometimes God's call is direct, face to face, without any middleman. When God called Moses, that was a direct call: "bush to

Bill Cullen, Th.D., is the former DCE Director at Concordia University Chicago. He currently serves as DCE at Mount Olive Lutheran Church, Rockford, Illinois.

Ken Krause, M.Div., serves as Pastor at Mount Olive Lutheran Church, Rockford, Illinois.

face," so to speak. No intermediary made the call. Today's calls are more often indirect or mediated, that is God calling by using an intermediary to extend His call.

Even when God does call immediately (without a "middleman"), God does it in many and various ways. He shows up in a burning bush with Moses, a bright light from heaven with Saul, or Jesus just walks by and says, "Follow Me!" However God communicates with you, whether directly or indirectly, it's wonderful to receive a message from God. Treasure it!

God calls us to various vocations. He calls one person to be a teacher, another to be a DCE, another to be an accountant, another to be a candlestick maker. No matter to what vocation God calls you, you have an important and indispensable function in the body of Christ (1 Cor. 12). No matter to what vocation God calls you, serve Him with all your heart. What an honor to serve God. What a privilege to serve our Savior.

Being called by God can be a scary thing. Moses is a good example. Moses came up with every excuse in the book why he could NOT do what God called him to do. You have to admit it would be a scary proposition to receive a call to go to Pharaoh, one of the most powerful men on earth, and ask him to do something he didn't want to do. You have to hand it to Moses: he is creative in his excuses. He doesn't know God's name, what if they want to know God's name? He says "They won't believe me that I saw God." He claims not to be able to speak well. Finally he just says (to God!) send someone else.

It's good for us to accept God's call, and not to think we have a better idea than the all-wise God. For all his arguing, Moses still goes to Pharaoh, and God does powerful things through Moses. God was clearly calling the Israelites to enter the Promised Land. Ten of the twelve spies thought they knew better, and there was suffering to endure for 40 years because of their refusal to follow God's call.

It's important to note that while it may seem scary to receive a call from God, God always supplies us with what we need to carry out our vocation. Isaiah recognized his limitations: he was a man of unclean lips. God cleanses him. Joshua had big shoes to fill since Moses had led the Israelites for more than 40 years. Now God called him to lead the people into the Promised Land. Imagine if you were called to a congregation where your predecessor had been with that congregation for 40 years and was respected and loved. While Joshua may have been scared, God provided what Joshua needed. God assures Joshua that He will be with him and tells Joshua to be strong and courageous (Josh. 1:1-9).

This of course reminds us that we must fulfill our calling in God's power. What He calls us to do may *seem* more than we can do. Whatever you are called to do, it *is* more than you can do…by yourself. With God, all things are possible. And when God calls you, He supplies the wisdom, the strength, the words and/or the abilities…in other words all you need to do what He has called you to do. When God calls it's not just possible that you'll be able to do it, it's not just probable; it's a sure thing. He will supply all you need…and so much more!

DCE BILL

When I taught at the university I taught my students what I called "God's Math." God's math is "Jesus + me = More than Enough." This equation is illustrated in John 6 where Jesus feeds 5000+ with five loaves of bread and two fish and after all have eaten to their full the disciples take up twelve baskets of leftovers. When Jesus is in the equation of our lives and our call, regardless of what we bring or don't bring to the table in innate ability, Jesus will provide more than enough. In our weakness we see and experience His strength (2 Cor. 3:4-6 & 12:8-10).

The purpose of this chapter is to talk about the calling into "the office of the public ministry." In the church we make distinction between ministries and ministers by talking about Lay Ministry in terms of the "Priesthood of All Believers" (1 Pet. 2:9), and the Office of the Public Ministry (Eph. 4:11). Within the Office of the Public Ministry we make further distinction between ordained ministers (pastors), and commissioned ministers (teachers, DCEs, deaconesses, DCOs, and DCMs). To help us understand these distinctions The Lutheran Church–Missouri Synod suggests that there is one office of the public ministry and that is the pastoral office. As extensions of the pastoral office there are auxiliary offices. The individuals who fill these offices are designated as commissioned ministers.

Understanding these distinctions and their implications is important if we are to function as a healthy team for the common good and for the advancement of the kingdom. In football, if a team is to function effectively, it is important that each team member knows and understands his role. The quarterback and the tackle are both important players, but to function effectively each player needs to focus upon the role for which he has been gifted and trained, and to which he has been assigned. Yet, even though the players have their primary focus; if the team is to be effective, team members also have to be alert and to be constantly adapting to the ever-changing situation at hand. Ordinarily, a tackle on a football team does not handle the football. However, if there is a fumble an alert tackle may need to do so. Likewise, ordinarily a quarterback is not going to be making a tackle. However, if there has been an interception the quarterback may be the last line of defense in preventing a touchdown.

The same is true in the church. All church staff members (as well as all members of the congregation) are a team. Scripture calls us a body—one body, Christ's body with Jesus being the head (Eph. 1:22-23). As members of the team, Christ's body, we each have a role to fill, each with its own primary focus. But like an effective football team we all need to be constantly alert and adapting to the ever-changing terrain and to the needs of both our teammates and of the world community to which God has called us to give witness and service. As we do so, from time to time, we may need to take on responsibilities that might lie outside of our primary focus (e.g. during a pastoral vacancy).

> Now to each one the manifestation of the Spirit is given for the common good (1 Cor. 12-7).

> From him the whole body, joined and held together by every supporting ligament, grows and builds itself up in love, as each part does its work (Eph. 4:16).

While these distinctions can be helpful, they can also carry with them some inherent dangers of which we need to be mindful in order to avoid the misunderstanding and misrepresentation they can unintentionally encourage. Chief among these misunderstandings and misrepresentations is the development of a hierarchy in ministry or in the valuing of one ministry over another.

> [21]The eye cannot say to the hand, "I don't need you!" And the head cannot say to the feet, "I don't need you!" [22]On the contrary, those parts of the body that seem to be weaker are indispensable, [23]and the parts that we think are less honorable we treat with special honor. And the parts that are unpresentable are treated with special modesty, [24]while our presentable parts need no special treatment. But God has combined the members of the body and has given greater honor to the parts that lacked it, [25]so that there should be no division in the body, but that its parts should have equal concern for each other. [26]If one part suffers, every part suffers with it; if one part is honored, every part rejoices with it (1 Cor. 12:21-26).

Both "lay ministry" and "the office of the public ministry" are biblically supported in Ephesians 4. According to Ephesians 4:11-13 a chief responsibility of those in public ministry is "to equip the saints for the work of ministry" (NRSV) or "to prepare God's people for works of service" (NIV). Those in public ministry (the "called" workers), have no more important role as ministers of the Gospel than do lay persons. According to Ephesians 4 a primary role of those in public ministry is to equip the laity—the people in the pews—to be co-ministers of Christ's Body, the church. With this understanding for those of us in "public ministry," we ought not to be gauging our effectiveness by how full our calendars are with Bible studies, events, and the like. Rather, we ought to be gauging our effectiveness by assessing how well we are mentoring, coaching, empowering, commissioning, and releasing our members, the laity, into ministry/service in order that together we might "complete what is lacking in Christ's affliction for the sake of his body, the church" (Col. 1:24).[25]

---

[25] What is lacking in Christ's affliction has nothing to do with the work of justification. Justification was fully completed through Jesus' death on the cross. What is lacking is in the work of proclamation, touching a hurting world with God's love and grace through our words and our deeds in order that people might fully experience and enjoy the life and salvation He offers and join us as lay or professional ministers of the Gospel.

PASTOR KEN

Two challenges come to mind. The first is when God has given us success, when we have seen God do powerful things through His word we've proclaimed, it's easy for us to think too highly of ourselves. It's easy to fall into the trap of thinking we are somehow accomplishing things by our own might or wisdom. As the proverb warns us, "Pride goes before destruction" (Prov. 16:18). Certainly we don't want to get the distorted idea that we're better than those who are not called to full-time ministry. We don't want to be among those who "lord it over others" (Mk.10:32-45). We are called to be servants. He who would be first must be slave of all. We don't want to think of ourselves as superior and requiring others in the church to serve us and our needs. It's better that we "not think more highly of ourselves than we ought, but rather think sensibly" (Rom. 12:3). Sensible, balanced thinking is to realize that by ourselves we are nothing. Yet God has given us certain gifts, and at His calling, by His empowering, God can and will do great things through us (2 Tim. 1:6-7). To Him be all glory and honor, now and forever.

DCE BILL

Good Point! Jesus graphically teaches us to take the posture of a servant in John 13 when He washes His disciples' feet. When He goes to wash Peter's feet, Peter objects, and Jesus tells him that he doesn't understand now, but later he would. What Peter didn't understand was why someone of Jesus' stature, whom he had called "the Christ, the Son of the living God" (Matt. 16:16) and whom he calls "Rabbi" and "Lord" (Jn. 13:13), would be washing feet. However, I believe Peter also objected for another reason, for something he understood all too well and that was the implications of Jesus' actions for himself (Peter). I believe that Peter understood that if Jesus (#1, Head Honcho, etc.) was washing feet, then he/Peter (who probably saw himself as Jesus' right-hand man) was being called to wash feet also and he is thinking to himself "This isn't what I signed on for." Jesus reinforces this understanding in John 13:12-17 & 34-35. We best exercise leadership and our offices as ordained and commissioned ministers not from the posture of lord, but from a posture of servant (Mk. 10:42-45).

But Pastor, you said two challenges come to mind. What is the second challenge?

PASTOR KEN

Sometimes people who work in the church get a little confused about their priorities. *God is to be first* is sometimes equated to *my vocation is first*. Where do spouse and family come into our priorities? When does my own personal well-being come into the picture? Certainly at times our spouse and/or family will have to sacrifice as we serve. Certainly there will be pressing ministry issues that will postpone our scheduled time off. But sometimes we'll need to say no to public ministry opportunities and yes to our family, to our friends, and even to ourselves. God has given us our body, and taught us to be good stewards (Rom. 12:4-8). We are to be good stewards of our souls: being at work at church does not necessarily equate with living closely with the Lord. We are to be good stewards of our spouse and family. This takes time: plenty of time with spouse, plenty of time with family. As good stewards we will also not neglect the work to which God has called us—perhaps long hours of work. There will certainly always be a tension here. Lord, help us work hard and to be properly balanced in each of the vocations to which you have called us.

DCE BILL

Lord, the tension is good as it is the tension that keeps us from straying and keeps us in a healthy balance. Amen!

CHAPTER 5

Directors of Christian Education

Telling the Family History

PAUL SCHOEPP AND THADDEUS WARREN

Most people love to hear stories about their families. Chances are pretty good that you've asked questions about your family as a child or answered them for a young person you know. Our stories matter. They help define us. The history of those who have gone before shapes and molds who we are and how and why we do the things we do today. That's true for us as individuals within our families of origin. It's also true for us as individuals within a profession or, if you will, the family of Directors of Christian Education (DCEs). This chapter will attempt to tell some of the stories and events which have shaped and defined DCE ministry over the past fifty years.

Paul Schoepp, Ph.D., serves as Associate Professor of Applied Religion and Director of Church Work Programs at Concordia University College of Alberta.

Thaddeus Warren, Ph.D., serves as Associate Professor of Education on the DCE Faculty at Concordia University, Nebraska.

FIRST TEACHERS OF THE FAITH

Many scholars have shown that, for centuries, the Christian faith has been shared and passed on from generation to generation finding its roots in the Jewish faith traditions and customs. In its earliest recorded history we see that faith was passed on from parents to children, from children to their children, and from family to family.

> These commandments that I give you today are to be upon your hearts. Impress them on your children. Talk about them when you sit at home and when you walk along the road, when you lie down and when you get up. Tie them as symbols on your hands and bind them on your foreheads. Write them on the doorframes of your houses and on your gates (Deut. 6:4-9).

Formal religious training can be traced back to the Old Testament with the prophets, priests, rabbis and even to and including the traditional practice of religious festivals designed to teach about the faith life of the people (Tidwell, 1982; Elias, 2002). The task of Christian education also figures prominently in the New Testament era. Christ, in addition to being Lord and Savior, also carried the title Rabbi, or teacher. The apostle Paul was also a significant teacher of the faith as he traveled around establishing new churches and providing follow-up instruction about the faith through the letters that have become part of our New Testament (Lawson & Choun, 1992; Stubblefield, 1993).

Many notable authors have documented the path of Christian education from the earliest of days to the present (Furnish, 1976; Tidwell, 1982; Gangel & Benson, 1983; Reed & Prevost, 1993; Pazmino, 1997; Elias, 2002). There is little question from the literature or from Scripture itself that Christian education has a long history. The majority of the literature speaks to the philosophical and theological constructs of the profession. For the purpose of this chapter we will be limiting our review to the literature concerning the development of the DCE profession in the Protestant Christian church beginning in the 20th century and to the specifics of DCE history within the LC–MS.

HISTORY OF THE PROTESTANT DCE

In England around 1780, Robert Raikes started the first Sunday school. The Sunday school was originally designed to reach out to the poor and uneducated children and youth on the streets. It was defined as a social experiment that used Christian tools for education (Reed & Prevost, 1993). The thought behind its inception came from recognizing that those who could not read and write or who were not educated would have trouble succeeding in society. It was out of this societal concern that the church adopted the idea and started Sunday schools with the dual goals of educating individuals to help them advance in society and to share with them the message of faith. This movement quickly spread and met with success among Christian churches in England. Similar Sunday schools were started in the United States but with a slightly different motivation. "Many of those who had settled in the New World came with deeply seated religious convictions. It was only natural that their concern for their children's literacy would join with a like concern for their children's religious training" (Reed & Prevost, 1993, p. 260). It was not long before the Sunday school became the primary teaching agency for communicating the faith in the United States among Protestant churches (Furnish, 1976; Reed & Prevost, 1993; Stubblefield, 1993; Elias, 2002).

During the early part of the 20th century a number of Christian congregations in the United States began to develop the profession of Director of Religious Education (DRE) out of a need for help in carrying out the ministry functions of the church. One of the primary reasons for the early establishment of the DRE role was to promote and administrate the Sunday school (Furnish, 1976; Stubblefield, 1993). As the Sunday school grew, more and more churches saw the need to hire full-time individuals to administrate and manage this agency of the church. Those initially serving in this role were referred to as "director of the Sunday school" or, more often, "paid Sunday school superintendent." Often times, if women filled the position, the title "Educational Secretary" would be used (Stubblefield, 1993).

DREs were identified in the first two decades of the twentieth century primarily in Congregational, Methodist, Presbyterian, and Baptist churches in major cities like Chicago, Pittsburgh, and Buffalo. The primary concern of these directors was religious training of children and youth (Furnish, 1968). These directors often decided curriculum, appointed teachers, and handled all aspects surrounding the administration of the Sunday school. By 1920 the director was not only responsible for the Sunday school but generally was in charge of most of the congregation's programs related to children and youth. With the changing roles came a modification of some of the director's titles to "education director" (Furnish, 1968, p. 16). Stubblefield (1993) points out that "for years the director of religious or Christian education went by the initials DRE or DCE" (p. iv).

During the next two decades, Vacation Bible Schools (VBS) and midweek schools were often added to the education director's workload. A shift in roles was emerging from being the hands on leader and administrator to more of a leader, trainer, and resource person. Along with this shift in role, came an expectation that the person serving as director be theologically trained (Schroeder, 1974). In the 1960s "denominations lifted the position of the DRE to a higher professional level and showed denominational support for their work" (Stubblefield, 1993, p. 31). Many denominations were starting to establish standards and more formal training for those wishing to serve as Directors of Religious Education.

Furnish (1976) identifies four periods of the history of the DCE. The first period 1906-1910 is identified as "A Profession is Born" and discusses the development of early directors and the role that the Religious Education Association, established in 1903, played in influencing the early days of the profession. The second period, 1920-1930, is identified as "The Future is Ours," which discussed the growth of the profession and some of the struggles of standardization and the issues of definition. The third period, 1930-1945, is titled "Disillusionment and Despair" and discusses more of the challenges of the profession, especially those which came as a result of the Depression and World War II. The fourth period, 1945-1965, is identified as "Recovery and Growth." This period discusses some of the changing dynamics of churches following the war and the growth of the profession because of and despite some of these changes (Furnish 1976; Stubblefield, 1993; see also Schoepp, 2003).

Stubblefield (1993) added a fifth period to the work of Furnish: 1965 to the present (i.e. 1993), referred to as "Clarification and Advancement." The challenge of a decline in church membership is discussed along with the shift to larger multi-staff ministries. During this time denominations became more proactive in developing more specific training for DCEs using a variety of approaches including the obtaining of a master's degree. Certification became a requirement in some denominations and several denominations attempted to "establish or revise their standards of certification for the educational minister" (p. 33).

THE DCE IN THE LUTHERAN CHURCH–MISSOURI SYNOD

The history of the DCE in the Lutheran Church–Missouri Synod (LC–MS) follows a somewhat different path. While the Sunday school had some influence on the DCE profession in the LC–MS, it did not define the roles and the preparation of early DCEs as it did in most Protestant churches. DCEs in the LC–MS find their history starting in the parochial school. When Lutherans settled in the United States, they developed day schools with the hopes of maintaining some of the heritage they brought with them from Germany. These schools provided a good academic education with the added benefit of daily religious education (Keyne, 1995).

The Lutheran church was well grounded in its practice of establishing and using day schools as a primary faith-shaping tool. Among some in the church there was a concern that establishing Sunday Schools might compromise the day school and their conviction that day schools were the best avenue to nurture the faith of children (Schroeder, 1974). Many congregations did however start to use the Sunday school in the late 1800s to supplement and/or provide Christian education to their children and youth. Lutheran churches were careful to place the Sunday school under the direction of a theologically trained or, more specifically, a synodically-certified person, typically the pastor or the Lutheran day school teacher. The first Missouri Synod congregations to conduct Sunday schools also had day schools, thus there were readily available trained teachers to teach and direct the Sunday school from as early as the 1910s. It is noteworthy that these individuals were often asked to serve as organist or as choir director in addition to establishing various forms of religious instruction in the parishes they served (Griffin, 1995).

The early beginnings of the DCE ministry within the Synod are sometimes difficult to trace because historical records are not clear. Often the records reference only the Lutheran teacher, even if the teacher was not serving in a traditional classroom but, instead, in the congregation's other educational agencies. Further complicating the process, the title "Director of Christian Education" was not used extensively until the 1950s (Schroeder, 1974). The first clearly recorded DCE as "teacher," A.W. Kowert, served a church in Sheboygan, Wisconsin, from 1916 to 1924 (p. 33). Kowert was called to serve the church in multiple roles as teacher, organist, and choir director. Schroeder indicates that by 1940 there were at least six congregations within the Synod that had teachers serving in director roles.

Schroeder (1974) claims that the DCE profession in the Lutheran church really did not find itself until the 1960s due to the synod's commitment to the Christian day school. Although there were some individuals serving in DCE roles, he asserts that the Synod as a whole really saw no purpose for the position of DCE as, traditionally, the roles now assumed by the DCE were performed by the male day school teacher. Keyne (1995) affirms that the role of DCE was often seen as a threat to the day school. It was this mindset that often limited the widespread acceptance of such a position in the Lutheran church.

Griffin (1995) records that as early as 1934 the Atlantic District, in convention, voted to "petition Synod at its convention in June, 1935, to make provision at one or both of its teachers' seminaries for the training of 'directors of Christian education,' who will be equipped to serve congregations that have no Christian day school, as instructors in week-day religion schools, as superintendents of the Sunday and Bible-schools, as church organists and choir directors, and as missionaries particularly to the children" (*Proceedings*, 1935, p. 98-99). The resolution to establish the position of DCE failed in large part due to the previously noted concerns that the position might undermine the viability of parochial schools but the matter was recommended for further study. Although the 1938 convention did not establish the position of DCE, a report came back outlining probable functions a DCE might serve and noted the status of the office as equal to that of teacher or assistant pastor. Additionally such persons should be synodically trained and should be listed on the Roster of Synod. As for professional preparation, "the training program offered by the two teachers' colleges of Synod under the revised curriculum is adequate for specialization in the field of religious education in the local church" (*Proceedings*, 1938, p. 45-46). In spite of not formally adopting the position of DCE, the number of non-certified DCEs in synod continued to grow throughout the 1940s and 1950s.

As new churches were established without a day school, they were inclined to search for someone with gifts and passions to help with the educational agencies of the church. By the 1950s, there were more and more demands by parishioners that churches provide programming for youth and children as congregations were experiencing the Baby Boom along with the rest of the country. These factors were instrumental in driving the church to seek a better way to meet the demands of the people with the result that in 1956 the Youth Leadership Training Program was instituted at Valparaiso University in cooperation with Synod's Board for Young People's Work, the Walther League, and the Lutheran Laymen's League (Schroeder, 1974, p. 35). This program was designed to focus on the youth ministry needs of the congregation, a cutting edge idea that would serve to change the face of DCE Ministry. Since Valparaiso University was not an official training institution of the Synod, having their graduates serving congregations in the LC–MS was revolutionary. With the onset of this program, more and more congregations saw the need for adding staff that might not be directly associated with the day school and might not be trained as classroom teachers.

In 1959 the LC–MS in convention, passed a resolution to include Directors of Christian Education on the Roster of Synod declaring these individuals as commissioned ministers under the heading of "teacher." The convention resolved that "the directors of music and education who are graduates of any one of our recognized teachers colleges, or have passed colloquy (a post baccalaureate certification process), and are eligible for a call (vocational work) in any one of our schools, be considered teachers with all the rights and privileges pertaining to this office" (*Proceedings*, 1959, p. 309-310). This formalized the position of DCE among the churches in the LC–MS and was a starting point for legitimizing the profession. This action led to the placement of students into parishes with the title of DCE starting in 1960 (Schroeder, 1974; Griffin, 1995). It was not until the 1962 convention that the Synod passed a resolution to establish specific training programs for DCEs at two of the synodical colleges; River Forest, Illinois, and Seward, Nebraska (*Proceedings*, 1962). Of note here was the fact that these training programs would operate within the framework of the existing teacher training programs for parochial schools thus requiring DCEs to be certified both as school educators and as parish educators. Evidence of these early roots of a dual certification requirement still existed at the time of this writing insofar as there are DCEs listed on the church roster with dual certification (*Lutheran Annual*, 2009). Several of the Concordias that certify DCEs continue to give students a dual certification option for their undergraduate degree (e.g. Concordia University, Nebraska and Concordia University Chicago).

In 1969 the Board for Higher Education (BHE) of the LC–MS commissioned Concordia College in St. Paul, Minnesota, with developing a training program that did not require students to obtain a teaching certificate. This, in turn, broadened the scope of the curriculum and changed what had been the norm of structuring the preparation of DCEs (Schroeder, 1974; Griffin, 1995; Keyne, 1995). Schroeder (1974) indicated that the three schools "programs differ significantly" (p. 38) with those in Seward and River Forest sticking with a core of traditional teacher education and the program in St. Paul taking on a broader focus in the area of parish education. This decision precipitated something of a crisis for DCE ministry since roster status was attached to teacher certification—DCE graduates of the program in St. Paul were not on the Synod's roster. At the 1983 convention fourteen years later, the Synod passed a resolution allowing DCEs to be rostered without completing a teaching certificate. "With this resolution, the office of DCE attained full maturity as an officially recognized ministry of the Synod in its own right and was to be included on the official roster" (Griffin, 1995, p. 145).

Over the ensuing years, three additional higher education institutions of the LC–MS have been approved to prepare DCEs for ministry: Concordia University in Portland, Oregon, and Concordia University in Irvine, California, joined in 1977 and most recently Concordia University in Austin, Texas, in 1999 (Schoepp, 2003). Each of the six institutions has brought to the profession a unique set of gifts and opportunities in the preparation of DCEs.

Additionally DCE ministry made its way north into Canada. The first DCE (a teacher who was later field certified as a DCE) was called into Canada in 1973 (Lobitz, personal communication, Feb. 11, 2009). When in 1988 the three Canadian Districts of the LC–MS became an autonomous church body, the Lutheran Church–Canada (Lutheran Church–Canada, 1988), there soon followed a decision at the second LCC convention to establish a church work position in addition to those of pastor and teacher (Lutheran Church–Canada, 1990). The position which grew out of this resolution became known as DPS (Director of Parish Services). The program is housed at Concordia University College of Alberta in Edmonton and teaches students to be lifespan teachers of the faith with a curriculum that parallels DCE preparation in the LC–MS. LCC and LC–MS have a memorandum of agreement recognizing each other's church work certifications and providing for movement of workers between both church bodies (Lutheran Church–Canada, 1987).

OTHER HISTORICAL DCE DEVELOPMENTS

As DCE ministry has developed informally over the past century and formally over the past 50 years it is noteworthy to consider other factors that have been at work in the growth of the profession.

Over time there have been a number of historical markers regarding the definition of DCE ministry. After initially establishing the DCE profession at the 1959 convention, the synod's next major definition of DCE ministry appeared in 1981:

> A Director of Christian Education is a professionally trained educator called by congregation to plan, organize, coordinate, administer, and promote the congregation's ministry of Christian education. As a member of the congregation's team of called ministers, the director works in close cooperation with the pastor particularly in the congregation's educational ministry. The work of the director of Christian education is in the ministry of God's people to build one another in the Christian faith and life (Griffin, 1981, p. 2).

Then, in 1999 a more concise definition was developed at the annual DCE Summit:

> A Director of Christian Education is a synodically certified, called and commissioned lifespan educational leader prepared for team ministry in a congregational setting (DCE Summit Minutes, 1999).

A cursory review of the history of DCE ministry and these two milestone definitions highlight the importance of:

- the training and certification of DCEs;
- the roster status for DCEs;
- the DCE function as a lifespan teacher of the faith;
- the reality of team ministry for DCEs;
- the local congregation as the target for most DCE ministry.

DCEs have always been collaborative in nature and have joined together with others who share similar ministry responsibilities. There have been various professional organizations, such as Pastors and Education Directors Association

(PEDA) established in the 1950s in the Midwest. In 1967 this organization merged with Lutheran Education Association (LEA) to form Department of Pastors and DCEs (DPDCE). In 1973 the name changed to Theological Educators in Associated Ministries (TEAM). In 2001 LEA restructured itself into a series of networks and TEAM became Lutheran Education Association-DCE Network (LEA-DCEnet). In 2009, in conjunction with the 50th anniversary of DCE ministry, another variation of the DCE professional organization was unveiled—the National Association of Directors of Christian Education (NADCE).

In terms of professional meetings of DCEs there have been National DCE Conferences held every three years since 1988. Further, an annual DCE Summit has brought together DCE leadership from congregations, the synod, and the Concordia University System DCE program directors since 1990. The Karpenko Institute for Nurturing and Developing Leadership Excellence (KINDLE) has also been a significant development in the history of DCE ministry. Pioneered in 1999, KINDLE it has been providing opportunities since 2002 for experienced field DCEs to gather for a year of extensive training and accountability "to enhance the church by fostering and multiplying servant leaders" (http://kindledce.org/). There have also been various informal DCE clusters in some LC–MS districts that have provided regular opportunities for face-to-face encouragement and equipping. All of these organizations and professional conferences have continuously operated in one way or another with the intent of supporting, providing resources and setting direction for DCEs. (Schoepp & Warren, personal communication, February, 2009). Throughout their history DCEs have learned to connect through conversation in various formal and informal ways.

Print resources related to DCE ministry have developed over time too. In 1965 the LC–MS Board for Parish Services established the *DCE Bulletin*. It ceased publication in 1990 and was replaced by TEAM with *DCE Directions* until approximately 2002 after which LEA established *Network DCE* and took up the task of providing print resources and written communication for DCEs.

Since 2007 *Christian Education Leadership* has been published as a quarterly electronic newsletter. This has been a cooperative effort of LEA-DCEnet, the DCE program directors, and KINDLE (Schoepp & Warren, personal communication, February, 2009). The *Ethical Guidelines for Directors of Christian Education* published in 2002 by the Lutheran Education Association has provided another significant benchmark resource for the development of DCE ministry. These guidelines clearly articulate the values of DCE ministry and the principles of sound doctrine, a life above reproach, and competency in practice.

The LC–MS has certified 1,756 directors of Christian education for the church since the inception of this particular office. Of that number, 630 are currently serving in DCE ministry in a congregational context. That number is significant because, in a synod of just over 6,000 churches, it can be stated that DCE ministry is currently making an impact on 10% of the church body in practicing quality Christian education and in equipping others to effectively share the Gospel.

So now you know a little bit more of the DCE family history. It's an exceedingly large family that has been on a long and eventful journey to this point. Our family journey promises to continue offering opportunity and challenge as we engage in the task of teaching the faith across the lifespan.

CHAPTER 6

Invited to the Big Dance

A Relational View

Tim Rippstein

Then God said, "Let us make man in our image, after our likeness. And let them have dominion over the fish of the sea and over the birds of the heavens and over the livestock and over all the earth and over every creeping thing that creeps on the earth. So God created man in his own image, in the image of God he created him; male and female he created them" (Gen. 1:26-27).

Relationships and the desire to be relational are divinely designed into our spiritual DNA. God, as Trinity, is relational. In the two verses above, throughout the whole creation account, and throughout the Bible, are glimpses of God-the-relational in action. God the Spirit is "hovering over the face of the waters" (Gen. 1:2). God the Father is speaking by way of God the Word, into existence, all that is created. The infinite truth of the Trinity and their interaction is not entirely clear to human, finite understanding, but throughout history, people have

Tim Rippstein, M.A., from Concordia Seminary in St. Louis, serves as Intern Site Coordinator and is on the DCE Faculty at Concordia University, Nebraska.

tried to better understand this phenomenon. One of my favorite illustrations to appreciate the Trinitarian relationship is a divine dance. Imagine (after all your imagination is also created by God!) three persons moving, flowing, exchanging leads, so very gracefully, never missing a beat, never stepping on toes, all together in one powerful dance. This is how some of our earlier church fathers, such as John Damascene (7th century) attempted to understand the unity of The Three Persons, as *perichoresis*.[26] Another exciting aspect of this perichoresis is that God has invited us to join this divine dance. To be made in His image, among other things, means to be relational, to dance divinely!

We see this spiritual DNA to be relational people at work throughout the Bible. One can scarcely read a chapter without running into relational language. "I will take you to be my people, and I will be your God, and you shall know that I am the Lord your God, who has brought you out from under the burdens of the Egyptians" (Ex. 6:7). "And because you are sons, God has sent the Spirit of his Son into our hearts, crying, "Abba! Father!" (Gal. 4:6).

"Now Adam knew Eve his wife, and she conceived and bore Cain, saying, "I have gotten a man with the help of the Lord" (Gen. 4:1). Here in the introduction of humanity, we see a most intimate relationship, sexual union between a husband and a wife. This intimate, relational act is described as 'knowing' someone. We see this also in the New Testament for example when Joseph "knew her not" and did not have intercourse with Mary until after Jesus was born (Matt. 1:25).[27]

Another example of the very central role of relationships all through our lives and the core of our being is the prophet Hosea and his "wife of whoredom," Gomer, which is a very real and very personal illustration of the relationship between God and His people which has been broken.

---

[26] Greek *peri* = around; *choresis* = dance. "*Perichoresis*, wrote Karl Barth, 'asserts that that the divine modes of existence condition and permeate one another mutually with such perfection, that one is as invariably in the other two as the other two are in the one.'" Karl Barth as quoted in Peterson (2005), p. 44.

[27] The Greek word used is *ginôskô* = know. It is the word of choice in the Greek Old Testament (LXX) and the New Testament for this relational and experiential knowledge.

These relational themes are all over our Scriptures describing and portray-ing life in all its trials, struggles, beauty, joy, pain, confusion and clarity, as hu-mans fallen from the image of God. Can we use our experiences in relationships to better understand and appreciate our relationship with Jesus Christ? Can we also use our relational experiences with parents, siblings, best friends, significant others, spouses, children, etc. to nurture our relationship to the Lord and to cul-tivate a maturing, healthy spiritual life in Him? Yes we can! In fact it is expected that we will learn from and mature in the Lord as a result of our human relation-ships. Jesus expects us to draw from them to better 'know' him.

My own relationships have, and continue to serve, as a never ending source of understanding and appreciation of the Lord and His work. I hope to draw upon some of these with you, not because my relationships are better, but be-cause I know them and their accompanying lessons best.

We will rely on this relational aspect designed into our spiritual genetics, using our experiences in relationships to explore how we as people who seek to serve as called church workers can cultivate a healthy, maturing spiritual life.

Drawing Near

And I, when I am lifted up from the earth, will draw all people to myself (Jn. 12:32).

Therefore, brothers, since we have confidence to enter the holy places by the blood of Jesus, by the new and living way that he opened for us through the curtain, that is, through his flesh, and since we have a great priest over the house of God, let us draw near with a true heart in full assurance of faith, with our hearts sprinkled clean from an evil conscience and our bodies washed with pure water (Heb. 10:19-22).

Submit yourselves therefore to God. Resist the devil, and he will flee from you. Draw near to God, and he will draw near to you. Cleanse your hands, you sinners, and purify your hearts, you double-minded (Ja. 4:7-8).

God our Father, desiring to be in communion with His own, invites us all into this union of divine dance, to be related to Him. He has, and continues to invite all people through His Son. This invitation is described as a dynamic movement, a drawing near to Him. The word used in these three grounding texts is 'draw.' It carries with it the understanding that there is continuous movement in His direction and with Him. Once a person has been invited and brought into this loving relationship, there continues to be a drawing near, a dynamic, maturing relationship.

When we identified our current house, after walking through numerous homes for sale, there was tremendous excitement. We had been searching and each house had its drawbacks until entering *the one*. Upon entering it, we knew it was special; it met our needs *and* our wants. Even before entering the front door we saw a yard to play in, trees to climb, and a porch where we could enjoy conversations on cool summer evenings. Once we were inside, the excitement grew as kids ran from room to room anticipating where furniture would go and which room might be theirs. As we searched around more, we discovered closets, storage cabinets, a back porch, a shed, and more and more neat things that made this house special. Outside were varieties of trees, bushes, flowers blooming, each uniquely giving color and fragrance at different times of the season. It took us a whole year just to learn about each plant, its blossoms, its hue and fragrance. We've been in the house many years now. We know the floor plan well, have had to clean windows, do some painting and some repair work, but we are still discovering nuances of our house appreciating its uniqueness. We are thankful for its basic protection from the outside elements, but also enjoying it as our home where we *do* family, enjoy company, eat, rest, laugh, cry, hug, yell, care for each other, forgive one another, and where life happens.

In our baptism, or when we responded to our Lord's gracious invitation to be in union with Him, we entered His house. Upon the cross he drew us in. We are in His salvation. This is what we call justification, a one-time, awesome, mysterious event, entirely accomplished by Jesus' life and work. Now we get to explore! There is much about our home and living together to learn, to experience, to enjoy. This living in Christ we call sanctification. It is dynamic and on-going. It is participatory; we get to participate in the 'drawing near' by cultivating an attitude of exciting exploration even taking some risks in living by grace together. This living in sanctification also means some pain, some sorrow. We will say and do things which hurt others and disappoint our Father. Others will say and do things which will hurt and disappoint us. Sanctified living in Christ requires forgiving and healing.

There are many days and weeks when we have to do tedious, hum-drum maintenance work around our house. The lawn needs mowing again, weeds need pulling, windows need washing, carpets need vacuuming, and the toilet gets plunged. I hate cleaning the gutters and can find almost anything else to do instead.

This, too, is not so different from living in sanctification. There are hum-drum, tedious times and times when we can find almost anything else to do but… (pray, go to worship, read the Bible, talk to others about my faith, stay faithful to my vocation as a student and do my assigned reading, you finish the sentence). The point is that it is participatory, and there are plenty of days, weeks, and months when there is more tedium than excitement.

Life together in our home takes commitment to 'drawing' together. We have to commit to eating together regularly, to listening to one another, to playing together. Life in salvation also requires commitment to 'drawing nearer.' It takes time and commitment without which any relationship will suffer. Two foundational practices that have helped God's people 'draw near' for over twenty centuries are prayer and study.[28] There is enough territory to explore for a lifetime, and growing anticipation in using these gifts to nurture and cultivate a healthy relationship in Christ. We'll briefly investigate them here, but we certainly won't exhaust their cavernous depths.

---

[28] These are two foundational practices among many such as regular worship, participation in the Lord's Supper, confession and absolution, tithing, acts of service, etc. We will focus on prayer and studying because we don't have space to focus on all of them adequately and because these two seem to be particularly challenging for called church workers to mature in and also model and teach.

What Were They Doing?

And they devoted themselves to the apostles' teaching and fellowship, to the breaking of bread and the prayers (Acts 2:42).

But we will devote ourselves to prayer and to the ministry of the word (Acts 6:4).

My wife and I are celebrating 25 years of marriage. Add to that four years of friendship and courtship, and we've got 29 years under our belts. We have spent many moments talking to each other, articulating needs, wants, hopes, dreams, and fears. There have also been times of listening, seeking to understand, to console, to appreciate the other. In the early years, much time and energy was devoted to learning about each other– favorite colors, favorite flavors of ice cream, music preferences, and preferred ethnic foods. In time, we spent more energy planning for a future together, making decisions about finances, purchasing furniture, squeezing in time together in the midst of work and preparing for the demands of starting a home. Then came children and the conversations turned more towards child-rearing issues: disciplining practices, teaching them and encouraging them, dreaming what they might be like as teenagers and adults. We have evolved and matured through the seasons of these 29 years, as any long-term relationship will. It has not been without mistakes–things said in anger and from fatigue, misunderstandings and miscommunications, decisions made and the nagging doubts from second guessing choices made. But the Lord has been gracious and steadfastly present all along the way honoring His commitment to us.

So much about our relationship with the Lord, living in salvation, drawing near can be learned and appreciated from relationships with others. Two times in Acts we read summative verses describing the disciples and the infant church in relation to the Lord and to one another (Acts 2:42, 6:4). In both of these texts, prayer is foundational. The disciples, who knew Jesus face-to-face, and the growing community of believers understood the central value of prayer in their maturing relationship to the ascended Jesus. The disciples were also teaching their flocks to pray. While the desire to be in relationship is innate, prayer is not. The disciples had to be taught, "Lord, teach us to pray," they implored (Lk. 11:1). And, as disciples, they had to teach others. To be sure these Jewish men had prayed before, they knew the Psalms and the stories of Abraham and Moses. Yet, Jesus prayed as one in a relationship with the Father, it was noticeably different. Emily Herman's description of prayer gets right to the core, "To know what prayer really is, we must study it from the centre…. Prayer in its essence is communion with God" (Herman, 1921, p. 24). Drawing near to God will impact prayer, yet prayer will impact one's drawing near to God.

There is much to learn about prayer, and it must be taught. Prayer is experiential in nature. One can read all about the theology of prayer, doctrines on prayer, how-to books about praying, but to 'draw near' one must be praying. One would think I was foolish if all I ever did was read about marriage, devoured books about how to communicate with a wife, learned the theories of communication yet did not actually talk with my wife or often spend time with her (Although she probably wishes I'd read those books!). An interesting development has been happening as the years of marriage add up; my quality of listening can decrease and become more of an effort. It seems after so many years it is possible to assume I have heard it all, can simply catch a few words, access memory files, and draw conclusions or simply put listening on sleep mode. To keep my self-serving, human nature interested requires new and novel information. But the routine seems… well… hum-drum. It takes more concentration, more energy to really hear with my heart and mind after the years. This is a reflection on my lazy, sinful nature, not my wife's. There is still much to explore and enjoy in this relationship after 29 years! Time and effort are required. What is needed is what Dr. Eugene Peterson calls "unhurried leisure." "[Listening] requires unhurried leisure…. Leisure is a quality of spirit, not quantity of time" (Peterson, 1989, p. 21). Can this "unhurried leisure," this "quality of spirit" be brought into our prayer life? I think so. We still cry, "Lord, teach us to pray!" Let's explore ways many people over the centuries have matured in prayer, and have learned the art of listening to the Lord. One must first practice 'quieting down.' When I get home from work my wife has graciously learned to give me 10-15 minutes of unwinding time before telling me the garage door isn't working again, or the freezer has stopped running. This transition time from one frame of mind – work, to another – home, is vital to how I am able to cope with new climates of issues and information. Quieting down before the Lord, centering on Him is also helpful in developing prayer. A suggested practice is to use an ancient and simple prayer dating back to about the 4th century, called The Jesus Prayer. It can be said rhythmically with breathing to relax your body and focus the mind. Sit comfortably with back supported and your feet on the ground, and close your eyes. Notice your breathing. Take a few long, slow breaths. Then as you inhale pray, "Lord, Jesus Christ," exhale "Son of the Living God," inhale "have mercy on me," exhale "a sinful being." Do this prayerful, rhythmic breathing for five minutes or until you notice you are no longer distracted by outside thoughts of whom you should talk to, what you forgot to do, what's on TV tonight, or your next homework assignment. When you find your mind wandering to the myriad activities simply focus on breathing this simple prayer to center your mind on the Lord.[29] After regular practice you will find it easier to relax and focus in this way. What a wonderful way to begin to pray and to study.[30]

Meditation and prayer have been a part of the lives of God's people ever since King David. I like the way Gordon MacDonald describes it, "The act of meditation is like tuning the spirit to heavenly frequencies" (MacDonald, 2003, p. 168). It is extended and focused attention. David said in the inaugural Psalm to the Judeo-Christian prayer book, "Blessed is the man... his delight is in the law [or instruction] of the LORD, and on his law [or instruction] he meditates day and night" (Ps. 1:1-2). The English word 'meditate' appears 23 times in our ESV Bibles, nineteen of these times in the Psalms. Over 80% of its usage appears in our God-given prayer book! Meditation is a very useful practice in prayer.

---

[29] It may be helpful to keep a pen and note pad nearby to record those things you need to attend to after. They can have a way of nagging at you while praying and in this way you can jot them down and let them go from you mind.

[30] This centering prayer can also be useful in other ways as well, such as prior to worship or even as an opening devotional practice before class.

Martin Luther knew this. He practiced and taught meditation as a valuable component to prayer. In 1535, his friend and barber, Peter Beskendorf, asked Dr. Luther to teach him how to pray. His response is available in a small booklet titled *How One Should Pray, for Master Peter the Barber* (Wolfmueller, 2006). In the introduction, Pastor Wolfmueller writes, "For Luther, prayer is bound to meditation on the Lord's Word. Studying and meditating on the Scriptures turns into prayer, and prayer likewise leads us back to the Scriptures where [the] Lord refreshes us with His gifts of life, salvation, and the forgiveness of all our sins" (p. 2). There are various meditation exercises to help develop this part of one's prayer life. We will look at one below.

Let it be clearly stated that the focus of meditation is the Lord. The Christian who wants to continue to 'draw near' in a relationship with God will stay focused on Christ. It is not a way to find truth by seeking inside one's self or looking inward for answers. While we are enjoying life in salvation, we are still sinful humans and that is what we can expect to see when we focus on self. To recap, in developing prayer, two useful practices are centering and meditation, as it was with Luther and God's people for 20 centuries.

Using the Mind to Study

And one of the scribes came up and heard them disputing with one another, and seeing that he answered them well, asked him, "Which commandment is the most important of all?" Jesus answered, "The most important is, 'Hear, O Israel: The Lord our God, the Lord is one. And you shall love the Lord your God with all your heart and with all your soul and with all your mind and with all your strength'" (Mk. 12:28-30).

Finally, brothers, whatever is true, whatever is honorable, whatever is just, whatever is pure, whatever is lovely, whatever is commendable, if there is any excellence, if there is anything worthy of praise, think about these things (Phil. 4:8).

The brothers immediately sent Paul and Silas away by night to Berea, and when they arrived they went into the Jewish synagogue. Now these Jews were more noble than those in Thessalonica; they received the word with all eagerness, examining the Scriptures daily to see if these things were so (Acts 17:10-11).

Studying the Word of God is the second foundational practice in the cultivation of a healthy spiritual life. The mind is an amazing gift-- most of which has yet to be understood. Yet its role in our drawing near has been identified in every generation. It has also been adversely impacted by sin and requires sustained effort and discipline to nurture and cultivate. "The mind must be *trained* to think, to analyze, and to innovate" (MacDonald, 2003, p. 108). MacDonald's observation of Christians who have not attended to this discipline is also true, "Some Christians appear to be afraid to think. They mistake the gathering of facts, doctrinal systems, and lists of rules for thinking. They are uneasy when dealing with ambiguity" (MacDonald, 2003, p. 114).

Studying the Scriptures is vital in the discipline of training the mind. Jesus recognized the value of using the mind to love God; the Bereans demonstrated the use of thinking and studying in their practice of "examining the Scriptures daily" (Acts 17:11). We, too, develop and discipline our minds, which are ours in Christ Jesus, by studying regularly the Scriptures.

One of the stimulating joys of spending over half my life with Kathy is the many scintillating conversations on a vast array of topics. She is a faithful thinker and often our conversations have stimulated new ideas, corrected immature or goofy ones, and best of all, revealed more about her and contributed to a very significant relationship. This, too, has been a lesson in appreciating a relationship with God.

It must be pointed out that studying the Bible is different from the devotional reading of Scripture. Both have value and encourage the 'drawing near.' Devotional reading is reading and listening to the message 'for me.' It allows the Spirit to nurture, to encourage, to convict if needed, so confession can happen. It is placing oneself before the Lord in a personal, listening posture. Devotional reading may lead to studying and often will. But for the most part, it will not engage the tools of study beyond reading the English Bible.[31]

Studying is more analytical in approach. It is developing and using one's rational skills to understand God revealed in The Word both incarnate and written. Developing these study skills uses exegetical tools and hermeneutical methodologies.

Even studying can be viewed in two ways according to its purpose. One can study *for others* in preparation to teach or proclaim. Here the focus is on how the truths can be useful for another person: a Senior High youth night, a confirmation class, an adult Bible class or a sermon. One can also *study for one's self.* Here the focus is on one's own nurturing and development. Both are vital to anyone wishing to serve effectively as a called church worker. One must not be sacrificed for the other or considered as a substitute for the other. To do so is to stymie either one's own spiritual nurturing or sacrifice the nurturing of those one is called to serve.

This studying, both *for me* and *for others* as well as devotional reading all serve to fill one's spiritual reservoir of knowledge (*ginôskô*) of God. Once this is in the reservoir, it can be accessed for a variety of purposes. And the Holy Spirit is master at helping His own people remember and understand God and the exciting relationship He has established. "But the Helper, the Holy Spirit, whom the Father will send in my name, he will teach you all things and bring to your remembrance all that I have said to you" (Jn. 14:26). However, it seems the flipside may also be true. Normally, if the studying has not been happening, and the reservoir is shallow, there is not much from which to draw for the Holy Spirit to bring to remembrance. In other words, He seems limited to drawing out only that which has been put in.

"No vital Christianity is possible unless at least three aspects of it are developed," wrote Elton Trueblood. "These three are the inner life of devotion, the

---

[31] This distinction and the one made later in studying is largely due the fact that those called to work with the Bible can easily fall into the temptation to combine devotional reading and studying when preparing for a Bible study, Sunday school lesson, sermon, etc. The distinctions help to identify this temptation and try to keep the various kinds of Bible reading and studying separate.

outer life of service, and the *intellectual life of rationality* [italics added]" (Mac-Donald, 2003, p. 109). The incorporation of these two foundational practices, prayer and study, in our 'drawing near' allows room for imagination and exploration. In his preface to the Large Catechism, Luther shares his regular practice of reading, conversation, and meditation. "As for me.... Every morning, and whenever else I have time, I read and recite word for word the Lord's Prayer, the Ten Commandments, the Creed, the Psalms, etc.... In such reading, conversation, and meditation the Holy Spirit is present and bestows ever new and greater light and fervor, so that day by day we relish and appreciate the Catechism more greatly" (Luther, 1959, p. 359). In the letter to his barber, Luther recommends reading, reciting, and praying.

Another practice common to the Christian church and currently enjoying a renaissance is *lectio divina*. *Lectio divina* combines our two foundational practices of prayer and the Word (more the devotional reading style) along with meditation on The Word. A Google search will land you about 1.5 million sites. Many of these sites have 'how-to' information. Essentially *lectio divina* has four parts or movements. First is *lectio* (reading). Identify a section of Scripture upon which to pray and meditate. One source might be to use one of the selected lectionary readings for the upcoming Sunday worship. Read it, preferably out loud, to yourself about three times, slowly. Next is *meditatio* (meditation). Here you silently allow the words of Scripture to ruminate in your heart and mind. Notice if a word or phrase catches your imagination or attracts your thoughts. Any images forming in your mind's eye? What may the Spirit be about in these? Allow about five minutes for this. If nothing comes to mind, no worries, move on to *oratio*. This is oration or conversation. As the reading and meditation guides your heart, mind and imagination, offer these in prayer. Any feelings surfacing? Bring these before the Lord as well. It is a time to respond to God in conversation. Allow at least five minutes here as well. Lastly is *contemplatio* (contemplation). This is simply enjoying the presence of the Lord. No words required, no expectations of visions, simply resting in the presence of The One who loves you without condition and more deeply than any person could. Allow five minutes here. This practice of *lectio divina* may take about 20 minutes or longer. In the beginning you may follow it as step 1-2-3-4. In time you may experiment allowing more flexibility and fluidity as the Spirit guides you. It is best if you do not digest too much text at a time. A whole chapter is a bit much. A few verses or even just one verse is enough. Many of the Psalms (ex. 1, 8, 23, 32, 100, 150) or portions of them are ideal for this. Philippians Chapter 2 is another favorite. Experiment with *lectio divina*, and enjoy this time of 'drawing near' through this ancient practice.

We have learned that at least three factors facilitate longevity in 29 years of relating together: discipline, routine, and rhythm. It takes commitment to not only stay together, but also to grow together. Commitment requires discipline. It certainly requires making the interests and needs of another a high priority and at times sacrificing one's own desires and needs. It is funny to watch people when the phone rings (or vibrates!). People will drop anything they are doing to answer the phone, even when it's obvious the caller can leave a message. This observation became an intrusion in our house at dinner time at least three times a week, and we would leave the dinner table, drop our conversation to answer the phone. We decided to discipline ourselves to not answer the intrusion and let them leave a message. We were amazed how challenging this was at first, even when we all knew most of the calls were from sales people who would call back. Discipline is required.

Routine has also been a positive factor over the years. There have been relatively few mountain top or Death Valley instances. Most of those years have been pretty routine: the daily brushing of teeth and the showering, fixing lunch and changing cat litter, dusting the shelves only to have to do it again next week (or next year! ;-). One routine I have enjoyed is eating lunch with Kathy. These are usually more mundane meals of leftovers and conversations about the morning's events or kids' activities. Over the years this routine has afforded the nurturing of two individuals, with unique sinful wills, into a union and relationship of 'knowing' one another. Routine forges strength in relationships over the long term.

Thirdly is the factor of rhythm. Closely related to routine are the drumbeats in life, the things which keep the beat of living moving regularly. Very early in my ministry career, Mondays were established as a day off, enjoying a more relaxed morning, attending to some 'honey-dos,' reading, enjoying the entitlements of 'day off.' Yet, Kathy still had to clean, do laundry, fix dinner, etc. So we decided to go out for dinner on Mondays to give her a break, too. As the kids grew, we alternated who got to select which fast food joint we'd go to each week. It has been 20 years now, and in hindsight this practice has been part of our family rhythm. We also have liturgical rhythms to add a beat of stability to lives which would otherwise be marching to other less spiritual drummers. We have such liturgical weekly beats as worship and Sunday school, seasonal beats such as Lent and Advent, and annual beats like Easter and Christmas worship services.

Discipline, routine, and rhythm, while challenging to establish and maintain, have served our relationship well over the years. They certainly also facilitate the maturing relationship in Christ.

A WORD ABOUT BUSYNESS

This kind of 'drawing near' takes time and patience. It requires learning to live in grace. "The person… who looks for quick results in the seed planting of well-doing will be disappointed. If I want potatoes for dinner tomorrow, it will do me little good to go out and plant potatoes in my garden tonight. There are long stretches of darkness and invisibility and silence that separate planting and reaping. During the stretches of waiting there is cultivating and weeding and nurturing and planting still other seeds" (Peterson, 1989, p. 3).

Quite possibly the most subtle and subversive intruder into any maturing relationship is busyness. It is a continual temptation for students and professionals alike to give in to the busyness syndrome. People like to appear important and somehow busyness has become the criteria for importance. The more committees one is on, the more hours one works, the more things and people who need one, the more important one appears to be. Peterson believes the church worker is busy for two reasons: vanity and laziness. "I am busy because I am vain. I want to appear important" (1989, p. 18). This is the reason alluded to above.

He also says, "I am busy because I am lazy. I indolently let others decide what I will do instead of resolutely deciding myself" (1989, p. 18). Lazy, busy people allow others to fill their time running roughshod over prime time for prayer and study. The answer: take control; prioritize your schedule according to the values important to you and your vocation. Might it be suggested you put these values and the things which support and cultivate them into your daily planner. Then when someone asks you if you can do something or go somewhere, you can plan around what is most important to you or you legitimately respond, "I'm busy then" or "I've got something scheduled already."

SUMMARY

God the Trinity is relational. Cultivating a healthy spiritual life with Him, over the long haul, will require relationship skills. These skills can be observed in our human relationships with family members and friends. All of us have had both poor relationship modeling and positive modeling. Two foundational factors in nurturing and 'drawing near' as we live in salvation are prayer and study. Prayer facilitated and enhanced through centering to better focus and meditate on Christ and His work. Studying both *for me* and in preparation for others, as well as on devotional reading to develop thinking skills and nurture the mind is important. *Lectio divina* brings both meditative prayer and The Word together in an ancient practice. There is much to explore in this relationship and many joy-filled times to have together. Developing discipline, routine and rhythm will be invaluable over the long haul.

CHAPTER 7

DCE: Generalist or Specialist...Revisited

MARK BLANKE

I wrote an article entitled "DCE: Generalist or Specialist?" for the March/ April 1995 edition of *Lutheran Education (LE)*. The premise presented in that article was that the DCE was both generalist and specialist: a "specialist" in that the focus of DCE ministry is specifically in the area of religious education and a "generalist" because we must make use of a variety of skills, some seemingly unrelated to education and some requiring a level of expertise, in carrying out Christian education in the church. So, the DCE who carries out religious education specifically aimed in youth ministry may find herself counseling a teen experiencing the death of a friend, managing a budget, coordinating a sporting event, writing a worship experience for use on a retreat, and publishing a monthly newsletter. This variety of responsibilities is one of the joys of DCE ministry, but perhaps it also poses a threat.

After writing the *LE* article I received more angry mail than for anything else I have ever written. The main theme in these letters was that I was being too narrow in my understanding of DCE ministry. Writers felt that DCE was

Mark Blanke, Ed.D., serves as DCE Program Director at Concordia University, Nebraska.

This chapter is based upon an article by Mark Blanke that appeared in the March/ April 1995 issue of Lutheran Education.

their title, but it was their job to do whatever the church wanted them to do and that they may be a "DCE who doesn't do education." One writer indicated that I was diminishing his role in music ministry by saying that the 1.5% of the DCE population (in a 1990 study) who didn't participate in parish education are "either not operating within a parish or they are not DCEs, despite the certification they hold" (Blanke, 1995, p. 197). He felt he was merely operating in the tradition DCEs have been known for – the malleable generalist able and willing to help the church wherever needed.

Today I believe even more strongly that the DCE is a religious education specialist first and foremost. Unfortunately, I have yet to see the clear emergence of the DCE as a religious education specialist in the Lutheran Church–Missouri Synod (LC–MS). I have not seen the DCE profession step forward to "claim" the responsibility of being *teachers* of the faith. I have seen the quality (and quantity) of religious education falter in our church body. I have seen the increase in the number of DCEs serving in our congregations and yet have not seen a renaissance in Christian education in the church. I have not seen the importance of religious education elevated as a priority in the church as a whole. Major educational ministries of our church—confirmation, Sunday school, Midweek, youth ministry, VBS, adult education—still have significant foundational problems that aren't being addressed by DCEs in a way that enhances these ministries in the church as a whole. Many DCEs continue to deliver a "programming" model that we know doesn't adequately equip disciples. We haven't emerged as advocates for education in our church at a level of real influence. While it may sound harsh, from what I have seen I can come only to the conclusions that DCEs either do not own the understanding of themselves as educational specialist, do not have an adequate power base to influence change, or do not have the necessary operational expertise and dedication to effectively carry out transformational educational ministry.

Educational ministry in the church isn't an option. Focusing resources to prepare disciples through education isn't adiaphora. When Jesus outlined the Great Commission to his disciples, he told them to make more disciples by baptizing them and teaching them. We have a directive and it is clear, teach people to obey what God has commanded so that they are able to carry out His work on earth. Why DCEs have been unable to elevate the importance of this ministry in our 50 years of existence is a mystery – perhaps it is because we have strayed from the role that we were intended to fill when our synod established our profession – that of a congregational Christian education specialist.

In 1959, the LC–MS established the position of DCE. The resolution passed by convention reads as follows:

> Whereas, The development of an organized and systematic program of Christian education is a necessity in every congregation; and
>
> Whereas, Many congregations would benefit from the services of a director of Christian education who would assist the pastor in providing the professional leadership for the Sunday school, Saturday classes, and other educational activities of the congregation; therefore be it
>
> Resolved, That congregations be encouraged to analyze their parish education program and, where needed, to establish the office of "director of Christian education" in order to provide additional leadership for the educational program of the congregation (*Proceedings*, 1959, p. 224).

Another resolution was passed in 1962 which designated the two teacher training schools of the time (in Seward, Nebraska, and River Forest, Illinois) as the institutions responsible for the training of DCEs. The choice of these two schools was not an arbitrary decision. "The question of the 1920s had finally been decided. Those best suited for DCE ministry came from a teaching background, not the pastoral background. This decision grounded the director of Christian education in education theory rather than in theology, an important determinant in how the DCE's education would be constructed" (Keyne, 1995, p. 131).

It is obvious from reviewing these documents that the intent our synodical leaders had in developing the position of the DCE in our church body was to enhance the ministry of Christian education in our church. "So what?" some of you might say. "Things change." "I can do multiple roles and not diminish my effectiveness or the perception the church has of DCEs." "Shouldn't our call to be servants supersede our particular focus on a specialization?" First and foremost we must retain the clear understanding that the church must carry out Christian education. We are not just risking some affront to our profession, we risk diminishing the importance of our task. History also provides some clues as to how a disregard for our role as religious education specialist might also risk our profession.

In 1995, Lisa Keyne submitted her doctoral dissertation entitled *Who do you say that I am? The Professional Identity of the Director of Christian Education in the Lutheran Church–Missouri Synod.* In it, she identified six characteristics that needed to be present for an occupation to be considered professional. The characteristics were: a common theory base, a distinctive culture, a code of ethics, involvement of the professional school, clarity of function and mission, and power. Dr. Keyne concluded that DCEs did not have enough power to make decisions about their future and, therefore, could not be considered fully professional. I believe that, because so many of us see ourselves as generalists, we also fail to fulfill the characteristic of having clarity of function and mission. Too many of us fail to aim clearly at our role as Christian education specialists, and that hurts our profession.

In a review of the history of the Minister of Education (M.E.) in other denominations (it is interesting to note that Stubblefield says that jokes about the initials "M.E." often focus on the M.E. as "ministers of etcetera"), Stubblefield writes of a period of decline that took place for M.E.s starting during the Great Depression. Stubblefield calls this the period of "disillusionment and despair." This decline was partially due to a lack of a clear understanding of the work of religious education. Stubblefield states," [Church leaders] expected the director to be involved in areas of the church that did not relate to educational training or specialization" (p. 28). He goes on to state that "the educational minister has always struggled with being required or assigned duties other than education… once additional duties were added to the educational duties, it became almost impossible to escape from them…" (p. 29, 30).

In speaking of the perception of M.E.s today, Stubblefield states that, "Many M.E.s are seen by their pastors, the church and themselves in roles other than that of educator" (p. 166). Stubblefield attributes this misperception to the fact that M.E.s oversee work in areas other than education. Stubblefield stresses that we should heed a warning made years ago by W.L. Howse when he cautioned that, "care must be taken in enlarging the supervisory activities of the minister of education so as to not weaken his opportunities for maximum service in his major field" (Howse, p. 7). Emler states that the DCE is a professional who is "in a specialized ministry of the church. The specialized ministry is the field of religious education in which the framework is education rather than religion or theology" (1989, p. 83).

In essence, our synod has developed a system of rostered positions that is predicated on an assumption of specialization. The "alphabet soup" of those in public ministry in our church has grown dramatically in the past 50 years. DCEs, Directors of Christian Outreach (DCOs), Family Life Ministers (FLMs), Lay Ministers, Deaconesses, Lutheran Teachers (LTs), Parish Assistants, Parish Workers, Directors of Parish Music (DPMs), all are eligible for rostering within our church body. The intent behind the development of each of these positions was to fill a specific congregational need, to provide an individual with specialized preparation to carry out specific ministries.

What does a fractured commitment to the role of Christian education specialist look like? It is first and foremost found in a diminished commitment to the art and science of being an educator. As counter-intuitive as it may seem, the so called "soft science" of education may be a much more complicated endeavor to master than the "hard sciences" of physics, chemistry, and the like. Education attempts to manage a process that is as complicated, and unpredictable, as the people it seeks to serve. Researchers and academics spend careers trying to understand every bit of minutia of how to best manage the educational experience. This has been going on since before Socrates, and yet we remain but novices in our efforts to master the mysteries of how to educate. How to educate is indeed a daunting task, but add to that the primary responsibility of the DCE to use education to help make disciples – to help facilitate the process of sanctification that is Spirit-led, unable to be measured, and not truly completed until one receives his or her final reward – and one can truly see how challenging the role of the religious education specialist. DCEs who add responsibilities outside of their calling as religious education specialists risk diminishing the difficult task of doing education effectively. For example, if a DCE is asked to assist the pastor in leading the congregational worship experience, he should consider doing so provided he felt he had fully mastered the role of religious educator and could continue to effectively develop disciples while focusing on these other significant responsibilities.

Too many in our church (including DCEs) see education as an art, a gift that some have and some don't have. They fail to also see the science behind the educational role, a science that demands our undivided attention and dedication – no matter how gifted one is as an educator. Often times, while other educators focus professional conferences and in-service efforts on enhancing personal teaching skills, DCEs will often focus on a broad range of learnings more or less related to congregational ministry. At a recent professional DCE conference, only six of the sixteen sectionals focused in any substantive way on enhancing educational competencies.

Of much more importance than the risk that we take on our profession by ignoring our primary role as Christian education specialist is the risk that we take on the mission of the church by diminishing the church's effectiveness in the task of preparing disciples. We shouldn't fear the possibility of sinking our profession into a state of "disillusionment and despair," we should fear that our inaction may lead to a church body that is even less effective in fulfilling the Great Commission.

Chaucer wrote, "The life so short, the craft so long to learn." This reminds us that we all need to continually focus on improving how we ply our craft—our vocation. DCEs who are asked by their congregations to move to a more generalist role need to ask themselves, "Do I practice my craft (carrying out religious education in the parish) adequately enough to devote energies towards an additional ministry area?" The need in our church for competent Christian education specialists has never been greater – my prayer is that all DCEs are seeking to enhance their competencies first and foremost in this vital role – the generalist responsibilities are of a lesser concern.

CHAPTER 8

DCE MINISTRY AS A PROFESSION

Lisa K. Keyne

Welcome to DCE Ministry! You are entering a profession that has a rich history, yet is still young, and you will contribute greatly to its ongoing development.

"I realize that this work is more than a job or occupation. It requires that I have a passion for the work. I have to think deeply about what I am doing, and the best processes to accomplish the goals. I am working toward a long-term vision – when I go home at night, my work isn't done. This is very different than when I worked at the video store."

This newbie DCE's observations reflect an understanding that there is a difference between a job and a work that requires legitimization before you can practice. The work of Directors of Christian Education (DCE) in the Lutheran Church–Missouri Synod (LC–MS) exemplifies the process of a work that has become professionalized throughout the years. Just what makes any occupation a profession?

Lisa K. Keyne, Ph.D., is the former Director of the DCE program at Concordia University–Portland. She currently serves as Executive Director of North Carolina Campus Compact.

WHAT CONSTITUTES A PROFESSION?

A professional is not an amateur. She has gained the requisite knowledge – the principles and theories – deemed necessary to enter that field. This can result in "occupational closure," barring others from the work because they do not have the requisite training.

The traditional professions were medicine, law, and theology. If one had the appropriate credentials, that doctor, lawyer or theologian knew what was necessary to practice. Consumers could confidently visit the professional, knowing they would get the help they needed, and which they were unable to determine on their own. Professionals were held in high esteem, well-respected for their invaluable contributions to the community.

There is a movement required to "professionalize" an occupation. What motivates initiating that movement is important. Particularly in the church, we know professionalizing is not about greater compensation or recognition. If considered a profession, there is assurance *for those being served* that those practicing are trustworthy. Members of that profession hold each other accountable–to good practice, to ongoing development, and to building the profession. In general, the public can have greater confidence in those practicing, and practitioners are held to higher standards. Pursuing professionalization demonstrates a field is pushing for the highest standards possible.

The professionalizing process ensures development of:

1. **A clear function and mission.**
   Not only do practitioners know their work's purpose and fit within the broader world, but the general population also accepts that contribution.

2. **A theory base.**
   Those entering the field learn that theory base, knowing they cannot do the job without that education. Once equipped, the practitioner can confront new, unique situations, building on the theory learned, rather than proceeding with a trial and error approach.

3. **Schools that equip for the profession.**
   Those schools build the profession by recruiting and equipping new professionals, and by supporting members of the profession through ongoing

development opportunities and through participation in national meetings. Their professors contribute to expanding research and theory.

4. **Established certification criteria.**
   Established criteria may also be established for preparatory programs (i.e., business school accreditation). Certification and accreditation prove to the public that the individual or the program adheres to high quality standards based on the latest research and on professional practice. Periodic reviews for recertification or reaccreditation are intended to identify continuing development and growth, as well as the maintenance of entry level standards or qualifications.

5. **A distinctive culture.**
   Culture includes stories passed down that help newcomers catch the spirit of the work; heroes that were the pioneers who started or stretched the field; lingo used with the work; communication patterns; ceremonies and celebrations; and behavioral norms, beliefs, values, and ideologies that guide the work. Culture evolves, but the professionalizing process assures there are ways to capture and share it. Professional organizations and conferences contribute to both developing and sharing a unique culture.

6. **A code of ethics.**
   Created by that profession, a code of ethics describes the behaviors and relationships integral to the work, describing what is and what is not proper. It needs to be strong enough so that practitioners will not choose to violate the code, while also being flexible enough to be generalized to the variety of settings in which the profession functions. Consequences for violating the code must be enforced. Only those within a profession are expected to conform to its code.

7. **An ongoing process of evaluation.**
   Leaders within the profession commit to the process of professionalizing. They regularly assess the progress of the field on the various criteria associated with professionalizing, and identify goals that will help strengthen that field.

8. **A professional organization.**
   Organizing can ensure the creation and enforcement of a code of ethics, bringing together the field for professional development, integrating feedback from the field in future planning, and providing an opportunity to connect with those doing the same work.

9. **Power.**

A true profession believes it has the power necessary to influence the profession's future. The source of power is the profession's knowledge. The professional has achieved a monopoly over a certain area of service, thereby receiving the respect, trust, and dollars (in some cases) of those seeking the service he or she can provide. Hence, that professional has considerable power.

LC–MS Directors of Christian Education have been taking the steps to build their ministry occupation into a profession.

THE LC–MS DCE AS PROFESSIONAL

The first LC–MS church calling a worker DCE was St. Mark Lutheran Church in Sheboygan, Wisconsin. When the church was dedicated in 1891, the church had 300 children in the only English-speaking Sunday School in the area. Weekday Bible classes were added in 1916, the same year Teacher A.W. Kowert, a 1912 graduate of Concordia Teachers Seminary, Addison, Illinois (now Concordia University Chicago), came to St. Mark to serve as teacher, organist and choir director, using the title of "director of education and music."

Even though St. Mark hired a "DCE" in 1916, the LC–MS was not promoting this new position. The Reverend William H. Luke, hired in the mid-1920s to serve the Lutheran Church–Missouri Synod as Superintendent of Sunday Schools, encouraged the LC–MS Board for Parish Education to develop the occupation of Director of Christian Education in 1928. The February 18 minutes of the General School Board and Sunday School Board discussed the topic of "calling teachers or candidates as educational directors in congregations without schools."

> In view of the great amount of religious instruction actually expected from Sunday Schools and other agencies, in view also of the missionary opportunities in these agencies together with their reflex influence upon teachers, in view also of the present trends

in other church bodies to employ full-time men as directors of religious education, the question presents itself to us: Are we ready to encourage or approve such positions for experienced day school men who would act as missionaries for the Christian day school in congregations where no day school exists at the present time, giving their full attention to a) the training of Sunday School teachers; b) the improvement of every opportunity for indoctrination of children and adults; c) of holding up the ideal of the Christian day school and working towards its immediate establishment?

Review of additional letters and articles written by Luke in the following years emphasized that this DCE would complement the work of the pastor with an emphasis on educational ministries of the church which, at that time, included Sunday School, week day school, summer Bible school, Saturday school, confirmation, Walther League or young people's society, as well as men's and women's groups (Luke, 1932).

Unfortunately, Pastor Luke died of Hodgkin's Disease on October 11, 1932, at 36 years of age. With him, it appears much of the impetus for promoting a ministry focused on parish-based Christian Education disappeared.

It was not until the 1959 convention that the LC–MS formally resolved "that congregations be encouraged to analyze their parish education programs and, where needed, to establish the office of 'Director of Christian Education' in order to provide additional leadership for the educational program of the congregation" (*Proceedings*, p. 224). The first DCEs were teachers, or they had received training through Valparaiso University's Youth Leadership Training Program (YLTP) undergraduate curriculum. At the 1962 convention, Concordia Colleges (now universities) in River Forest, Illinois, and Seward, Nebraska, were "encouraged… to intensify the program for training Directors of Christian Education in their curricula, within the framework of their training teachers of Lutheran parish schools" (*Proceedings*, p. 84).

According to researcher Paul Ebensteiner (1977), "the office of Director of Christian Education gained credibility as a ministerial role within the LC–MS with its official implementation by the Synod and by the active involvement of Synodical schools and agencies in developing a support system" (p. 399). In the 1960s and 1970s, tasks outside of the parish for DCEs and other leaders included forming a mission statement, and designing initial DCE curriculum, as well as creating a professional niche within the LC–MS.

In 2009, the LC–MS celebrated 50 years of this ministry profession. The Reverend Dr. Gerald B. Kieschnick, president of the LC–MS, signed a proclamation that, prior to giving thanks for the ministry of DCEs, states that "Directors of Christian Education have been serving the church with vibrant energy and tireless dedication since the office was originally designed... and our Church remains as much in need of ongoing effort in the area of Christian education as it was 50 years ago..." (Kieschnick, 2009). This public acknowledgement is evidence that the DCE profession is well-established in the church.

Through the 50-year history of DCE ministry in the LC–MS, leaders in the field – early DCEs, their teammates, program directors, Synodical and district leaders, those elected to lead the networks, and parish-based DCEs – all contributed to the professionalization process. Table 6.1 provides a brief synopsis of some of the key indicators that LC–MS DCEs have grown in professionalizing their ministry position.

TABLE 6.1

Indicators of DCE Professionalization

Profession Characteristic	Evident for LCMS DCEs?	Description
A clear function and mission	Since Luke's call for "missionaries for the Christian day school," there have been several official definitions. Most widely and recently accepted was adopted in 1999 after a definition-building process with leaders in the field.	**Definition:** A director of Christian education is a synodically certified, called and commissioned lifespan educational leader prepared for team ministry in a congregational setting. **Mission:** Empowered by the Holy Spirit, the DCE plans, administers and assesses ministry that nurtures and equips the Body of Christ for spiritual maturity, service and witness in home, job, congregation, community, and the world.
Theory base	Established preparatory programs differ, but all point toward a similar, common theory base	Theory derived from theology, Christian education, educational psychology, and lifespan development; some original research building understanding of LCMS DCE practice. A yearlong, parish-based internship overseen by a pastor and mentor DCE ensure that new graduates make the bridge from theory to practice.
Preparatory schools	Six programs established and officially designated to equip DCEs	Concordia Universities in Austin, Irvine, Portland, River Forest , St. Paul, and Seward. Colloquy and post-baccalaureate programs provide means for second career folks to pursue DCE ministry.
Certification or accreditation process	Certification process for DCEs; no DCE program accreditation process	Since 1983, DCEs have received certification from the LCMS that they have met established requirements to be a DCE. The six DCE baccalaureate programs are independent with no off-campus oversight.
Distinctive culture	While more difficult to point out, DCEs do have a culture distinctive from pastors and teachers in the LCMS.	On-campus fellowship groups enable DCE networking to start in college; DCE cluster groups foster local fellowship; stories are told, a unique lingo is used; awards honor "heroes" that model best practices.

TABLE 6.1 (Continued)

Indicators of DCE Professionalization

Profession Characteristic	Evident for LCMS DCEs?	Description
Code of ethics	Formally created in 2000	Those new to the field become familiar with the Code of Ethics through their preparatory program and through the professional organization -- (http://www.lea.org/deprtmnt/dcenet/ethics.pdf). As far as is evident, there is no incident in which the professional organization has "enforced" the code.
Process of evaluation to develop the field	Yearly Summits have been held since 1990 with DCE program directors, the TEAM board, former TEAM presidents, and invited DCE and Synodical leaders to, among other goals, "Develop and implement the processes to enhance and maintain high standards of quality for DCE ministry" and "Work to safeguard the integrity of DCE ministry as a valid ministry of the Church . . ."	These Summits have held conversations with seminary professors about team ministry, helped create the current mission statement for the LCMS DCE, initiated a Code of Ethics, and plan a new professional organization.
Professional organization	PEDA first met in early 1960s. Next three iterations were networks of the Lutheran Education Association: DPDCE (1967-1973); TEAM (1973-2001) and DCENet (2001-2009).	Efforts underway in 2009 to establish the National Association of Directors of Christian Education (NADCE), an independent association to address DCE needs in advocacy, connections, and resources
Power	While not able to vote at the Synodical convention, evidence demonstrates DCEs are influencing their future.	Evidence of their power to build the field includes all steps above, and continued growth and development (such as creation of NADCE), rather than stagnation.

Other indicators that LC–MS DCE ministry is professionalizing include:

1. **Conferences.**
   Since 1956, conferences have been held regularly for professional development, networking, and building of team ministry. The first nationwide conference was held in River Forest, Illinois, in 1961. DCEs and their pastors could join PEDA, Pastors and Education Directors Association.

   PEDA affiliated with Lutheran Education Association in 1967 and became DPDCE, the Department of Pastors and DCEs. The department had its own officers. National meetings were held in conjunction with the LEA convention, with regional meetings held as well. In 1973, the name changed from DPDCE to TEAM, Theological Educators in Associated Ministry. In 2001, TEAM became DCEnet.

   Between 1971 and 1986, inter-Lutheran conferences were held more regularly than TEAM conferences. In 1988, the Board for Parish Services of the Lutheran Church–Missouri Synod sponsored the first National DCE Conference in Denver, Colorado. A national DCE conference has been held every three years since.

2. **Synodical support.**
   When DPDCE was created, stated purposes all indicated professionalizing the ministry profession. The Synod's Board of Parish Education supported those efforts and maintained a central, current listing of all serving as DCEs. Throughout the years there has been a close relationship with and concrete support from district and Synodical officials. As the position has matured, DCEs have taken on significant roles within the Synod, furthering connections that have built an understanding of the ministry position Synod-wide.

3. **Professional publications.**
   The *Bulletin for DCEs* was started in October 1965 by the Board of Parish Education. The quarterly promoted resources, conferences, and articles which fleshed out DCE ministry. *Issues in Christian Education*, published three times a year by Concordia University Nebraska, has highlighted topics specific to DCE ministry. The Lutheran Education Association's publication, *Lutheran Education*, has annual DCE issues. From 1992 to 2000, *DCE Directions* was the official journal of LEA-TEAM. Its purposes included "the dissemination of theological and educational articles that reflect the growing knowledge base of our profession. Since 2001, *Network DCE* has linked and equipped DCEs.

4. **Continuing education.**
    Options have increased for field-based DCEs to pursue continuing education. Concordia Universities offer advanced degrees, demonstrating expansion of the theory base upon which DCEs can practice. KINDLE, the Karpenkpo Institute for Nurturing and Developing Leadership Excellence, was founded in 1999 "to enhance the church through the ministry of DCEs who foster servant leaders." This rigorous year professional development process incorporates research-based content, and connecting via residency and technology.

CHALLENGES

As the DCE profession matures and develops, there continue to be challenges that may prevent the DCE vocation from becoming a fully-developed profession.

Congregations continue to hire their own educational workers, granting the title of Director of Christian Education to non-certified, non-trained personnel. There is no official oversight that prevents anyone from utilizing the title.

DCEs are currently disenfranchised and cannot vote at the Synodical convention where many decisions that influence their work are made.

Certification is "for life." There is no formal requirement to continue professional DCE development, or to seek recertification, once one has entered the field.

While there is a common preparation for DCEs, once in a congregation the title and tasks vary. Field DCEs and laypersons need to understand DCEs operate from a theory base that allows generalizing into new areas of practice–but from the common foundation of serving as a lifespan educational leader.

ENTERING THE PROFESSION

You can have confidence that what you are studying in your program will equip you to serve effectively in a congregational setting. Members of the congregation you serve will know that you have met long-established criteria for preparation, and they will trust you are prepared to serve within the job description assigned. You will help to build the profession as you clarify your work for others, meet with fellow DCEs, and contribute to research. Your interactions with prospective DCEs will help them have a better understanding of what is entailed when serving.

It is a precious, rewarding ministry to which you are called – to contribute to the faith formation of children, youth and adults, serving as a lifespan education leaders prepared for team ministry in a congregational setting. Professionalizing the field will help continue to seek better and more effective ways to live out this calling. How do you contribute? When in your parish:

Keep in front of you

- The definition and mission of the LC–MS DCE – what you have been prepared to do

- Your job description – how your congregation is asking you to specifically live out your mission

Nurture your faith

- Continue your professional education – grow as a lifespan Christian educational leader

- Participate as an active and supportive member of your parish's called team

- Periodically review your mission, job description, and goals

- Seek out DCEs – learn together, nurture each other

- Participate in NADCE – contribute your gifts and skills, learn through opportunities presented

CONCLUSION

DCEs encounter factors similar to those impacting other developing occupations, and so there is justification in evaluating with criteria characteristic of secular professions. However, additional consideration must be given to the fact that the worker who fills the position of DCE is a *commissioned minister* of the Lutheran Church, an individual called to serve in ministry in a specific congregation. That fact has numerous implications for the culture of the Director of Christian Education.

Ultimately there is only one goal that matters in a ministry profession: Is our Lord and Savior, Jesus Christ, being held up as our Master, and are our communities learning more of Him, maturing as His people in this place? Are we being effective in the work taken on? The late James Michael Lee eloquently expressed the value of being "professional":

> To paraphrase the Bible, 'be professional and all these things will be added to you.' Because if you're professional that means you get tremendous training, you'll keep up with the field, you'll keep up with reading, you'll analyze your own teaching behavior constantly, you'll work to improve it and things like microteaching situations. You will always try to do the very best every time. Everything follows with being professional (1992, p. 10).

When the DCE is properly prepared for her work, greater participation by members in education, service and worship is inevitable. When trusted with such important work as nurturing the faith of God's people, let us pursue paths that have demonstrated increasing growth and development resulting in a much higher quality of work. To God be the glory!

CHAPTER 9

DCE Ethical Guidelines

RICHARD CARTER

A DAY IN THE LIFE OF...

Interesting discussion at dinner with a friend. "So," he and his wife asked," how did it go last year when you tried to reduce your work week to fifty hours?" I could say truthfully that I had succeeded some in working down from sixty or seventy hours. But I could also feel the challenge that comes with this: "The DCE manages himself or herself in such a way as to maintain an appropriate relationship with regard to time commitments between personal, family, and professional responsibilities" (Principle 2.01).[32]

For me, the choices to participate more in the Citizen's League of the Twin Cities and to get to our block's National Night Out event in part come from remembering that "The DCE is a responsible and active member of the civic community" (Principle 2.03).

I much appreciated, though I report it here with some caution, the feedback from a presentation I made to youth and mission workers in Eastern Europe, that I rated well as a teacher both because I used

---

[32] The Principles cited in this chapter refer to those of the Ethical Guidelines for Directors of Christian Education (2002) found at http://www.lea.org/deprtmnt/dcenet/ethics.pdf.

Richard Carter, Th.D., serves as Professor and Director of Pre-Seminary Studies at Concordia University, St. Paul.

interactive teaching methods and because my humility was evident. In part the humility was easy: what could I seriously pretend to know about what it is to be a church worker in a country with forty years of communism under its belt? I was also reminded that "The DCE leads in the congregation and the larger church by demonstrating both initiative and humility in service" (Principle 3.10).

The concluding numbers from each vignette come from "Ethical Guidelines for Directors of Christian Education," available here and on the website of the Lutheran Education Association. The vignettes suggest correlations between those guidelines and my life as a DCE. The challenge and opportunity of this chapter in your studies is your use of the Ethical Guidelines in your practice of Gospel ministry.

HISTORY

The "Introduction" to the Guidelines, supported by the "Credits" near the end, gives you some sense of the history of the Guidelines. DCE ministry has been visible in the Lutheran Church–Missouri Synod (LC–MS) for more than half a century (Schoepp, 2009). A natural consequence of years of good professional work was a concern in the DCE community for professional ethics (Keyne, 1992). (You don't like the sound of "professional" because you love Jesus and are going into "ministry"? Loving Jesus and going into ministry are good things, but so is becoming a professional. Read on.) Written drafts, review of other codes of ethics and conference conversations came throughout the 1990s. 1999 featured a National DCE Leadership Summit that clearly articulated the definition, mission and values of DCE ministry for the LC–MS. In that context it was possible to create a committee to take the next step in professional development, the clear articulation of ethics related to mission and values.

It might seem strange in a textbook about professional development to encounter first and second person pronouns, e.g., "I much appreciated..." and "your studies." I propose that ethics and ethical guidelines are not neutral, objective materials about which one can debate abstractly. We are never not in ethical situations, though most of those are taken for granted and we make ethical choices routinely. With this chapter I invite you personally to join the continuing conversation about ethics and ministry in the Church. [Note that "Church" is a plural noun; you cannot be the Body of Christ all by yourself (Ratzinger, 98-100).]

In the Ethical Guidelines document you can read the names of the committee who drafted the Guidelines. They entered the ethical conversation in earnest in 2000; I am grateful for their help again as I have prepared this chapter. If you did some historical and geographical research you would detect that at the time the committee was formed its members were all DCEs located in the Twin Cities metropolitan area. The document was tested by DCEs around the country, including Listening Posts in Texas and Iowa, but the committee was blessed by the opportunity to struggle in person, face-to-face, to articulate the "Principles" and "Ethical Implications" that would become the document. One challenge they faced was to keep the whole forest in view, not just individual trees. They risked writing a list that was merely rules and regulations, a location for legalism; you face a parallel risk as you read the document. The implications needed grounding in the principles; the principles needed grounding in Scripture and the mission and values of DCEs.

"The DCE seeks professional review of programs under his or her purview" (Principle 3.02). Not least the committee, finishing its work on what it called "Ethics of the DCE," needed to do just that. For this document the "professional review" included legal counsel. "Ethics" became "Ethical Guidelines," in part to avoid lawsuits for future DCEs.

The development of the Ethical Guidelines for DCEs was a demonstration of, a practice of, what the guidelines describe. The team leader was respected and honored (Principle 2.09). The committee of DCEs worked for the Church at large in developing the guidelines (Principle 2.04). Those selected for the committee brought with them "present or emerging professional competence" and lead the larger church by demonstrating initiative in preparing the document (Principles 3.05 & 3.10). They contributed "time and professional expertise to activities that promote the value of, integrity of, competence of, and respect for the Director of Christian Education ministry" (Principle 3.21).

USE

Are you aware of the differences among (LC–MS) pastors, those who work regularly with the original Hebrew and Greek languages of the Scriptures and those who seek to be faithful without that particular effort? You might discover a similar use among DCEs of the Ethical Guidelines. Can a pastor preach a good sermon on Sunday without a review of the Greek? Perhaps, or even probably, for a while. Can a DCE serve well in a congregation or other setting without a review of the guidelines? Perhaps, or even probably, for a while.

If a minister of the Gospel is actually seeking excellence, however, "for a while" is not enough. As careful Biblical study may refresh pastors (and DCEs!) in their ministry, so also thoughtful attention to and later review of the Ethical Guidelines for DCEs may help keep them focused, aware of an appropriate style with which to approach the never ending array of tasks that comes before DCEs. Consider, for example, that a DCE is never not ministering. While handling her or his tasks, the DCE:

> "refrains from inappropriate and unwarranted criticism of [fellow students and] colleagues..." (Principle 2.11)

> even in public planning meetings, "respects and encourages the individual to move towards a Spirit-led life of self-direction in learning and decision-making" (Principle 2.24)

> "teaches and administers in such ways as to equip people as the Body of Christ for spiritual maturity, service, and witness... " (Principle 3.08)

There's more. Ministry as a DCE, even growth in ministry as one studies, will be filled not just with some array of tasks but with responsibilities and quandaries. As Guideline No. 7 points out, "Ethical dilemmas are part of functioning as a professional and ... every professional practitioner must make judgments with regard to propriety" (Lutheran Education Association, p. 4). Growth in ministry includes growth in this capacity to recognize when an ethical challenge is arising. Consider hunting: it is not enough to be skillful at firing the gun. A successful hunter must also develop the skills to walk through the fields or woods quietly and to see the animals, to see what is coming or developing.

Perhaps you are already acquainted with dilemmas, challenges, and troubles. Are you yet acquainted with the gift of others to walk with you through such things? A DCE "seeks personal, spiritual, and professional support" (Principle 2.06) as appropriate to sort things out. As a member of the Body of Christ, "the DCE lives in the context of community and in the course of life, will both give and receive support from that community" (Principle 3.16). Certainly one reason I treasure DCEs is the support I received from them in the dark first months of my ministry, at one point in a conference appropriately and literally surrounded by three of them.

If the implications of the Use of the Guidelines is beginning to "pinch," to make developing professional life seem more difficult or complicated, or even accusing, you are in the midst of the challenge experienced by the committee as they worked on the guidelines. Couldn't they have made it simple and just borrowed guidelines from some other profession? They certainly studied them, as the "Bibliography" makes clear, but you can only borrow some other profession's guidelines if you are that profession. DCE ministry is defined as people who are "Synodically certified, called and commissioned lifespan educational leader[s] prepared for team ministry in a congregational setting." None of the other guidelines covered that territory. To care about the Ministry of the Church, in its institutional form and personally, is to care in a particular way that no other field cares: God uniquely instituted the office of ministry so that the Gospel could be heard (Augsburg Confession, Article V).

Couldn't the committee have settled for a couple relevant Bible verses and trusted us to love Jesus enough to figure out the rest? The committee trusted that you would love Jesus, but "figuring out the rest" is what we do together in team ministry for the church. Here I think of my (in)competence in sailing, even with a motorboat, yet alone with one of those things with masts and jibs and sheets. The DCE that knew how to sail knew also that I wanted to be out on the water, but my "loving" to sail was not good enough grounds to let me out on the water alone. Especially when the gusts of wind came up I was grateful for the partnership, able to learn, to follow his guidelines. Here we are touching on what it means to be professionals. A professional is trusted not simply to act, but to act competently, safely, wisely on behalf of others; in ministry to act as well so that the love of God in Jesus Christ is not simply a motivation but an evident part of the content and conduct of the ministry. Ever sat through a sermon, Bible study, or camp devotion that was simply too long? Professionals learn through self-evaluation and professional review (Principles 3.01 & 3.02) to shape their ministry to make evident the Scriptural Gospel of freedom and forgiveness in Christ. If you are reading this text, you are somewhere on the journey to being a professional, to being publically and officially responsible for the Word of God to get heard in the world. As you attend to the guidelines welcome the company of sisters and brothers and their conversation with you about how it all might work in the complex situations we are bound to face. These guidelines can be good coaching.

That these guidelines might raise questions of sin or at least of poor behavior means that one gets close to the questions of legalism or the sense that the guidelines are one more set of rules, one more set of hoops to jump through. As if the Ten Commandments aren't enough, there are the requirements of a DCE Program to fulfill. Do we really need more rules? Are we really going to measure the quality of DCE ministry by measuring adherence to rules? I don't think so. There are rules for driving and for boating–safely–but the satisfaction or significance of driving or boating is not measured by the rules. Indeed, the Ten Commandments themselves are not quite rules in our usual sense that someone is trying to control us or spoil our fun. Have you looked at the Commandments in Ex. 20? The first words are of God's deliverance. "I have set you free. Now let me tell you how freedom works." Have you yet done enough study in psychological development to know that a child matures better in a clear framework of expectations? That DCEs can be more comfortable in their ministry when the directions and the boundaries are clear? So it is that these guidelines "give expression to and facilitate dialog about our commonly held values that are rooted in the Holy Scriptures and the Lutheran Confessions" (Lutheran Education Association, p. 3). As we consider the definition, mission, and important values of DCEs, these guidelines do just that – guide.

But perhaps the pinch of the guidelines is not simply professional or behavioral. The complex situations we encounter may relate to our own weakness, even our own sin. Perhaps we don't like ethical guidelines because we know that in some ways, great or small, we are not ethical. If we don't look at the guidelines–after all, we love Jesus–we don't have to confront our guilt. Well, that does work for a while, kind of like avoiding the doctor so that you don't have the definite information that you have a deadly disease. You'll go on dying anyway, but you don't have to think about it or discover the risk of healing.

Note that the essence of sin is not immorality but personal opposition to God. While our usual examples likely qualify as sin–adultery and getting drunk–other examples may including working for a 4.0 GPA, being totally committed to acts of service, or seeking to be or find the perfect spouse. The fruit on the tree in Eden looked good; particularly for those in the service of the Church not pressed by the "big" immoralities, the reality of the sin of our good work may be missed. The more clearly we see our pervasive sinfulness–the disease that we share–the deeper may be our valuing of the Gospel. We really are valued by God, given life with God (Emmanuel means "God with us") in Christ, power and potential over against sin.

Scripture and the Confessions have much to say on this Gospel, this power of God for salvation. One explicit proposal from Luther's Exhortation (1959) concerns individual confession: go for the sake of the absolution! The DCE's Ethical Guideline No. 5 has the same purpose, to "Foster the opportunity for Confession and Absolution leading to reconciliation and forgiveness" (Lutheran Education Association, p. 3). [I refer in particular to individual confession and absolution not because it is in the books somewhere but because for forty years it has been changing my life, liberating me as those absolving words have been spoken quietly to me.] To read, review and live with the Ethical Guidelines for DCEs is the opportunity to know more deeply still that one is a forgiven sinner. No doubt people stay away from serious (individual) confession for fear, perhaps for "the terror of the absolution," as one colleague calls it (Michael Walcheski, personal communication, August 14, 2009), that such full forgiveness can be so powerful. It could be that people stay away from the Guidelines for the same reason.

To see the guidelines as a guide puts us in the neighborhood, in Lutheran language, of what is called the Third use of the Law; the other two uses are curb and mirror. The Third Use is mentioned in the guidelines. You may know that there is some discussion among Lutherans on the topic. One phrase says it well, that we live no longer under the law but in the Law (Formula of Concord, Epitome, Article VI:2). The structure and stability of the law remains, but in Christ the curse and guilt are removed. Of course, until they lay us in the grave the desire of sin will continue to plague each of us, so any time we have contact with God's Law, even in such a form as Guidelines, the curse and guilt of the Law may raise their heads. The freedom to live in the law can be claimed by conversations like this: "You're correct, Satan, that I am a sinner and have sinned. But you have forgotten that Jesus carried my sin on the cross. You will have to take up the question of guilt with Him, while I set about doing the things He's asked me to do today."

"Freedom to live in the law" is perhaps not a common Christian concept. Many see Christian living as a burden, something close to the rules and legalism mentioned above. For all people, including Christians and DCEs, there are responsibilities in life, as professionals, as siblings, as neighbors. For Christians, in view of Christ's death under sin and life after the grave, there is also freedom to carry out those responsibilities. This is one form of the discussion of sanctification: whether leading a great, deep Bible study or changing diapers, the context is God's love for us. I do not need to check over my shoulder to see whether a wrathful God is going to "get me" for saying the wrong things about a Bible verse or choosing the wrong (cloth or plastic?) diaper. In the freedom and power of the resurrection I can look straight ahead at the people who need God's care through me, the infant or the Bible Class.

We do have roles, relationships and responsibilities on our shoulders, but this is Christian living as we live them daily related to God in Christ. One understanding of vocation is "freedom in Christ for service to the neighbor." Service to the neighbor is inescapable for all of us; again, we are never *not* in ethical situations, whether we are Christian, Buddhist or agnostic. To keep looking over your shoulder is safe neither in Christian life nor in driving. Look ahead, confident that God is still saying "You're mine." God baptized most of us as infants; most of us are still little children in our faith; but God has seen to it that we are *His* children.

One last thought on the use of the guidelines by DCEs. It may be simply that one finds the value in them, as stated in No. 10, because they "serve as an expression of the core values necessary for functioning as a servant leader in public ministry" (Lutheran Education Association, p. 4). And as No. 11 points out, they also "promote behavioral goals to which the individual DCE, as well as the profession, can encourage one another with Christian love" (Lutheran Education Association, p.4). Guidelines that help us to give and receive Christian love are not such a bad deal.

CHAPTER 10

CROSS-CULTURAL CHRISTIAN EDUCATION

CHRISTINE M. ROSS

Which of the following statements best aligns with your present view of your future as a Director of Christian Education (DCE)?

I am looking forward to working with people of a similar culture as my own as this is where I can best communicate God's love through Christ and equip the saints for ministry.

God has given me the desire to work with people of cultures different from my own and I am looking forward to connecting this desire with my passion for educating and equipping the body of Christ.

Both statements are appropriate and justifiable! This article is not intended to persuade those of you interested in serving in your own cultural context to change your views; rather the primary purpose is to reveal the fact that all Christian educators *will* be involved in cross-cultural ministry in some form. Con-

Christine M. Ross, Ph.D., serves as DCE Program Director at Concordia University Irvine.

sider these Christian educator's experiences (names have been changed, but the experiences are true):

> Teresa's church hosts an older but vibrant Caucasian community, a younger Chinese community, and an elementary school. When she began her ministry she was surprised to discover that all of her youth were of Chinese descent. Over time her congregational youth events have become more multi-cultural as Korean and Hispanic youth from the church school have joined. As Teresa learned about each culture she discovered that there are differences between the first, second, and third generations as the younger generations assimilate to US culture. She sometimes feels that she is the "common bond" between parents and youth and between the Caucasian and Chinese churches and she is learning how to manage this role in a way that brings unity to all members of Christ's body.

> Jacob serves a large wealthy suburban congregation. The different ethnicities which make up the church family are united by their common economic standard so there is little diversity within the congregation itself. However, Jacob has encouraged international mission and local service activities within his congregation. As a result, Jacob is teaching himself and his parishioners to understand, love, and share the Good News of Jesus with people who are culturally different from themselves.

> David thought his internship was exactly what he wanted – at a congregation and community that was similar to what he grew up in - except for the fact that it was 1500 miles away from his home-town. However, during the internship retreat he stated, "I feel like I'm working in a cross-cultural environment even though everyone looks just like me!" David discovered that the culture of a southwestern vacation, gambling community is very different from the culture of his midwestern home-town. David is slowly growing accustomed to the different ways of parenting, the different types of activities children enjoy and the different views of a DCE's responsibilities that he's encountered in his internship congregation.

Allison's congregation is the stereotypic mid-western Lutheran congregation with little cultural diversity and much commonality amongst the German-heritage farmers. Yet even here, women sew quilts for the local shelter which serves mainly migrant farmers, and each month families travel to the nearest city to work on Braille Bibles, and the missions committee works through Vacation Bible School (VBS), youth group activities and congregational events to raise money for a relative of the congregation who is a Lutheran Church–Missouri Synod (LC–MS) missionary. These varied events provide Allison with the opportunity to educate the congregation about God's desire that all people know of salvation in Jesus and enable the congregation to both support missionaries serving in other countries and to consider how they themselves can be the light of Christ to people they come in contact with each day.

CULTURE

Having grown up on a dairy farm in the Pacific Northwest, a move to Philadelphia caused me to experience the phenomena known as *culture shock*. Learning to rely solely upon public transportation rather than my own automobile caused anxiety and disorientation until I learned the public transportation system. Living in close contact with many people created stress until I became more accustomed to the urban lifestyle. My students looked incredulous when they learned I had never eaten water-ice and they laughed when I joked about drinking pop and wearing tennis shoes at the beach (on the East Coast one drinks soda, wears sneakers, and vacations at the shore). Many of the differences in the way I grew-up in Washington State compared to how I learned to live in Philadelphia highlight *culture*.

The *American Heritage Dictionary* defines *culture* as "the sum total of ways of living built up by a group of human beings and transmitted from one generation to another" (Culture, 2000). This definition indicates the breadth of what makes up culture: beliefs, values, and assumptions about the world as well as customs and material objects that are part of everyday living. The way in which we grow up provides our foundational culture and becomes "second nature" to us and may cause difficulty when becoming accustomed to (assimilating) or understanding alternative ways of life. *Ethno-centrism* is when we judge the behavior of other cultures by our own standards. For some Americans not owning a car and depending solely upon public transportation seems strange, yet the majority of the world is comfortable with this custom.

People in the United States often have trouble understanding the power of culture because of the high value we place on individualism. We think that everyone is unique and special in some way. However, individualism itself is a cultural value (Kottak, 1994, p. 43) which may hinder us from fully understanding Scripture and from sharing the Good News of salvation in Christ with people of different cultures.

CROSS CULTURAL

While in Philadelphia I lived amongst and worked with predominantly African Americans. I had to learn both the *sub-culture* of the East coast urban lifestyle and the African American culture. I suspect that most people would understand ministry with African Americans as *cross cultural* ministry yet may not have thought about the *cross cultural* aspects of ministering to people who seem like themselves but are accustomed to living in very different ways. This cross-cultural distinction is fundamental to the premise of this writing for I believe that some Christian educators will be called to ministry with people of another ethnicity but all Christian educators will be involved in *cross-cultural ministry*. A simple example of a cultural difference between Christians and non-Christians occurred recently when a barista at a Starbucks coffee shop near my pastor-husband's church asked him what he was writing; to his response "my sermon" she asked "what's a sermon?" Even though the people who live near one's church may look like you, if they have not been raised in the Christian *sub-culture* they will not understand the customary language and activities of Scripture and the church. Consider the implications of this for DCE ministry. A DCE may convince her VBS staff that they need to reach out to the neighborhood through this year's program. The staff hangs promotional signs prominently so drivers by can read the information and they even go door-to-door handing out 500 flyers in the congregation's immediate neighborhood. The promotional work brings in a handful of children whose families attend other local congregations, but no un-churched or non-Christian children come. Why? Possibly it is because the un-churched families do not speak Christian church language. They are unfamiliar with the term "VBS," the teaching, the games and the music a church offers so they do not even consider pulling the children from the summer program provided by their school. The DCE and her volunteers wonder why their sincere attempts to "reach-out" were relatively fruitless but they do not understand that when un-churched people have no understanding of church culture and no re-lationships with anyone in the congregation, there is little likelihood that they will attend even a well-publicized church event.

There are Christians who label ministry to people of the same ethnicity as "mono-cultural missions" and the term cross-cultural ministry is used strictly for work with people of other nationalities (Barrett, *et al.*, 2003, p. 672). However, as missionary strategist David Hesslegrave (1991) points out, Biblical Christi-anity requires a cultural change in values, beliefs and worldview; thus a DCE's work to educate newly churched, un-churched and non-Christians about Christ and His church is cross-cultural ministry (p. 102). One reason for the recent de-velopment of *missional church* theory is that church workers and congregations realize that they are "increasingly out of touch with the rapids of cultural change and the real world in which their neighbors lived (Minatrea, 2004, p. 7)." Per-ceiving the distance between themselves and the unchurched mainly through declining church attendance, *missional* congregations seek to understand the non-Christian culture of their neighborhood in order to determine how to serve their neighbors in ways that will be meaningful and how to share the Gospel in ways that may be better understood. Another DCE, understanding that VBS will not make sense to the congregation's Vietnamese neighborhood, works with his Christian education committee to provide a weekly evening tutoring program in place of VBS. His neighbors understand "tutoring" and the parents appreciate the opportunity for their children to receive homework help by native English speakers. A few un-churched neighborhood children attend the summer tutoring program and the church is able to build positive relationships with these children and their parents. These families verbally promote the program to their neighborhood friends and the attendance of the neighborhood children doubles by the end of the school year.

When Christian educators acknowledge that relationships with people outside of the church are cross-cultural relationships they may begin to: understand why fewer people than hoped for attend a traditional church activity; to see the need to deliberately consider the culture of the people they desire to reach; to become more intentional in providing activities that would serve their un-churched neighbors; begin to learn and teach their parishioners about cross-cultural mission theory; and begin to practice becoming better prepared to share through Word and deed the Good News of Jesus.

SCRIPTURE AND MISSION IN RELATION
TO CROSS CULTURAL MINISTRY

Christianity and the Bible are not culturally "western." The Biblical setting is present day Iraq, Iran, Syria, Israel, Egypt, Turkey, Greece, Italy, and their surrounding countries. Studying Middle Eastern culture and visiting Biblical cities can help Westerners better understand Scripture. For almost the first thousand years after Christ's ascension the majority of Christians were non-white (Barrett, 1987, p. 28) and presently there are more Christians—and Christianity is growing faster—in Africa, Asia, and Latin America than in Europe or North America.

Despite national or cultural differences and the communication obstacles these create, God desires for all people to know Him through His Son, Jesus (Jn. 3:16) and this has been His desire since He told Abram to "be a blessing for all families of the earth" (Gen. 12:3). Although throughout the Old Testament and through Jesus' first and final words to His disciples (Matt. 4:19; 28:18-20) God affirms His desire for all nations to know Him; the "mystery of God's will" (Eph. 1:9) was not revealed until after Christ's ascension to heaven. God's revelation is that all nations are "fellow heirs, members of the same body, and partakers of the promise in Christ Jesus through the Gospel" (Eph. 3:3-6); and that the church is given the confidence to proclaim the message that by Christ's blood He "has ransomed people for God from every tribe and language and people and nation..." (Rev. 5:9). It is with this foundation that God calls church workers "to equip the saints for the work of ministry, for building up the body of Christ, until we all attain to the unity of the faith and of the knowledge of the Son of God..." (Eph. 4:11-13).

At the first Pentecost after Christ's ascension God's Spirit broadcasted the Gospel to people of many cultures (Acts 2:9-11). Having revealed His mystery, God used both natural and super-natural means to motivate His people to spread the Good News of Jesus to all nations. God's hand is evident in the dreams that spurred Peter to witness to the Gentile Cornelius (Acts 10-11), in the conversion of the greatest missionary, Saul, and in the persecution that forced Christians to leave their homes and spread the Gospel wherever they went (Acts 8:1, 4).

For a variety of reasons the urgency to spread the Gospel among all nations declined after Constantine: Christianity became the State religion placing "conversions" in the hand of the army; the catholic church grew in power and placed the Scriptures in the hands of the priests, monks, and nuns; the dark ages inhibited the spread of knowledge and the increase of rural life with the subsequent decrease of urban life-styles inhibited cross-cultural communication. The Protestant Reformation did little to increase the zeal for cross-cultural missions. People of the Reformation period generally lived amongst those of similar culture, travel was difficult and Christians were focused upon the changes within the church (Barrett, 1987). Even so, Luther did address the need to share the Gospel with others when he taught that "one must always preach the Gospel so that one may bring some more to become Christians. The kingdom of God stands in becoming, not in being" (Stolle, p. 26); and when he preached that confidence in one's own justification will motivate a Christian to good works toward and teaching the Gospel of Christ to our neighbor (Luther, p. 360).

The traditional approach to missions as we know it, where a "missionary" is a vocational call to take the Gospel from the Christian West to people in distant lands and different cultures wasn't born until the 1800s, which global missions statistician David Barrett calls "The Great Century of worldwide Christian expansion" (1987, p. 41). During this time-period, a small group of German Lutherans left Germany to forge a life in America where they could worship God and teach the Scriptures according to their beliefs. Although many people in the LC–MS today speak as if their fore-fathers cared only for preservation of their German culture, the first president of the LC–MS, C. F. W. Walther preached that

> the entire congregation should be a holy nation, a royal priesthood; every Christian is to be concerned about the soul's misery of his neighbor and help along that the saving Gospel win constantly more victories over men, that Satan's kingdom in the world be destroyed, and Christ's kingdom promoted. Oh, how much different the outlook would be, how much greater and more wonderful the blessing of God's Word would be, if every Christian would recognize his holy calling and discharge his office of royal priesthood (Walther, p. 272)!

Early in the Synod's existence the German immigrants began work among Native Americans, then Blacks (resulting in the establishment of Concordia College in Selma, Alabama). Later their sons and daughters started ministries to deaf, blind, and handicapped persons. Each of these ministries provides an example of how the LC–MS has been involved in cross-cultural ministry within the United States. The LC–MS World Mission board, Lutheran Women's Missionary League, Lutheran Laymen's League, Lutheran Hour Ministries, and other organizations were created to share Christ with all people, of differing or similar culture both near and far and they continue to do so today. Recent changes at the LC–MS seminaries indicate the Synods continued commitment to share Christ with the various cultures within our borders: (1) The Center for Hispanic Studies provides pastor and deaconess training in Spanish; (2) the Deaf

Institute of Theology provides alternative teaching-learning opportunities for deaf and hard of hearing persons who desire to train for pastoral or deaconess ministries; and (3) the Ethnic Immigrant Institute of Theology provides on-line education for pastoral leadership in immigrant based churches and the Cross Cultural Ministry Program, a partnership between the St. Louis Seminary and Concordia University–Irvine, provides training for men interested in ethnic specific or cross-cultural specific ministry contexts.

By voting to adopt the LC–MS World Mission's vision for the 21st Century as a church-wide vision, the 2004 Synod convention sought to unite its congregations and members around the proclamation of the Gospel of Jesus to all people in a mission movement titled *Ablaze*. The three major Ablaze goals adopted in Synod conventions are:

1. share the Gospel with 100 million unreached or uncommitted people, including 50 million in the United States, by 2017 (the 500th Anniversary of Luther's nailing of the 95 Theses to the Castle Church door in Wittenberg)

2. plant 2,000 new missions in the U.S. (and work with our partners toward another 3,000 in Africa, Asia, Eurasia, and Latin America)

3. assist 2,000 LC–MS congregations in mission revitalization

Perhaps the most significant goal for DCEs was the conventions resolution that every LC–MS congregation and institution should grow in its understanding of itself as a mission outpost, as a community of believers in the midst of a wilderness of unbelief, prepared to go out into that wilderness to share the life-giving Good News of Jesus (Ablaze, 2005).

THE ROLE OF A CHRISTIAN EDUCATOR
IN CROSS CULTURAL MINISTRY

Review the experiences of the four DCEs described at the beginning of this article and consider the various ways these DCEs are involved in cross cultural ministry. Objectives regarding how to accomplish Ablaze goals indicate that DCEs will work to expand cross-cultural ministry at home and abroad by guiding the saints of their church to understand their mission responsibilities through prayer and the study of the Scriptures; by encouraging individuals to learn the languages and cultures of the people around them; by encouraging and equipping the laity to view themselves as missionaries prepared and sent out by the congregation to share the Good News of Christ; by preparing resources that will teach and enable the laity to live out their missionary call in their home, work and community and by encouraging their congregation to adopt at least one new mission goal concentrating on the unreached of its own community (Ablaze, 2005). As a DCE is called by God to equip the saints for the work of ministry, DCEs will be involved in enabling congregational members to understand and be involved in God's plan of salvation for people of every tribe, language, people, and nation who live near and far from the church's community.

You can begin to prepare yourself for this awesome opportunity of equipping God's people to take part in His part plan of salvation for people of every culture. Even now, get to know the culture of the unchurched in your congregation's neighborhood. Learn the history of the community and of the congregation you attend. Ask the pastor if the church has completed a demographic study of its neighborhood and ask him questions about what he knows about the lives of the unreached in the community. Talk to a student of another ethnicity who attends your school. Ask her what she sees as the major differences in her culture and the Christian culture at the university. Be involved in service and mission opportunities your school or church provide, take time to get to know the beliefs and values of the people you serve. Educate yourself about other cultures. If your university or church is near a retirement center, learn about the Civic, Adaptive, and Boomer generations. If Mexican immigrants have moved into the community read multi-cultural material about this people group. Adopt a missionary, communicate with him to obtain prayer requests for him and for the people he serves. Study missions theory and cross-cultural communication techniques. Most of all pray that God would give you His heart for people who are different from yourself, the book *Operation World* (Johnstone & Mandryk, 2001) provides information about the history and culture of people groups and it provides specific prayer needs for each culture. The ways to be involved in cross-cultural ministry are myriad and dependent mainly upon our own education, imagination, and ability to observe the lifestyles and listen to the needs of the people around us.

I remember few songs from my childhood VBS days, but one that I learned in fifth grade imprinted itself on my heart and mind:

Jr. Missionary Theme Song

Be a missionary every day.
Tell the world that Jesus is the way.

Be it in a town or country, or a busy avenue,
Africa or Asia, the task is up to you!

So be a missionary every day.
Tell the world that Jesus is the way.

The Lord is soon returning,
There is no time to lose.

So be a missionary, God's own emissary,
Be a missionary – today!

Today our church proclaims that "whatever our life roles, we live as a missionary—a witness to God's love in Jesus—reaching out, engaging people, and proclaiming the love of God through good deeds done and in words of Gospel spoken" (LCMS World Mission, 2010, p. 3). As you engage with the uncommitted and unchurched people that God has placed in your community and look for opportunities to share Christ through Word and deed, you will be involved in cross-cultural ministry.

CHAPTER 11

Invisible Christian Educators

A Look at LC–MS Lay Practitioners of Parish-Based Christian Education

PAUL SCHOEPP

It has always been the task of people of faith to pass on their beliefs to succeeding generations. Scripture commands it (Deut. 6:4-9). At its most basic level this task will always belong to families but, as people of like mind have gathered together, other teachers of the faith have figured prominently. Since its inception in 1847 the LC–MS has assigned this role to pastors, and then to teachers (Schmidt, 1972), and more recently to directors of Christian education (DCEs).

Schroeder (1974), Giles (1983), Griffin (1995), and Keyne (1995) traced the development of the DCE profession within the LC–MS. DCE ministry first began in the second decade of the 20th century when a few Lutheran teachers moved from the classrooms of the parochial school setting into the congregational setting. Rather than teaching a narrow age range of students multiple subject areas, they began to serve people of all ages with a singular Christian education focus. Growth of the profession was initially slow but in 1959 the DCE position was ap-

Paul Schoepp, Ph.D. serves as Associate Professor of Applied Religion and Director of Church Work Programs at Concordia University College of Alberta.

proved by synodical convention (*Proceedings*, 1959) and over the next four decades six synodical institutions of higher education were approved to train and certify DCEs. Keyne (1995) reported that DCE ministry had gained acceptance and visibility in the LC–MS and was on its way to becoming an established profession.

Yet, there remains another group of parish-based Christian educators who are largely invisible to the institutionalized church. In addition to certified DCEs some congregations also identify and select lay people to join the paid staff and direct the congregation's Christian education ministry. These individuals have varying degrees of education and training for their ministry and are given various different titles by the congregations they serve.

While they carry out valuable ministry tasks for the local congregations they serve, lay practitioners are invisible to the larger institutional church because it takes no formal responsibility for their training or oversight. Decisions regarding engaging them for, and releasing them from, ministry are made at the congregational level—often without the larger institutional church's awareness. While the LC–MS maintains a roster of certified workers and publishes it annually (e.g. The Lutheran Annual, 2001), there is no such listing for lay practitioners. Further, while DCEs have been relatively well studied (Schaeffer, 1972; Davison, 1978; Karpenko, 1978; Giles, 1983; and Keyne, 1995) lay practitioners have not had the same scrutiny.

Prior to the work of Schoepp (2003) there was no empirical research published regarding the work of lay practitioners in the LC–MS. The time had come for a closer look. Schoepp's quantitative study focused on full-time lay practitioners of parish-based Christian education ministry in LC–MS congregations and explored variables in three broad areas. First, demographic variables were explored to develop a clear picture of the lay practitioner population in comparison to the DCE population. Second, the amount of time that lay practitioners spent in ten major parish ministry roles was measured and compared to similar data for certified DCEs. Lay practitioners were also asked to assess their perceived need for additional training in each of the ten ministry roles. Finally, since some lay practitioners have moved to formal certification, a last set of variables explored lay practitioner interest in pursuing

DCE certification as well as restraints to that certification and preferred methods of course delivery as enhancers to certification. This article chronicles Schoepp's findings and the work of lay practitioners of parish-based Christian education—paid staff members of a congregation carrying out Christian education ministry without having gone through a synodical certification program.

METHODOLOGY OF THE STUDY

The target population for Schoepp's (2003) quantitative study was identified through the use of an annual district survey that attempted to identify and enumerate both certified DCEs and lay practitioners. This survey was started first by Karpenko in the mid 1970s (W. O. Karpenko II, personal communication, July 11, 2002) and then continued by Cullen (2001). Another listing of both DCEs and lay practitioners from DCEnet (D. J. Broten, personal communication, April 25, 2002) was used to supplement the aforementioned list as was the participant list for the LC–MS-sponsored Youth Ministry 2002 Conference. The compiled list was checked against official records of DCEs (Concordia University System, 2002; *The Lutheran Annual*, 2001) to remove certified DCEs from the list.

The resultant accessible population of 513 lay practitioners was invited to take part in the survey through a five-contact protocol (Dillman, 2000). Participants were sent a pre-notice letter, a survey, and contact letter with a self-addressed stamped envelope, and a follow-up postcard. Then, as necessary, participants were contacted by additional follow-up mail and by telephone. The issue of informed consent followed the protocols of the Institutional Review Board of the University of Nebraska-Lincoln. Consent was addressed in the survey cover letters with completion and submission of the survey indicating consent.

The above noted rigorous implementation and follow-up procedures, as well as a wave analysis (Creswell, 2002) comparing early and late respondent groupings, resulted in no significant difference (alpha=.01) on several key variables reducing concerns about early/late response bias and respondent/non-respondent bias.

FINDINGS

Of the 513 surveys administered, 474 surveys were returned either through mail or telephone follow-up for an overall response rate of 92.4%. After certified workers, volunteers, and individuals who served in areas other than Christian education were winnowed from the responses, 158 respondents met the criteria of serving as lay practitioners of parish-based Christian education but only 112 of these were full-time. This represented an eligible response rate of 21.8% from the original survey administration but supported the largely invisible nature of the population and the difficulty in identifying them.

LAY PRACTITIONER DEMOGRAPHICS

Results for both Part I and II of the survey were calculated based on n=112 full-time lay practitioners. Part I of the survey (the demographic portion) studied 26 different factors that are summarized as follows. Lay practitioners came to their ministry positions from a widely divergent set of former careers ranging from homemaker to student to teacher to tractor-trailer driver. Most lay practitioners served a congregation where they had previously been members and all full-time lay practitioners had Lutheran backgrounds (almost all from the LC–MS). The ministry positions in which lay practitioners served were developed in a variety of different ways from initiating a new area of ministry, to covering ministry formerly done by volunteers, to replacing existing lay practitioners or certified workers. There was no dominant method of developing the position. The vast majority of lay practitioners only served in one congregation and had a mean tenure there of 5.84 years. Mean total years of service for lay practitioners was 6.89 years and mean anticipated years of future service in the lay practitioner role was 10.80 years.

The congregations where lay practitioners served had an average attendance of 567.51 and an average of 9.61 full-time and 5.07 part-time staff. These relatively large staff sizes were accounted for by the fact that almost two-thirds of the congregations where lay practitioners serve operated a parochial school. Twenty-seven of the 35 districts of the LC–MS had lay practitioners serving in them with a disproportionately high percentage of them serving in Michigan and Minnesota-South districts. Lay practitioners had mixed levels of contact with certified DCEs. About one-third of lay practitioners had a high school or associate degree as their highest educational level while two-thirds of lay practitioners had a bachelor's degree or a master's degree. Major areas of study for undergraduate degrees covered the spectrum with about one quarter of them falling into the area of education.

There were slightly more female than male lay practitioners, and the average lay practitioner was 40 years old. The vast majority of lay practitioners was married and most lived in households of three or more. Very few lay practitioners serve in rural areas or in cities with a population under 10,000. The majority of lay practitioners served in cities with a population of over 50,000. Over three quarter of the lay practitioners were satisfied or very satisfied with both their ministry positions and their relationships with other staff. Lay practitioners earned an average salary of $32,831.05, worked an average of 49.6 hours per week and were an average of 6.38 hours of driving time to the nearest DCE certifying institution.

Statistical testing (Mann Whitney U; Chi Square, and Independent-Measures t) at the.01 level of significance was also undertaken to compare lay practitioners and certified DCEs on several of the demographic variables where DCE data were available (Karpenko, 1997). In summary the demographic comparisons indicated no significant difference in regard to tenure at their current congregation with lay practitioners serving an average of 5.84 years and certified DCEs serving an average of 5.36 years. The average total length of service was significantly shorter for lay practitioners at 6.89 years compared to 10.18 years for DCEs. This was probably due to the fact that most lay practitioners do not move on to serve another congregation. Though congregational worship attendance was larger for lay practitioners (567.51) than for DCEs (466.34) the difference was not statistically significant. On average lay practitioners (40.00 years) were significantly older than DCEs (36.67 years) but both lay practitioners (49.60 hours) and DCEs (51.22 hours) work about the same number of hours per week.

As might be expected because of certification requirements, lay practitioners had significantly less post secondary education than DCEs with about one third of lay practitioners not having completed a bachelors degree. The ratio of female to male lay practitioners (53.2% to 46.8%) was significantly higher than the ratio of female to male DCEs 31.0% to 69.0%). Marital status between lay practitioners and DCEs appeared to be similar though it could not be tested statistically. By percentage, lay practitioners and DCEs worked in similar-sized communities. Lay practitioners and DCEs expressed similar levels of satisfaction with their positions but lay practitioners ($32,831.05 per year) were paid significantly less than DCEs ($37,131.54 per year).

LAY PRACTITIONER MINISTRY ROLES

Part II of the survey addressed lay practitioner ministry roles. Multiple frameworks exist for defining the roles or functions of parish-based Christian educators (Beal, 1976; Brantsch, 2001; Elmshauser, 2001; Emler, 1989; Furnish, 1968, 1976, 1984; Giles, 1983; Harris, 1976; Karpenko, 1986, 1990, 1997; Kraft, 1957; Lawson & Choun, 1992; Lines, 1992; and Stubblefield, 1993). Schoepp (2003) used Karpenko's (1986, 1990, 1997) framework since it was developed within the LC–MS context and was used to define critical ministry roles for the parish-based Christian educators known as DCEs. The role definitions that follow were transferred verbatim from Karpenko's 1997 research with only one exception: the term "DCE" was replaced with the term "lay practitioner" since lay practitioners were the subject of this study.

- **Leader**
  The role of leader is defined as that role which involves lay practitioners in bringing direction and change to various ministry areas by influencing individuals, groups, committees, boards, and assemblies to take action to realize the congregation's vision, mission, and goals.

- **Administrator**
  The role of administrator is defined as that role which involves lay practitioners in the day to day managing, coordinating/directing, promoting,

and evaluating the various parish ministry areas (e.g., education, youth, music, etc.), activities, projects, programs, and agencies.

- **Age Group Resource**
  The role of age group resource is defined as that role which involves lay practitioners in spending time with, leading, or speaking on behalf of, a person of a particular age, either individually, in small and/or large same-age groups or in intergenerational groups.

- **Care Action Minister**
  The role of care action minister is defined as that role which involves lay practitioners in ministering to a person, family or group through nurturing and/or crisis visitation activities (e.g., home, hospital, etc.), community organization efforts, or counseling experiences.

- **Church Professional**
  The role of church professional is defined as that role which involves lay practitioners in developing and maintaining of their sense of identity, purpose, devotional life, code of ethics, staff relationships, church-at-large commitments, peer support, and continuing education activities.

- **Educational Program Resource**
  The role of educational program resource is defined as that role which involves lay practitioners in providing the educational resources, or being the educational resource for the boards, committees, etc. in one's congregational-assigned ministry areas.

- **Music Facilitator**
  The role of music facilitator is defined as that role which involves lay practitioners in facilitating individual and group use of music (soloist, Sunday School music, etc.) and/or performing within the formal music ministry of the congregation (choir directing, organ playing, etc.).

- **Pastoral and Staff Support**
  The role of pastoral and staff support is defined as that role which involves lay practitioners in working with the pastor(s) and/or other staff in other parish ministry areas such as evangelism, stewardship and congregational worship.

- **Parish Teacher**
  The role of parish teacher is defined as that role which involves lay practitioners in serving the congregation as a teacher of the faith and a theological resource in classes, courses and/or programs in the day school and/or the parish.

- **Volunteer Specialist**

  The role of volunteer specialist is defined as that role which involves lay practitioners in identifying talents/gifts of individuals, as well as recruiting, training, supervising, sustaining, and evaluating volunteers who may assume various roles within areas of ministry such as education, youth, music (i.e., Sunday school teacher, youth counselor, etc.).

Lay practitioners were asked to indicate the number of hours they spent in each of the ten ministry roles and were also given an opportunity to identify new ministry roles. The rank order of time spent in each ministry role from largest amount of time to smallest was: (1) administrator; (2) leader; (3) age-group resource; (4) church professional; (5) educational program resource; (6) volunteer specialist; (7) parish teacher; (8) care action minister; (9) pastoral & staff support; (10) self-identified role; and (11) music facilitator.

Clearly administrative tasks were deemed to consume the largest amount of lay practitioners' time (25.1%). The role of leader was next with 18.3% lay practitioner's time investment. Third on the list was the role of age-group resource (10.8%). Taken together, the first three items (administration, leadership, and age-group resource) comprised over half of the time (54.2%) invested by lay practitioners.

The role of church professional received 9.2% of lay practitioner's total time. The role of educational program resource received 6.7%. The role of volunteer specialist received 6.6%. The role of parish teacher received 6.3%. The role of care action minister received 6.1%. Taken together these next five items (church professional, educational program resource, volunteer specialist, parish teacher, and care action minister) comprised about one-third of the time (34.9%) invested by lay practitioners.

The last three items were much spottier in the responses with many respondents leaving them blank or indicating that they spent no time in that role. The role of pastoral and staff support received only 4.1% of lay practitioner's time. Self-identified roles received only 4.1%. The role of music facilitator received only 2.8% of their time in this ministry area. Taken together the last three items (pastoral & staff support, self-identified roles, and music facilitator) only comprised about one-tenth of the time (11.0%) invested by all lay practitioners.

A Mann Whitney U-Test comparison of time spent by lay practitioners in ministry roles to time spent by DCEs in ministry roles revealed five significant differences at the .01 level of significance. Lay practitioners spent a significantly larger percentage of their time (18.3%) in the leader role than did DCEs (12.8%). Lay practitioners spent a significantly larger percentage of their time (25.1%) in the administrator role than did DCEs (18.9%). Lay practitioners spent a significantly smaller percentage of their time (6.7%) in the educational program resource role than did DCEs (8.4%). Lay practitioners spent a significantly smaller percentage of their time (6.3%) in the parish teacher role than did DCEs (13.4%). Lay practitioners spent a significantly smaller percentage of their time (6.7%) in the volunteer specialist role than did DCEs (9.7%).

Regarding their need for training, lay practitioners expressed a moderate perceived need for additional training in nine of the ten ministry areas. Lay practitioners expressed a low level of need for training in the area of music—an area where they spent very little of their time.

It was worthy of note that the three areas with the strongest perceived need for training were in roles where there was a significant difference in the time invested between lay practitioners and DCEs. The strongest perceived need for training was in the volunteer specialist role. Lay practitioners spent less of their time (6.7%) in the volunteer specialist role when compared to DCEs (9.7%). The second strongest perceived need for training was in the leader role. Lay practitioners spent more of their time (18.3%) in the leader role than did DCEs (12.8%). The third strongest perceived need for training was in the parish teacher role. Lay practitioners spent less of their time (6.3%) in the parish teacher role than did DCEs (13.4%).

LAY PRACTITIONER CERTIFICATION INTEREST

Part III of the survey addressed lay practitioner interest in DCE certification as well as restraints and enhancers to certification. There was one item on the survey that specifically asked "How much interest do you have in pursuing coursework through one of the Concordias that would lead to certification as a rostered Director of Christian Education?" Twenty-nine respondents (25.9%) indicated no interest in pursuing certification while 83 respondents (74.1%) indicated some level of interest in pursuing certification. Twenty-one respondents (18.8%) indicated a slight interest, 29 respondents (25.9%) indicated a moderate interest, 22 respondents (19.6%) indicated a strong interest, and 11 respondents (9.8%) indicated that they were already pursuing DCE certification. Responses to the remainder of the questions for the survey were based on n=83 (the number of lay practitioners expressing some level of interest in DCE certification).

Use of a Spearman correlation to find relationships between certification interest and other demographic variables indicated only two significant relationships. Increased lay practitioner interest in DCE certification was related at the .01 level of significance to regular contact with DCEs ($r=+.246$) and to higher overall perceived needs for training by lay practitioners ($r=+.440$).

Of those interested in pursuing DCE certification the vast majority (91.6%) would pursue DCE certification on a part-time basis. Part-time coursework appeared to be the only way lay practitioners would consider pursuit of certification. This made perfect sense when one took into account several of the demographic variables in the survey. These individuals worked full-time as parish-based Christian educators and putting in an average of 49.6 hours per week; 76.8% were married; and 55.4% had households of three or more persons. It was quite clear that there was not time for lay practitioners to pursue DCE certification as full-time students due to other responsibilities in life.

When asked how they would pay for the tuition costs of certification 23 respondents (28.0%) indicated that the full amount of their tuition would be covered by outside support. Twenty respondents (24.4%) indicated that outside support would cover 75% of their tuition costs. Nineteen respondents (23.2%) indicated that their tuition costs would be split evenly between themselves and outside support. Six respondents (7.3%) indicated that they would be covering 75% of their tuition costs on their own, and eleven respondents (13.4%) indicated that they would have to bear the entire cost of their tuition.

Lay practitioners were asked to indicate restraints to certification. From greatest to least, the restraints to certification were: 1) inability to relocate due to family/child concerns; 2) inability to relocate due to spouse's job; 3) high financial cost of certification; 4) length of time for certification; 5) distance from a DCE certifying institution; 6) lack of a favorable impact on salary; 7) little certification encouragement from congregation; 8) little certification encouragement from staff; 9) the demanding nature of Christian education ministry; 10) a perception that no new competencies would be gained; 11) a perception that certification was unnecessary since the lay practitioner was already involved in Christian education ministry; 12) different career goals from Christian education ministry; 13) the perceived difficulty of certification coursework.

The first three items were considered strong restraints to certification. Lay practitioners appeared to be geographically immobile and unable to relocate to pursue certification even if interested in that course of action. This fit well with the demographic that showed most lay practitioners have only served one congregation. Finances were also strong restraint to certification.

Moderate as restraints to certification were the next eight ranked items. Of interest were the items ranked ten and eleven—both had a bi-modal distribution. For rank number ten, it appeared that one group of lay practitioners tended towards the belief that they had all the necessary competencies for parish-based Christian education ministry while another group tended toward the belief that they could still learn new competencies or grow in their existing competencies. For rank number eleven it appeared that a group of lay practitioners saw DCE certification only as a door to enter parish-based Christian education ministry. Since these individuals were already involved in parish-based Christian education ministry, certification held little value. It appeared that the other group valued DCE certification for more than its ability to provide an access point to serving in parish-based Christian education ministry.

The last two items were deemed weak restraints to certification. This paralleled nicely the responses in the demographic section of the survey where lay practitioners indicated a mean of 10.80 years of additional anticipated service—most lay practitioners anticipated serving as Christian educators for an extended period. As regards the difficulty of certification coursework lay practitioners were clearly not daunted by the academic rigors necessary for certification as DCEs.

Finally, lay practitioners were asked what types of course delivery would be enhancers to pursuing certification. In rank order of preference from highest agreement to lowest they were: 1) computer/internet courses via the world wide web; 2) independent study courses via regular mail; 3) television courses via cable TV; 4) compressed multi-weekend courses via extension in the lay practitioner's geographic area; 5) on campus courses in a compressed one week format; 6) television courses via satellite TV; 7) semester long courses via extension in the lay practitioner's geographic area; 8) on campus courses in a regular semester format.

The first four ranked items were considered strong enhancers to certification. What each of these delivery methods shared in common was that instruction was taken to the lay practitioner rather than asking the lay practitioner to come to the instruction. A feature that was shared by the top three preferred methods of course delivery (internet-based courses, mail correspondence courses, and television course via cable TV) was the asynchronous nature of the interaction that could occur with those instructional formats. That is to say that the instructor and students could still interact with one another but do not need to do it in real time.

Items ranked five through seven were considered moderate enhancers to certification while the item ranked eight was not considered an enhancer. It was clear that regular on campus course delivery did not meet the needs of lay practitioners.

There were no significant correlations between method of course delivery and certification interest. Stated another way, lay practitioners with low levels of interest in certification were likely to be as favorably disposed to any given type of course delivery method as lay practitioners with high levels of interest in certification.

CONCLUSIONS AND RECOMMENDATIONS

Despite their invisibility to the institutionalized church, considerable numbers of lay practitioners of parish-based Christian education are engaged in ministry in congregations of the LC–MS. In many ways their roles as Christian educators parallel the roles undertaken by certified DCEs yet there are some significant differences. Lay practitioners spend significantly more time than certified DCEs in the areas of leader and administrator. Lay practitioners spend significantly less time than certified DCEs in the areas of educational program resource, parish teacher, and volunteer specialist. This research also indicated that lay practitioners have the strongest perceived need for training in the roles of volunteer specialist, leader, and parish teacher.

DCE undergraduate training in the LC–MS has been guided by Karpenko's (1986, 1990, 1997) work on ministry roles and sub-roles and the LC–MS national DCE definition (Lutheran Education Association, 2002). An area worthy of further exploration would be to study whether the specific training received by DCEs contributed to the significant differences in the amount of time invested in particular ministry roles. It could be that since two of the main areas of preparation for DCEs have been in the enabling and equipping of volunteers and in providing educational resources that DCEs had less need to spend time in the leader and administrator role—congregational volunteers may have been picking up some of the leadership and administrative tasks for DCEs while lay practitioners may have been carrying out these tasks on their own. A stated value among DCEs is "lead to equip leaders" (Lutheran Education Association, 2002, p. 3). DCEs may have spent more time in the role of parish teacher because of the greater amount of formal training they received in that area during their undergraduate education in comparison to lay practitioners. Further study is needed to verify these suppositions about the training received by DCEs and its impact on expenditures of time in ministry roles.

This research identified that half of lay practitioners were not encouraged by their congregation or their staff to pursue certification. This raises the question of what value congregations and other certified workers in synod (pastors, teachers, DCEs, district presidents, and district education executives) place on DCE certification for the parish-based Christian education role. Why did congregations choose lay practitioners of parish-based Christian education rather than certified DCEs? Was it related to the significant differences in salary between lay practitioners and certified DCEs? Was it related to the current and impending shortage of certified church workers (Barry, 2000; Klaas & Klaas, 1999)? Was it related to congregational or staff dissatisfaction with certified DCEs? Or, were there other factors at work?

This study confirmed the ministry of lay practitioners within congregations of the LC–MS and as such also confirmed the discrepancy between the synod's normative structure, "the way things should be," and its behavioral structure, "the way things are" (Scott, 1998). The LC–MS constitution (The Lutheran Church–Missouri Synod, 1998) notes that only certified workers should serve congregations. It may be important for the LC–MS to address the discrepancy between normative and behavioral structure as related to parish-based Christian education ministry.

To do this the LC–MS needs to become more intentional about identifying and tracking its lay practitioners of parish-based Christian education. Official accountability to the normative structure can only be monitored and encouraged when there is information available about how closely individuals and congregations are adhering to the normative structure. The LC–MS needs to develop and maintain a list of lay practitioners of parish-based Christian education ministry. This is not a recommendation to make lay practitioners members of synod as ordained or commissioned ministers—only a recommendation to be aware of who lay practitioners are and where they are serving. Once the LC–MS has an official awareness of how closely its congregations conform to its normative structure, several options exist to address the discrepancy.

One option that exists to address the discrepancy between normative and behavioral structure for parish-based Christian educators is for the LC–MS to enforce conformity to its normative structure and remove from synodical membership congregations which persistently violate the requirement to use only certified workers (The Lutheran Church–Missouri Synod, 1998). Censure of congregations by synod is NOT a recommendation of the researcher based on the results of this study. The data from this study showed that lay practitioners of parish-based Christian education ministry have served many congregations for many years. The current and impending shortage of certified church workers (Barry, 2000; Klaas & Klaas, 1999) has put many congregations into the situation where they have had to augment their staffs with uncertified workers who have not been trained via the traditional college, university, or seminary route.

Further, Article VII of the synod's constitution (The Lutheran Church–Missouri Synod, 1998) notes that synod may not exercise "legislative or coercive powers, and with respect to the individual congregation's right of self-government it is but an advisory body" (p. 11). Given LC–MS polity, censure would likely do more to fracture practice rather than unite practice.

Another option that exists to address the discrepancy between normative and behavioral structure regarding parish-based Christian educators is for the LC–MS to recognize the discrepancy as inevitable and perhaps even desirable. Theological reasons exist for the tension (Carter, 2002; Commission on Theology and Church Relations, 1981; Janzow, 2002; Koehler, 1952; Kolb, 1993). On the one hand, the LC–MS recognizes the doctrine of the priesthood of all believers (1 Pet. 2:9ff) and the reality that all of God's gifts of grace (the Office of the Keys) are available to all Christians anywhere and at any time. All Christians are engaged in ministry (sometimes called service or vocation) in the broad sense of the term. On the other hand, the LC–MS recognizes the office of the public ministry and the right and obligation of congregations to call certain people to carry out a distinct public ministry by order of and on behalf of the congregation. Public ministers of the Gospel preach, and teach, and administer the sacraments, but their task does not end there. The task of public ministers is also to "prepare God's people for works of service, so that the body of Christ may be built up" (Eph. 4:11).

When the local congregation and its public minister(s) are effectively doing their job, it follows that lay people will be equipped to carry out their volunteer ministry more effectively. In some cases, based on their fitness and competency, these volunteer lay people may be identified by their congregation and requested to join the paid staff and serve in public ministry. One respondent shared an example of this in a write-in section of the survey. "I did not choose this career but the Lord and the pastors in the parishes I served saw something in me and put me to work."

As stated previously, lay practitioner ministry does not conform to the current practice of preparing individuals for the office of public ministry. The normative structure for the LC–MS has been that individuals leave their home congregations and go to a centralized college, university, or seminary to receive their training and then are called into a different congregation to fill an office in the public ministry. However, such practice has not always been the case for the Christian church. In early church practice, the apostle Paul was quick to identify natural leaders within the congregations he established and put them into official positions of ministry (Allen, 1956; Titus 1:5). He then went on to start other new congregations but as he was doing so, he kept in contact with the already established churches by providing training in written form. Much of the New Testament consists of Paul's epistles of instruction and encouragement to these congregations and the leaders who served them.

The reality that most lay practitioners joined the staff of the congregation they already belonged to suggests there is still something to be said for the early church model of moving people into public ministry directly from within the local congregation. There may be multiple paths to service in public ministry in the church. What is needed are ways to acknowledge that possibility. Perhaps some lay practitioners will never be desirous of certification but will still continue to minister effectively in the congregations they serve. Perhaps some lay practitioners who are interested in certification need an alternative form of equipping and training that does not rely on a geographically centralized institution. Perhaps, since lay practitioners are already involved in public ministry, they need an in-service route to certification rather than the traditional pre-service route of certification followed by public ministry.

This leads to the last, and best, option that exists to address the discrepancy between normative and behavioral structure. The LC–MS should lower the restraints (but not the requirements) to certification; to make it easier for lay practitioners to obtain professional credentials for their role in public ministry. This option implicitly values certification because of the theological knowledge, the theoretical knowledge, and the practical training that go along with it. Such an education is one of the marks of a profession. Parish-based Christian education is more than a craft. It is a public ministry of service; but it is also a profession. "A craft is something which can be observed, imitated, learned by experience. The craftsman's knowledge has been developed through trial and error. A profession has skills and theory that must be taught" (Keyne, 1995, p. 80).

The LC–MS holds that professional training is necessary in order to serve in public ministry as a pastor or a teacher. That same standard is becoming more prominent for parish-based Christian educators and is the story of the development of the DCE as a profession. Generally speaking lay practitioners had a desire to serve in parish-based Christian education ministry for the foreseeable future and had some level of interest in certification. Lay practitioners of parish-based Christian education were not opposed to certification or concerned about the difficulty of coursework for certification—they were simply unable to access certification because of multiple restraints. Many of the restraints can be addressed via distance education methods of course delivery.

The two strongest restraints to certification for lay practitioners were family or spousal job concerns that prevented relocation. These may be combined into a single issue of geographic immobility. A quote from one of the lay practitioners stated succinctly how the issue of geographic immobility could be overcome: "The internet has reduced the need for the university as an institutional 'place'—start using congregations as the training ground!" As Willis (2003) noted in an online definition, distance education addresses the restraint of geographic immobility: "At its most basic level, distance education takes place when a teacher and student(s) are separated by physical distance, and technology (i.e., voice, video, data, and print), often in concert with face-to-face communication, is used to bridge the instructional gap." The LC–MS, and its DCE certifying institutions, need to affirm distance DCE certification options. Such distance education options already exist for teachers to be certified within the LC–MS (CUEnet, 2003; First graduates, 2001) and for some pastors in special situations through a program called Distance Education Leading to Ordination or DELTO (DELTO, 2003; Isenhower, 2002). A similar option for distance DCE certification of lay practitioners has been established at Concordia in St. Paul, Minnesota (Brons, 2002), and experienced modest success. Distance DCE certification for lay practitioners should be supported throughout synod and enhanced through the cooperative work of all DCE certifying institutions.

Another strong restraint to DCE certification was cost. Distance education already begins to address the issue of making DCE certification more affordable since lay practitioners need not quit their paid ministry positions and relocate their families. Distance education also reduces the cost of certification by requiring less travel for education and the attendant food and accommodation costs. While those cost savings are true and realizable through the efficiencies of distance education, more congregations should support the certification process for lay practitioners by providing financial incentives. Such financial incentives might be in the form of paying all or part of tuition costs for certification (addressing a strong restraint), it might be in the form of increased salaries after certification (addressing a moderate restraint), or both.

Other moderate restraints to certification can also be addressed by distance education. Distance education addresses the moderate restraint of length of time for certification by allowing lay practitioners to work at certification at the same time they are carrying out ministry. Distance education also allows lay practitioners to work over extended time periods towards certification. Distance education nullifies the restraint of distance from a DCE certifying institution.

There is no panacea to address the needs of congregations who request lay practitioners to minister among them; to address the needs of lay practitioners who minister in those capacities, and to address the needs of the larger synod for uniformity of practice and professional credentialing. Yet, there is no doubt that lay practitioners of parish-based Christian education are meeting ministry needs within the congregations of the LC–MS. Though lay practitioners are invisible to the larger institutionalized church they are very visible to the congregations they serve and are engaged in important ministry roles that further the expansion of God's church. Lowering the restraints to certification and providing lay practitioners with the opportunity to further build their knowledge and skills for ministry can only enhance their already valuable ministry.

CHAPTER 12

Job Satisfaction and Educational Needs

Among Directors of Christian Education in the Lutheran Church–Missouri Synod : A Summary

JAMES H. MCCONNELL

INTRODUCTION

The purpose of this study was to investigate the sources of satisfaction and dissatisfaction among Directors of Christian Education (DCE) in the Lutheran Church–Missouri Synod (LC–MS). One specific intent was to determine what variables might influence or determine satisfaction or dissatisfaction in DCE parish ministry. Another intent was to determine if any of these variables might be predictors for likelihood to leave ministry in future years. The final intent was to determine what, if any, additional educational needs in ministry preparation might be needed.

RATIONALE

The rationale for this study was to provide an opportunity to survey DCEs throughout the United States who were actively serving congregations and give

Jim McConnell, Ph.D., is the former DCE Program Director at Concordia University Texas and currently serves there as Dean of the College of Education.

them an opportunity to respond to issues of satisfaction/dissatisfaction in their ministry. The gathering of such information provided information to help the Concordia University System evaluate curricula in the area of DCE preparation, to improve competency skills, and to support the LC–MS and congregations in the retention of these workers and to increase job satisfaction. The following three research questions guided the survey:

1. Are DCEs satisfied with their job?

2. What additional educational needs might be addressed through the Concordia University System Director of Christian Education preparation programs to promote job satisfaction?

3. What is the ability to predict satisfaction and likelihood to leave the DCE ministry during the next three years?

To address issues of satisfaction/dissatisfaction, questions were developed that would elicit comments to determine:

- The degree of satisfaction experienced in ministry through the work environment, relationships with congregational members, congregational leadership and staff, support and services provided by the district and Synod, and overall satisfaction with one's present ministry;

- The degree of satisfaction related to workload and compensation, opportunities for continuing education, personal spiritual needs, and time available for personal life;

- Competency/skill level satisfaction in areas of ministry such as Biblical knowledge, singles, small groups, evangelism, parents, marriages, diversity, crisis management, team members and children/youth;

- Satisfaction or agreement with statements related to commitment to ministry, effectiveness in ministry, support of family, balance between work and personal life, fulfillment through the ministry, salary and finances, and calling;

- Satisfaction with the work environment concerning a positive climate, trust, a sense of professionalism and teaming, clarity and flexibility regarding responsibilities, adequate work space, and communications;

- Satisfaction with the pastor/administrator in regards to approachability, respect, administrative skills, professional relationship, support, and mentoring;

- Satisfaction with parents and students and their expectations of the DCE;

- Overall job satisfaction level as increasing, decreasing or staying the same;

- Satisfaction in dealing with feelings of isolation, self-doubt, depression, discontentment, anxiety, anger, disillusionment, frustration and inability to relate to others;

- Areas that provide the most satisfaction and dissatisfaction in ministry;

- Biggest issues being faced in ministry; and

- Likelihood to leave DCE ministry in the next three years.

Two types of data were collected in this study: questionnaire and written response. The survey was largely composed of questions using a Likert scale. However, thirteen questions regarding demographics, specific elements of satisfaction and dissatisfaction, issues of concern, and likelihood to leave the DCE ministry provided an opportunity for the respondent to state an opinion in his/her own words.

DATA COLLECTION

The survey was distributed by mail to all LC–MS DCEs who were actively serving a congregation. That list, totaling 514, was derived from the official listing of DCEs maintained and published by the Concordia University System. For the purpose of this study, the survey did not include lay-practitioners or others actively serving as Directors of Christian Education without certification. In total, 394 surveys were returned via mail or through telephone follow-up providing an overall response rate of 76.7%. Of that number, 361 surveys were completed with usable data for a usable response rate of 70.2%. Thirty-three surveys were returned from individuals no longer serving in ministry positions they once filled and 120 surveys were not returned at all. The surveys of those who left ministry positions and missing surveys were all treated as missing data.

MAJOR FINDINGS

Demographic Data

- About 50% of the DCEs actively serving congregations are under the age of 36, yet almost 10% are over the age of 51.

- 60% are male, 75% are married, 3% are divorced or widowed.

- 78% are the primary wage earner and slightly over 50% have children at home or in college.

- About 85% are graduates of a synodical university, the majority from the campuses in River Forest, St. Paul, or Seward.

- 57% have been in ministry 10 years or less, and over 85% have been at their present church for ten years or less.

DCE Job Satisfaction

- DCEs are very satisfied in ministry, especially with the work environment, relationships with the pastor(s), relationships with parents, and relationships with the children and youth.

- Skills and competencies in the areas of office management, outreach, counseling, evangelism, effectiveness as a DCE, sense of direction in ministry, and opportunities to update or develop skills also bring satisfaction to the DCE, but on a somewhat lower level.

- Satisfaction is also stated in support services provided by the District and Synod and time available for personal life and family.

- The response of DCEs to the degree of satisfaction in their jobs shows 82.78% somewhat or very satisfied with their position and only 8.33% somewhat or very dissatisfied. There is no significance in regards to gender, age, marital status, university attended, years in ministry, or years at present church.

- In the area of compensation, continuing education, and personal/spiritual needs, DCEs are very satisfied with salary and benefits and felt there was adequate opportunity for continuing education. However, there is uncertainty as to whether or not their congregation had a plan to encourage on-going education.

- Concerning achieving a balance between professional and personal life and their relationships with staff, DCEs are very satisfied with the level of achievement in both of these areas. The same is true in the attainment of personal/spiritual needs.

- DCEs view the job as a ministry and a calling from God, and they have a strong sense of commitment to ministry.

- There is strong agreement when it comes to being treated as a valued professional--having a voice in decisions that affect them and having their overall needs met.

- In the area of pastor/administration, DCEs feel confidence, respect and recognition from the pastor. There is also strong agreement that the pastor needs to be sensitive to the needs and abilities of the DCE, is approachable, is flexible and is a strong advocate for the DCE and the staff.

- Concerning parent's attitudes and the relationship between parents, youth, and the DCE, there is great satisfaction with the respect, the supportive nature, and the appreciation shown by parents.

- There is no strong evidence of dissatisfaction created by unrealistic expectations of parents or the relationship between the DCE and the parents.

- Concerning the pivotal questions asking for the level of satisfaction with DCE ministry, the vast majority (82.27%) state a satisfaction level that is either increasing or staying the same.

- Only 17.73% of those surveyed state a decrease in the satisfaction level of ministry. While no significant difference is noted in gender, age, marital status, etc., further research shows that the 32-36 year olds are growing in their increasing satisfaction level and have a lower rate of decreasing satisfaction than the 22-26 year olds.

- Concerning feelings experienced in ministry, DCEs report not struggling with feelings of depression, disillusionment, anger or inability to relate to others. However, concerns are expressed with being overwhelmed, frustrated, isolated, discontent, anxious, and experiencing self-doubt.

- When examined more closely, results showed that female DCEs who have no children at home or in college express more concern about self-doubt and stronger feelings of anxiety in ministry. Females, as a whole, state stronger feelings of being overwhelmed in ministry and in an inability to relate to others.

- In the area of self-doubt, the youngest DCEs (22-26) experience less, while the oldest (52-62) experience the most. At the same time, the youngest express the highest level of discontentment while the oldest express the least.

- Over 50% of the DCEs who have been in ministry 1-5 years experience anxiety, while fewer than 5% of those in ministry 26-30 years experience anxiety.

- DCEs ages 52-62 state the lowest level of frustration, while those 22-26 years old state the highest.

- Concerning inability to relate to others, those 22-26 years old express a high level compared to those 52-62 years old. Those in ministry 6-10 years state much less inability to relate to others compared to those in ministry 1-5 years.

What additional educational preparation do DCEs need?

- DCEs feel highly competent and adequately prepared by their universities in areas of children/youth ministry, teaching the faith, dealing with congregational responsibilities and expectations, ministering to team members, ministering through small groups, ministering to parents, managing personal spiritual growth and, dealing with conflict.

- DCEs express less confidence in their skill and preparation in dealing with stress, ministering to non-members (evangelism), and ministering to those in crisis.

- They express low confidence and a lack of preparation in ministering to singles, ministering to those from diverse backgrounds, ministering through contemporary worship/music, and ministering to marriages.

- It is interesting to note that those with 11-15 years in ministry express a much higher level of competency in ministering to non-members than those with over 31 years in ministry.

- Nearly 25% of the respondents focused on dissatisfaction due to responsibilities in the congregation without adequate training or education.

What is the ability to predict satisfaction and likelihood to leave the DCE ministry within the next three years?

- Concerning the likelihood of leaving ministry in the next three years, 20.78% are somewhat or very likely to leave, and 72.02% are not very or not at all likely to leave ministry in three years. Additional testing failed to show any significance based on gender, age, marital status, university attended, years in ministry, or any other variable.

- "Overall satisfaction with present ministry" is not a strong predictor of likelihood to leave.

- While 8% state a somewhat or very dissatisfied view of ministry, another 27.89% stated they were somewhat or very likely to leave ministry in the next three years. This research indicates that 3 in 10 certified DCEs will leave the ministry over the next three years.

- Overall satisfaction and the likelihood of leaving are not simple effects that can be attributed to single causal factors. However, there are factors and demographic variables that affect satisfaction/dissatisfaction and whether or not DCEs are more or less likely to leave.

- No specific age group or gender is more likely to leave. In fact, "likelihood to leave" is a common thread woven throughout all ages groups in similar proportions:

Ages	Percent Likely to Leave
27-31	33.7%
22-26	32.8%
32-36	26.0%
42-46	26.0%
47-51	24.0%
52-62	23.5%
37-41	22.5%

Qualitative Responses of Respondents

- What three things provide the most satisfaction in ministry?

Youth/family ministry	31%
Teaching	19%
Serving	12%
Equipping	11%
Relationships	10%
Teaming	9%
Specific roles	7%

- What three things provide the least satisfaction in ministry?

Duties/responsibilities	25%
Volunteers	25%
Staff	19%
Ministry frustrations	15%
Financial	7%
Politics	5%
Personal	4%

- What is the biggest issue faced in ministry?

Future	27%
Skills	21%
Environment	19%
Volunteers	14%
Finance	9%
Staff	8%
Education	2%

- Those who stated that they are somewhat or very likely to leave in the next three years were asked to state the specific reason for leaving. They were:

Career change	27%
Personal concerns	20%
Family issues	18%
Salary	15%
Pastor/staff relations	15%
No reason	4%

- Reasons for leaving most often listed according to age are:

Age	Top Reasons for Leaving
22-26	Marriage, starting family
27-31	Salary, changing careers, family demands, job issues
32-36	Family demands, salary
37-41	Unclear/demanding job expectations, finances, seminary
42-46	Synodical issues, seminary
47-51	Seminary, age, career change
52-62	Issues with pastor, age, career change

RECOMMENDATIONS

While this study indicates satisfaction among Directors of Christian Education, it also provides an abundance of data that can be acted upon to make a difference in ministry by addressing the reasons for satisfaction/dissatisfaction, the reasons for leaving, gender concerns, and age-related issues.

Measures to increase satisfaction in the career can be undertaken quickly and economically by educating congregations and staff on the value of positive, supportive relationships, emphasizing boundaries between ministry and personal life, providing clear job descriptions, recognizing varying lifestage needs of the DCE, and encouraging a personal spiritual life for DCEs. Sharing this research with congregations will enable them to evaluate and compare their situations with this study and help them explore ways to enhance a supportive environment for younger DCEs. Congregations may also be able to identify ways to support and retain older DCEs in parish ministry.

These survey results will also help congregations understand the importance of continuing education and skills development for DCEs. Districts may also be encouraged to provide a mentoring program for DCEs new to the area.

Over half of the DCEs who plan to leave the profession indicated that they are doing so for personal reasons associated with life stage or lifestyle change. Measures should be taken to retain these workers through incentives such as bonuses tied to years in ministry or years at present church, considering reduced workloads for new parents, providing raises related to life stage levels such as college, continuing education, loans for home purchase, and creating flexible job descriptions to allow the DCE to remain in the ministry.

SUMMARY

While the findings of this study indicate that Directors of Christian Education are generally satisfied with their ministry, there are specific variables that do affect their satisfaction and likelihood to leave ministry. While there is no way to guarantee the retention of these workers, evaluating the educational curriculum and integrating needed competency skills and training can enhance the profession and ministry longevity. At the same time, improving relationships in the parish and taking preventative action regarding factors that create dissatisfaction can help both the DCE and the congregation.

REFERENCES

Arches, J. (1991). Social structure, burnout, and job satisfaction. *Social Work, 36*, 202-206.

Babbie, E. (1990). *Survey Research Methods* (2nd ed.). Belmont, CA: Wadsworth.

Board for Congregational Services. (2003). *Certified DCEs serving congregations.* St. Louis, MO: Author.

Bobbitt, S. A., Leich, M. C., Whitener, S. D. & Lynch, H. F. (1994). *Characteristics of stayers, movers, and leavers: Results from the teacher follow-up survey.* (Publication No. 94-337). Washington, D.C: National Center for Education Statistics.

Bobek, B. (2002). Teacher resiliency: A key to career longevity. *Clearing House, 75*(4), 202- 208.

Choy, S. P., Bobbit, S. A., Henke, R. R., Medrich, E. A., Horn, L. J. & Lieberman, J. (1993). *America's teachers: Profile of a profession* (Publication No. 93-025). Washington, D.C: National Center for Education Statistics.

Commission on Ministerial Growth and Support (2000). *Teacher 2000: A survey of teachers in the Lutheran school system.* St. Louis, MO: Author.

Concordia Publishing House. (2001). The Lutheran annual 2002 of the Lutheran Church–Missouri Synod (2001). St. Louis, MO: Author.

Concordia University System. (2003). *Directors of Christian education who have been certified by a synodical school of the LC–MS: 2003.* St. Louis, MO: Author.

Creswell, J. W. (2002). *Educational Research: planning, conducting, and evaluating quantitative and qualitative research.* Upper Saddle River, NJ: Merrill.

Durkin, E. & Montague, J. D. (1995, February 11). Surveying U.S. nuns, *America Press, 172*(4), 11.

Elmshauser, J. M. (2001, February). *DCE ministry competency survey.* Survey results presented at the DCE Summit, Austin, TX.

Ewen, R. (1966). A theory of human motivation. *Psychological Review, 50*(4), 370-396.

Ferguson, D. B. (2000). NSTA teacher survey lists teachers' dissatisfactions. *Curriculum Administrator, 36*(7), 18.

Festinger, L. (1957). *A theory of cognitive dissonance.* Evanston, IL: Row, Peterson.

Feuerherd, J. (2002, September 20). Job satisfaction high among Catholic clergy. *National Catholic Reporter, 38*(40), 13.

Gall, M. D., Borg, W. R. & Gall, J. P. (1996). *Educational research: An introduction.* New York, NY: Long Publishers.

Herzberg, F., Mausner, B., & Snyderman, B. (1959). *The motivation to work*. New York, NY: John Wiley & Sons, Inc.

Hugick, L., & Leonard, J. (1991). Job dissatisfaction grows; "moonlighting" on the rise. *Gallup Poll News Service, 56*, 1-11.

Jayaratne, S. & Chess, W. A. (1985). Factors associated with job satisfaction and turnover among child welfare workers. In J. Laird & A. Hartman (Eds.), *A handbook of child welfare* (pp. 760-766). New York, NY: Free Press.

Karpenko, W. O. II. (1986). *A brief summary of the pertinent findings from phase I and II of the DCE curricular development and validation project involving directors of Christian education (DCEs) of the Lutheran Church–Missouri Synod*. Unpublished manuscript, Concordia College, Seward, NE.

Karpenko, W. O. II. (1990). *A brief summary of the pertinent findings from phase III of the DCE curricular development and validation project involving directors of Christian education (DCEs) of the Lutheran Church–Missouri Synod*. Unpublished manuscript, Concordia College, Seward, NE.

Karpenko, W. O. II. (1997). *The identification of the roles and subroles in which most directors of Christian education (DCEs) engage*. [Unpublished raw data].

Kay, W. K. (2000, January). Job satisfaction of British Pentecostal ministers. *Asian Journal of Pentecostal Studies, 3*(1), 83-97.

Keyne, L. K. (1995). *Who do you say I am? The professional identity of the director of Christian education in the Lutheran Church–Missouri Synod* (Doctoral dissertation). University of Southern California. UMI No. 9614035.

Kristof, A. L. (1996). Person-organization fit: An integrative review of its conceptualizations, measurement, and implications. *Personnel Psychology, 49*(1), 1-49.

Linville, P. W. (1987). Self-complexity as a cognitive buffer against stress-related illness and depression. *Journal of Personality and Social Psychology, 52*(4), 663-676.

Maslach, C., & Pines, A. (1988). Burn-out: The loss of human caring. In A. Pines & C. Maslach (Eds.), Experiencing social psychology: Readings and projects (2nd ed., pp. 246-252). New York, NY: Random House.

Maslow, A. (1943). A theory of human motivation. *Psychological Review, 50*(4), 370-396.

Masten, A. S., Best, K. M., & Garmezy, N. (1990). Resilience and development: contributions from the study of children who overcame adversity. *Development and Psychopathology, 2*, 425-444.

Moore, D. W. & Newport, F. (1995). People throughout the world largely satisfied with personal lives, *The Gallup Poll Monthly, 357*, 2-7.

Moreira, H., Fox, K. R., & Sparks, A. C. (2002). Job motivation profiles of physical educators: Theoretical background and instrument development. *British Educational Research Journal, 28*(6), 845-861.

Olson, L. (2000). Finding and keeping competent teachers. *Education Week, 19*(18), 12-18.

Palola, E. G. & Larson, W. R. (1965). Some dimensions of job satisfaction among hospital personnel. *Sociology and Social Research, 49,* 201-213.

Pamperin, B.F. (1987). Creative school social workers and job satisfaction. *Social Work in Education, 10*(1), 60-71.

Perie, M. & Baker, D. P. (1997). *Job satisfaction among America's teachers: Effects of workplace conditions, background characteristics, and teacher compensation.* (NCES Publication No 97-471). Washington, DC: National Center for Education Statistics.

Porter, L.W. (1963). Job attitudes in management: Perceived deficiencies in need fulfillment as a function of size of company. *Journal of Applied Psychology, 47*(6), 386-397.

Schroeder, T. W. (1975, April). A history of directors of Christian education in the Lutheran Church–Missouri Synod. *Directors of Christian Education Bulletin, 9*(2), 4-16.

Schoepp, P. W. (2003). Lay practitioners of parish-based Christian education ministry within the Lutheran Church–Missouri Synod: A survey of demographics, ministry roles and certification interest (Doctoral dissertation). University of Nebraska–Lincoln.

Spector, P. E. (1997). *Job satisfaction: Application, assessment, causes, and consequences.* Thousand Oaks, CA: Sage Publications.

Sweet, L. I. (1999) *Soul tsunami.* Grand Rapids, MI: Zondervan Publishing.

Tracy, E. M., Bean, N., Gwatkin, S., & Hill, B. (1992). Family preservation workers: Sources of job satisfaction and job stress. *Research on Social Work Practice, 2*(4), 465-478.

Unsworth, T. (1998, February 6). He visited 450 parishes, finds morale at low ebb. *National Catholic Reporter, 34*(14), 15.

Vinokur-Kaplan, D. (1990). Job satisfaction among social workers in public and voluntary welfare agencies. *Child Welfare, 70*(1), 81-91.

CHAPTER 13

Role of Women in DCE Ministry

Debra Arfsten | Audrey Duensing-Werner

William O. Karpenko II

As we celebrate 50 years of the Director of Education (DCE) ministry in the Lutheran Church–Missouri Synod (LC–MS), we take a look back at the role women have played in its history and the significant impact that their presence has made. We will also take a look at the unique characteristics and challenges that DCE women have faced throughout the five decades that they have been serving.

First let's take a look at the role women have played as servant leaders and in team ministry situations throughout the Bible. There are many references in Scripture where there are women serving in team ministry leadership roles. One of the earliest mentions of a woman serving in team ministry

Debra Arfsten, Ph.D., serves as Director of the DCE Program at Concordia University Chicago.

Audrey Duensing-Werner serves as DCE at Faith Lutheran Church in Topeka Kansas. She is also Chairperson-elect for the National Association of Directors of Christian Education.

William Karpenko II, Ph.D., served as DCE Program Director at Concordia University, Nebraska and Concordia University, St. Paul. He currently serves as Administrative Executive of KINDLE.

to the shepherd of God's people is the character, Miriam. Miriam, sister of Moses, served alongside Moses and Aaron and is mentioned in Ex. 15:20 as a prophetess. The Greek word for prophet is *prophetes*. The meaning of *prophetes* is one who declares to men what he/she has received by inspiration from God – he/she is speaking "for" God or on God's behalf. In all cases, prophets deliver divinely inspired messages from God that relate to the cause and kingdom of God and to human salvation.

Other examples include Esther and Ruth (books of Esther and Ruth), Huldah (2 Kings 22 and Chron. 34), Isaiah's wife (Isa. 8), Anna (Lk. 1), Phoebe (Rom. 16), and Priscilla in her ministry with her husband Aquila and Paul (Acts 18).

One favorite story that emulates the role of the DCE woman, however, is tucked away in an obscure corner of the Old Testament. It is not a very long story, but it makes a powerful connection. This story is of a mighty prophetess and judge named Deborah. The political structure at the time was very patriarchal and Deborah's responsibilities were those typically held by men. In fact the prophetess Deborah was the only woman judge among the twelve judges who ruled between the times of Joshua and Samuel. She was used by God to bring the people back to God and the nation acknowledged her as its leader. She was both a national and a spiritual leader. A judge, at that time, was more than one who settled disputes; a judge was equal to a governor holding executive and legislative authority as well as military authority. In her high position, Deborah was a mediator between God and His people and the proclaimer of His Word while communicating insight, wisdom, and the knowledge of God with love to her people.

In Judg. 4-5, we are told that Deborah ruled about 8-10 miles outside of Jerusalem. People would travel to her to hear her wisdom. Judge Deborah was known for her closeness to God and that God spoke to and through her. When the time came to fight the war, Deborah knew she should not be the appointed person to lead the fight because she was a woman, however, God told her who the right person was. She commanded a man by the name of Barak to do so.

She had been praying for the freedom in her country for many years, but knew that someone else should have the lead role in the fight. Deborah demonstrated shared leadership in a significant way with Barak. Although she was the first among her people, she did not place herself over Barak. Instead, she placed herself next to him and worked to inspire him in his leadership. Barak responded by accepting the challenge, but only if Deborah was with him. He knew God was with her and he wanted to have God's presence with him while he led the battle so he asked Deborah to accompany him to war. He knew he needed her wisdom from God. He showed respect for her as the leader and together they carried out God's orders with no sense of competition between them. Not only were they looking out for one another but they were also looking out for the welfare of the country.

The story of Deborah shows us that God does not always work in a set pattern; instead, he chooses people for leadership who are willing to be used as his instruments. Deborah was a great leader not only because she fulfilled her job responsibilities with excellence, but she was also a woman of enormous spiritual strength. She continually acknowledged that her strength and power came from God, rather than through any power of her own. Deborah showed a heart of a true servant leadership by not placing honor upon herself, but instead loving and caring for the people that God entrusted to her. She showed the unlimited possibilities of what women in ministry can do when God has complete control over their life.

Like Deborah, the role of the female DCE has been in serving within a patriarchal model. Deborah remained connected to God, respected among the people, did her work with excellence, walked alongside Barak in team ministry, and looked out for the entire community. Her role as a servant leader provides an excellent example for all women who seek to serve in team ministry.

Let us take a look at some of the research findings that show how women have served as DCEs in the LC–MS and the many and varied roles they have played.

CERTIFIED FEMALE DCEs IN THE LC-MS FROM 1972 TO 2010

From 1972 to 2010, approximately 1,175 women have been certified as DCEs by the programs of six Concordia Universities. The vast majority chose to be certified as DCEs by graduating from one of the six undergraduate DCE programs. Others took one of the following three routes: 1) a post-baccalaureate program, 2) a DCE colloquy program, or 3) being field certification through a special process created in 1984-87 to "grandmother" in women who had served in full-time DCE positions for seven years or longer (six women chose to do so).

According to the 2010 DCE Directory, the first two women certified as DCEs graduated from Concordia College in St. Paul, Minnesota, in 1972. By September 1988, there were 272 certified DCEs who were women, and they represented 35% of the total (787). As of September 2010, the number of certified women had reached 882 (46% of the total), reflecting the extensive growth of women being certified for DCE ministry. However, of the 659 individuals serving in congregations of he LC–MS in September 2010, the number of women and men was more evenly divided: 306 women (47%) and 353 men (53%).

A HISTORICAL GLIMPSE AT THREE SOURCES OF
RESEARCH INVOLVING CERTIFIED FEMALE DCES

As the number of women in DCE ministry became more prevalent, more questions about their service arose. Three questions that surfaced regularly over the past three decades are:

1. How would one describe the ministry of certified female DCEs in the LC–MS?

2. Are the congregational roles for women the same as for men?

3. As a female DCE, how would you characterize your relationships with pastors and other staff based on gender?

When questions like these arose, there was a stimulus to find answers. Here are glimpses at various efforts to address these questions.

A 1974 - 1996 COMPARATIVE LOOK AT
WOMEN IN DCE MINISTRY WITHIN THE LCMS

The following information comes from an unpublished teaching resource entitled *Women in DCE Ministry within the LCMS* and from the 1996 DCE Directory.

TABLE 13.1

Comparison of the Demographic Statistics of Female DCEs: 1974 vs. 1996

	1974	1996
Current Class		
Total*	19	159
Married*	5 (26%)	83 (53%)
Certified	7 (37%)	132 (83%)
Accepted a Call*	3 (16%)	52 (44%)
ALL DCEs		
Serving 10+ years*	1 (5%)	53 (33%)
Serving 15+ years*	0 (0%)	13 (8%)
Certified	11 (50%)	405 (38%)
Certified and Serving	6 (55%)	129 (29%)

Certified and non-certified.

A 1978 MATCHED-PAIR STUDY AND
MEN AND WOMEN IN DCE MINISTRY

In 1978, a matched-pair demographic research project designed to answer a 36-item questionnaire was conducted that would lead to an increased
awareness and understanding of female DCEs in the LC–MS. At the time
of the project, 40 women were identified as serving in DCE positions. Thir-
ty-eight (95%) of these women returned their questionnaires and 33 were
deemed useable. One hundred and twenty male DCEs were invited to participate and 104 (87%) of them responded. Given the surplus of men respondents, the 33 male DCEs were selected by matching four factors: 1) the same
number of years in their present DCE position; 2) the same number of years
in DCE ministry; 3) the same number of parishes served; and 4) a similar type
of professional background.

The final section of the report captured the following noteworthy demographics regarding women and men in DCE ministry in 1978:

- The demographic similarities between women and men in DCE ministry far exceed the differences when examining their age, educational
  background, call experience, title or age and tenure of pastoral teammate. These same similarities also existed in the percentage of time
  invested in the major congregational responsibilities, including planning, organizing, administering parish program, and working in youth
  ministry.

- Major differences between female and male DCEs focus in areas where
  synodical history and cultural traditions have tended to enforce a difference. These issues include earning less salary, receiving a non-tenured call,
  and little involvement in public worship, all of which have long been present with female LC–MS teachers and have tended to migrate over into
  DCE ministry because of local congregational decisions.

Since women have been serving as DCEs for less than a decade, and men for less
than two decades, many questions are just being formulated about women and
men in DCE ministry.

The profile of a female DCE serving a congregation in 1978 would include a person who was

- 28; frequently single; synodically-trained; usually teacher-trained

- just as likely to be certified as a DCE as not; in DCE ministry for three years or less

- serving her first parish; located in the Midwest and upper Midwest regions of the synod

- serving a congregation with 720 communicants, which usually does not have a school, and which is found in a suburb, town (1,000-49,999) or a small city (50,000 - 199,999)

- working with a pastor who had been in the congregation 7.6 years and was 18.1 years her senior

- interviewed on-site prior to accepting her 'call without tenure' and given the title of DCE

- earning around $10,500; and spending 50 hours per week 'on the job'

- spending the majority of her time planning and organizing programs with boards and committees, administering those programs, teaching various classes and doing youth ministry

- involved in public worship mainly through music and special worship events

- accountable to the pastor and some congregational board(s)

In short, it would appear that the female DCEs in this study were Directors of Christian Education – not part-time secretaries, musicians, or parochial school teachers who happened to have been given the title of DCE. Most of their time, much like their male colleagues, was spent in planning, organizing, and administering programs, in teaching in various parish education agencies, and in ministry to young people.

Building upon this 1978 study, the unpublished *Women in DCE Ministry within the LCMS* included comparative data between the percentage of time female and male spent in common DCE roles during 1990 and 1997, indicated in table 13.2.

TABLE 13.2

Percentage of Time Spent in Common DCE Roles

Role	Approximate Percentage of Time*			
	1990		1997	
	Female	Male	Female	Male
Administrator	21.0	22.7	18.6	19.0
Age Group Specialist	15.9	14.4	11.8	10.4
Care Action Minister	7.2	7.0	6.2	5.7
Church Professional	8.7	7.9	8.7	7.2
Educational-Program Resource	11.2	11.3	8.6	8.2
Musician	6.8	4.0	4.5	5.4
Organizational Consultant	3.2	4.3	changed to leader	
Organizational Leader	changed from consultant		11.1	13.4
Pastoral/staff Support	5.6	6.8	5.7	6.7
Teacher/Theological Resource	12.8	14.1	13.1	13.5
Volunteer Specialist	7.8	7.5	11.0	9.0

Not all columns add to 100% due to rounding.

When comparing these two years of data, as well as each year's differences, the following observations regarding female involvement in common DCE roles seems noteworthy. When comparing the 1990 data with that from 1997:

- Female DCEs' time investment in three "secondary roles" like pastoral/staff support, care action minister, and church professional remained relatively constant while three "primary roles" like administrator, age group specialist, and education-program resource reflected significant variation.

- Female DCEs invest two-thirds of their time in the five "primary roles" of a DCEs ministry: administering, working with specific age groups, providing leadership in various areas of the congregation's life, being a teacher/theological resource, and serving as a volunteer specialist.

- Female and male DCEs during each year, and over both years, dedicated at least two-thirds of their time in the five "primary roles" of their ministry.

1992 SYNOD STUDY ON STAFF RELATIONSHIPS
WITHIN CONGREGATIONS AND SCHOOLS

The Project on Team Ministry was initially convened in the fall of 1987 under the joint sponsorship of the LC–MS Board for Higher Education Services (BHES), the Board for Parish Services (BPS), and the Lutheran Education Association's Department of Theological Educators in Associated Ministries (LEA-TEAM). The initial endeavor of the Project was a Synod-wide Team Ministry survey in February 1989 in which 459 pastors and DCEs participated. The focus of the final phase of the Project was upon strengthening the capacity of district leaders to serve the various types of congregational and school staffs at work within their districts.

In 1991, a survey was conducted of District Presidents and Education Executives regarding the state of staff relationships throughout the Lutheran Church–Missouri Synod. The significance of the findings presented in the report related to the general perception in the 1970s and 1980s that female DCEs and male pastors were not able to work effectively together and that numerous congregations were experiencing extensive gender-related conflict. Specific findings from two sections of the Report present a different picture:

Focus of Congregational and School Interventions

1. For both district leaders (President and Education Executive), pastor-pastor and pastor-principal staff relationship were perceived as most frequently troubled.

2. Even though it may be a function of the prevalence of such relationships in some districts, those staff relationships perceived as least frequently troubled involved principal-DCE and pastor-deaconess.

3. Across districts, both district presidents and education executives perceived the number of gender-related staff problems to be significantly less.

4. Within a district team, three trends emerged when comparing now to three years ago:

    a. The number of strong teams was growing.

    b. Less time was being spent in responding to problematic staff relationships.

    c. The number of gender-related staff problems was much less than three years ago.

Number of Gender-Related Staff Problems Compared to Three Years Ago

- Presidents perceived the number of gender-related staff problems to be much less (2.5 on a 7.0 scale - "greater" = 7 or 6).

- Similarly, education executives also perceived the number of gender-related staff problems to be less (2.9 on a 7.0 scale - "greater" = 7 or 6).

- Within a district, this same perception held true between the presidents and the education executive (80% experience less gender-related staff problems).

A 1997 PERSPECTIVE ON THE INFLUENCES
OF BEING A FEMALE DCE UPON ONE'S MINISTRY

An additional section of *Women in DCE Ministry within the LCMS* contained the following composite of reactions from female DCEs when asked what "gender-related hindrances and helps" had been experienced in day-to-day ministry:

Gender-Related Hindrances

- "I'm not permitted to attend meetings of the elders or council."
- "It would be easier if you were a deaconess."
- "I have to work extra hard to prove myself."
- "It is hard to find visible ways to prove myself."

- "Pastor is threatened by my competence."

- "Pastor does not seem comfortable relating to me in an open, caring way."

- "Boys don't respond well to my efforts to discipline them."

- "Single moms convey a subtle disappointment that I'm not a male DCE."

- "Macho male youth—athletic and otherwise—seem to be less involved."

Gender-Related Helps

- "I am able to put pastor at ease; I pose no threat to him in preaching."

- "Pastor and I are able to model a healthy relationship."

- "I am able to bring a female sensitivity and perspective to our efforts."

- "I am seen as approachable, easier to talk to by many."

- "I am able to respond to certain women who are not comfortable talking to a man about their concerns."

- "I am providing youth, especially young women, with a professional ministry model."

- "Lay women of the parish feel affirmed by my presence."

- "There is lots of public affirmation of the 'gender balance' that our staff has."

THE LATEST RESEARCH FINDINGS:
PHASE I OF THE DCE CAREER PATH PROJECT

In February 2008, the largest research project involving certified DCEs was launched under the sponsorship of the DCE Summit of the LC–MS. The purposes of the project were to: (1) determine the predominant career paths for certified DCEs in the LC–MS, and (2) communicate to the church the results of this study.

Phase I of the DCE Career Path Project involved 802 certified DCEs who responded to 17 generic items and another 17-19 items that were specific to one of eight status categories of certified DCEs. These status categories included congregational DCE, non-congregational DCE, teacher/principal, other commissioned minister, pastor, retired, certified for rostered ministry status, and no longer on the Synod's roster. Among the numerous findings from Phase I, the following ten questions were addressed by the results:

1. **Among the 308 female certified DCEs who participated in Phase I, how many of them were in each of the eight status categories?**

TABLE 13.3

Female Certified DCEs by Status Category

Congregational DCE	170	55%
Non-congregational DCE	16	5%
Teacher/principal	21	7%
Other commissioned minister	8	3%
Pastor	0	0%
Retired	4	1%
Certified for rostered ministry status	20	7%
No longer on the roster	69	22%

2. **Was DCE ministry in a congregation a viable long-term career for women?**
   Among the 291 female certified DCEs who shared their career paths in the survey, three were still serving in congregation after 30 years; twenty-one still serving after 20 years; and 84 still serving after 10 years.

3. **If there were female DCEs whose career spanned 20 or more years, what helped it to happen ?**
   Although no specific item focused on this question, DCE career paths of the 291 females suggested that four factors played a significant longevity role: the women's desire and determination to pursue a long term career, their overall competence in fulfilling the DCE role, their congregation's flexibility in permitting a reduced or more flexible work schedule during the family raising years, and, if married, a supportive spouse.

4. **What percentage of the 170 females in the survey were serving a congregation while also raising a young family?**
   Thirty-one percent (52)

5. What percentage of the 170 female congregational DCEs was single?
   Thirty-two percent (55)

6. How many of the 170 female congregational DCEs were married to another certified DCE?
   Thirteen were married to another certified DCE, of whom two were also
   currently serving as a congregational DCE.

7. What were the predominant career path patterns for congregational
   DCEs who were female?
   The predominant career path patterns (or how these women began their
   professional career) of the 163 certified female DCEs who submitted a
   career statement were fourfold: congregational DCE only (61%); one or
   more other non-church-related positions and congregational DCE (15%);
   career path interlude (7%); and congregational DCE and one or more
   other church-related positions (6%). Among the 16 career path patterns,
   these four reflected 89% of the women.

8. What were the predominant global career path types for congregational
   DCEs who were female?
   The predominant global career paths of the 163 certified female DCEs
   who submitted a career statement were also fourfold: congregational DCE
   only (61%); DCE and non-church profession (17%); DCE and other
   congregational/school ministries (7%); and DCE and interlude for family/
   personal/professional concerns (7%). Among the seven global types, these
   four captured 92% of the women who responded.

9. What were the predominant specific career path types for parish DCEs
   who were female?
   The predominant specific career paths of the 163 certified female DCEs
   who submitted a career statement were fivefold: congregational career just
   launching (28%); short-term career congregational DCE (22%); mid-term
   career congregational DCE (10%); DCE and business/industry (8%); and
   DCE and marriage/family interlude (6%). Among the 30 specific types,
   these five described 74% of the women.

10. What other germane findings related to female DCEs did Phase I surface?
    a. The percentage of female DCEs who were no longer on the roster of
       the synod or were on candidate status was higher than male DCEs pri-
       marily because of fewer ministry role options and a greater need for a
       professional ministry interlude due to family considerations.

b. By 2008, there were 24 female DCEs who had served as a congregational DCE for 20 or more years.

c. Two additional female DCEs who were deceased at the time of the study also served as a congregational DCE for 20 or more years. All of the above statistics in this section need direct explicit citation. Are they taken directly from a number of pages, or is each answer on a separate page?

LOOKING AHEAD: RESEARCH QUESTIONS
RELATING TO WOMEN IN DCE MINISTRY

While the questions meriting new or renewed research are somewhat endless, the following questions hold promise to enrich one's understanding of the life and well-being of women in DCE Ministry:

Female DCEs' Congregational Role

1. Do the congregational roles of female and male DCEs still mirror one another or has there been significant change since the 1978, 1990 and 1997 studies?

2. Do the congregational roles of certified female DCEs differ from those who are not certified?

3. What are the salient characteristics of those congregations in which female DCEs continue to serve during the child-rearing years?

4. How have, if all, the roles of a female DCE altered if she continued working through her child-raising years?

5. Are there significant role differences among female DCEs who are single, married, or married with children?

6. What role changes take place, if any, in a female DCE's career path as she serves into her 50s and 60s?

Females in DCE Ministry

7. What impact will the increasing percentages of women in DCE ministry have upon the profession?

8. What are the key attributes of female DCEs who choose to serve in a paid congregational position while raising a family?

9. Once a female DCE "steps out" of the public ministry, how many have chosen to return to a congregational position? If so, what are the most productive avenues back into such positions?

10. What have been the experiences of those female DCEs whose spouse has simultaneously served in either the same or a separate congregational ministry?

11. What is the career path experience of female DCEs who have chosen to serve the local congregation in a role other than as a DCE? Or in a role beyond the parish?

12. What is the relationship between females who call themselves DCEs, DCM, and DFL?

13. What opportunities have female DCEs had to serve at the district and/or national levels? Has that experience been positive?

Staff Relationships

14. Do female DCEs tend to experience more conflict with their pastor than do male DCEs? If not, what areas of conflict are female DCEs still prone to experience with their pastor?

15. Is there a qualitative difference in staff relationships between female DCEs and pastors who once served as DCEs and those who never served in the DCE role?

16. What impact, if any, will the exodus of male DCEs into the pastoral office through the Specific Pastor Ministry (SPM) have upon women in DCE Ministry?

Support Processes for Female DCEs

17. How do women in DCE ministry still stay healthy emotionally, spiritually, intellectually, physically, and financially?

18. Are support processes different for female DCEs than their male counterparts?

19. What support processes are most commonly used by female DCEs when in conflict?

Single Female DCEs

20. What have been the most successful ways that single women have overcome being so consumed by "the job," in ways that it does not decimate one's social life and lead to a sense of isolation?

21. What have been the most effective means of maintaining regular visibility within the life of the congregation?

22. How have sexuality issues with one's pastor been worked through in order to maintain an honest level of gender respect and appreciation?

In 2009, Dr. Debra Arfsten and DCE Audrey Duensing-Werner sent out forty questionnaires to women who had been serving in the DCE ministry for five or more years. The questionnaire asked the participants to name three to five gender-related issues they faced as women in ministry and how they dealt with those issues in a positive way. Table 13.4 lists some of the specific responses noted on the questionnaires that were returned.

These responses are similar to those reported in the 1997 article *Women in DCE Ministry within the LCMS* and the 2007 article *Celebrating as Women in DCE Ministry.*

When the original research on women in ministry was completed in 1974, little was known about the challenges and experiences of women who were serving in DCE positions, nor what the future of DCE ministry would look like for female DCEs. Subsequent studies have shown that while many of the challenges and obstacles for women in ministry remain the same, there has been a tremendous increase in women serving in DCE positions very successfully. Gender issues will always remain, but team ministries that value the God-given gifts of each team member will not see gender as an issue, but instead embrace the diversity of the team. It is clear from the growth of female DCEs in the last 50 years that there is still a need and desire for women to serve in full-time ministry, and that God continues to gift women for this very purpose.

TABLE 13.4

Gender-related Hinderances & Helps

Hindrances
"The tension between juggling ministry and family time is overwhelming."
"The older I have become the more the church uses me in all kinds of leadership roles…finding Sabbath and balance is impossible."
"There is a glass ceiling that we'll never be able to overcome."
"I have to prove myself more than it seems male colleagues do."
"As a single female I sense the church expects me to work longer and harder because I don't have a 'family'."
"I serve nationally in leadership positions but my own parish does not allow me to lead at the same level."
"Things are said to me that would be considered 'sexual harassment' that would not be said to males."

Helps
"The Pastor and I team teach classes and it models positive male/female ministry relationships."
"The church and pastor use me to bring a female perspective to situations."
"For other women and young girls I am easier to talk to and listen."
"It shows women and young girls that there are positive leadership roles for women in the parish."
"I bring to the staff a 'nurturing' component that would not otherwise be there."
"I help nurture young women to fully live out their calling."

REFERENCES

Arfsten, D. J., & Seifert, V. (2006, Winter). Celebrating as women in DCE ministry. *Shaping the Future, 3*(4), 34-36.

Karpenko, W. O. II. (1975, Spring). 1974 DCE Call Trends, *DCE Bulletin.*

Karpenko, W. O. II. (1980, Fall). Women and men in DCE ministry: A comparative study. Part I: A demographic profile. *DCE Bulletin.*

Karpenko, W. O. II. (1992). *Findings and interpretive comments based upon a Survey of district presidents' and district education executives' perceptions regarding staff relationships within congregations and schools of the district they serve.* St. Louis, MO: LCMS Team Ministry Project.

Karpenko, W. O. II. (1997). *Women in DCE ministry within the LCMS.* Unpublished manuscript, Concordia University. Chicago, IL.

Karpenko, W. O. II. (1997). *Influences of being a female DCE upon one's ministry.* Unpublished manuscript, Concordia University. Chicago, IL.

1988 DCE Directory, Concordia University DCE Program Directors. Seward, NE: Concordia University, Limited edition publication, 1988.

2008 DCE Career Path Research Project-Phase I, NADCE-National Association of DCEs, 2010.

2010 DCE Directory, Concordia University DCE Program Directors. Seward, NE: Concordia University, Limited edition publication, 2010.

CHAPTER 14

Team Ministry: Traveling Together to Travel Far

JULIE JOHNSTON HERMANN

When you hear the word "team" what images come to mind? What do you think of when the phrase "team ministry" is used? What makes a team different from a group? What difference does a team really make when it comes to ministry? This article considers the characteristics of team ministry, as well as the personal awareness needed by a DCE when becoming part of a ministry team in a congregation.

WHY IS A TEAM SO IMPORTANT?

If you want to travel fast, travel alone; if you want to travel far, travel together. This African proverb indicates the benefit of traveling through life together with others. The meaning is that we can get much farther with others – traveling alongside us, working with us, supporting us – than if we are out on our own. This can be as true for our progress on a long road trip as it is for our

Julie Johnston Hermann, M.S. in Family Life Ministry, serves as Assistant Professor of Education and Director of International Education at Concordia University, Nebraska

work organizing a special event. When we can work alongside others the tasks are divided and the burden is shared.

We see many examples in nature of groups traveling together through life. Geese flying in formation, penguins huddled on the edge of an ice flow, junior-high girls gathered together at a youth event – all illustrate the need for support, encouragement, and direction that are found in being together with others. Life is not meant to be traveled alone. Traveling through life is much easier and more meaningful with the support of family, friends, and teams. Traveling together is especially important for the journey that is church work.

Any ministry vocation can become a very isolated situation if approached with a "lone ranger" mentality. We just cannot do it all alone, and we should not think we can. There is space for individuality that can be brought to the job, but there needs to be the opportunity for community, support, and accountability in order for anyone to have a healthy, long-term ministry. A strong team ministry situation can help provide those necessary personal and professional safeguards.

A TEAM IS BETTER THAN ONE

When Jesus began His ministry He gathered a team– His disciples– to expand His efforts. Since Christ had a limited time on this earth, He modeled for His team what they would need to know and do when He was gone. Author C. Gene Wilkes (1998) provides a number of Biblical examples of how Christ led to illustrate how we can lead as Jesus did. One of those examples refers to how Christ worked with His team. In Mark's Gospel we read that Jesus built a team in order to carry out His vision.

> Jesus went up on a mountainside and called to him those he wanted, and they came to him. He appointed twelve – designating them apostles – that they might be with him and that he might send them out to preach and to have authority to drive out demons (Mk. 3:13-15).

Jesus shared responsibility and authority with those He called to His team. The principle here is we can work together with others, empowered by God, to meet a greater purpose. It is not about us and what power or authority we claim for our individual efforts, it is about what Christ has entrusted to us as we serve as part of His team.

The wisdom of Ecclesiastes can also be considered in outlining the value found in teamwork.

> Two are better than one, because they have a good return for their work: if one falls down, his friend can help him up. But pity the man who falls and has no one to help him up! Also, if two lie down together, they will keep warm. But how can one keep warm alone? Though one can be overpowered, two can defend themselves. A cord of three strands is not quickly broken (Eccl. 4:9-12).

This passage illustrates the strength and encouragement that can be found in working and serving with others. We can consider further the implications for ministry teams found in specific sections of this passage.

They have a good return for their work. When we work with others the tasks can be shared and the benefits multiplied. Team intelligence activities show that more can be accomplished by a team working together on an activity than what individuals can do alone. In these team situations, more ideas are generated and additional perspectives for decision-making and problem solving can be considered. Teamwork can multiply the effect of individual efforts.

If one falls, the other can help him up. In a team, we are not alone. There is comfort knowing we have others who can assist us when we need it. In addition, it is not possible to always be "up," so team members can provide encouragement and support if someone happens to be having a "down" day.

If two lie down together, they will keep warm. People are made for relationships, not isolation. Teams can provide a place of community and comfort that humans need.

Two can defend themselves. Team members are able to work together toward common goals. Because of this connected purpose and understanding, team members can provide encouragement to each other in frustrating or discouraging situations. Knowing they are in this together can provide a sense of security and camaraderie to team members.

A cord of three strands is not quickly broken. Teams are stronger together than individuals are by themselves. Individuals who function as independent superstars can be detrimental to the team – it will fail if members continue to operate as individuals. True teams thrive when they develop a sense of interdependence, with each team member bringing skills, abilities, knowledge, or perceptions to the group that make the entire team stronger.

WHAT CAN A TEAM PROVIDE?

The nature of a team means that a group of people is working together toward a common goal. Each team member brings individual abilities to the group and can use those skills to build up and further the efforts of the team. You will come to a congregation with certain responsibilities stipulated in your job description. Other team members will have specific responsibilities that fall under their job descriptions as well. But beyond these pre-determined job responsibilities, team members bring who they are and what they can do to the team, allowing for creative and collaborative efforts to support the work of others. Ministry teams can provide a place for members to experience accountability, feedback, truth-telling, trust, communication, support and encouragement, and relationships of influence.

1) **Accountability:** There can be enormous freedom and flexibility in how church workers spend their time and resources – in the office, out of the office, at home, visiting with youth, participating in events, and so on. No one wants to have their intentions or motivations called into question. Proverbs 11:14 (NIV) notes the need for accountability, stating, "where there is no guidance, the people fall, but in the abundance of counselors, there is victory." Ministry teams can be one way of establishing accountability for church workers. Ken Blanchard and Phil Hodges (2003) advocate that one of the crucial habits practiced by any leader is establishing relationships of accountability. Being part of a ministry team can provide a group you can be accountable to for personal, professional, or spiritual goals. Team members can covenant with each other on how they will

function together and how they will hold each other accountable for their goals, decisions, or actions.

2) **Feedback:** Leaders need to hear honest feedback on their ideas and efforts. According to Blanchard and Hodges (2003), self-serving leaders may see feedback as a threat to their power or position. Therefore, they may ignore or avoid feedback in order to continue their efforts without having to change or consider the concerns of others. In contrast, a servant-leader can see feedback as an opportunity for growth. These other-focused leaders understand that feedback can provide vital information in order to improve one's decisions, actions, skills, or communication. Ministry teams can be a safe place to ask for and receive specific feedback. Ministry teams can also be a good place to practice giving appropriate feedback to teammates.

3) **Truth telling:** In addition to accountability and feedback, Blanchard and Hodges (2003) point out the need for truth telling in the lives of leaders. For example, Jethro was a truth teller for Moses. In Exodus 18 we read how Moses spent long days judging the people. Jethro observed this process and suggested that Moses select and train additional leaders to take over some of his responsibilities so more could be accomplished. Jethro encouraged Moses to take a team approach to his duties rather than operating as the sole authority who was on track to burn out from his initial solitary course of action. Moses listened to Jethro, took his advice, and found competent men of integrity he trained to serve the people. Ministry teams can provide the ideal setting for truth telling to take place – for team members to hear from fellow team members if there are other decisions or actions that they should be considering. Truth telling can be especially effective within teams that have developed high levels of trust.

4) **Trust:** Moses might have been caught up in doing it all for some of the same reasons we do it all rather than sharing responsibilities and working as part of a team. Lone ranger type leaders will keep responsibilities, tasks, and information to themselves. Students often express how they prefer to do a project on their own so they know it will be completed how they want it done. Does that happen with you? Do you ever feel like you are the only one who knows how something needs to be done? Are you able to trust others to follow through? Pride, ego, fear, or jealousy can get in the way of trusting others. Team members must be able to trust each other, especially when sharing ideas, perspectives, hopes, and dreams. A ministry team can provide a place to develop trusting relationships with others and to build trust for the team ministry process.

5) **Communication:** According to George Bernard Shaw, "the biggest problem with communication is the illusion that it has taken place" (Caroselli, 2000 p. 71). Just as clear and honest communication is necessary for any relationship, it should also be a goal of any ministry team. Miscommunication and misunderstanding can happen when we do not listen to others or assume we know what others think or feel. Team members need to talk with each other. Team members need to listen to each other. If there are concerns about actions, decisions, or ideas, these concerns should be shared directly with each other, not dropped into meeting agendas or sprinkled into comments to others. Conversations can move into emotional territory when differences of opinion or preferences occur (and they will occur). Therefore, it is imperative to handle any communication within the team with care and respect to keep crucial conversations from escalating into attack or escape responses toward others.

6) **Support and Encouragement:** Team members can be supportive of their teammates in a number of ways. For example, team members can participate in events led by other members, they can speak on behalf of a teammate in a meeting, or they can pray for concerns raised by teammates. Encouragement can also happen in various ways such as through personal words of praise, thank you notes, or acknowledgement of a teammate's efforts in church announcements. Every person is motivated differently so it is important to personalize the types of support and encouragement used, finding out what means are most appreciated by each individual team member.

7) **Relationships of Influence:** Leadership can be considered a relationship of influence. That being said, the relationships developed within a ministry team of leaders can provide natural relationships of influence. I was able to pick up "by osmosis" valuable leadership and ministry lessons by observing the reactions and responses of my teammates. Ministry teams present ideal settings for mentoring in the moments of real life.

MINISTRY TEAMS LOOK
AND FUNCTION DIFFERENTLY

You might have a picture in mind of what an "ideal" ministry team would be like – efficient and focused weekly meetings, stimulating conversations over theology and practice, with an abundance of warm chocolate chip cookies to nibble on – maybe, maybe not. Every church worker is unique so of course every church and every ministry team will have diverse qualities and operate in various ways. Ministry teams all look and function differently.

The first ministry team I was part of was very small (a pastor, a church secretary, and me) and truthfully, we were fairly nonfunctional as a team. The pastor was not very adept at fostering collaborative efforts and I was too inexperienced to provide direction in building the team relationship from my end. In essence, we each did what we were tasked to do according to our job descriptions with little or no mutual support from each other. Periodically, I would catch my pastor in his office, ask if he had a few minutes, and would then share what I was doing in my specific responsibility areas. While I gave him an update, he would listen absently, preoccupied with opening his junk mail. He tolerated my "interruptions" as long as they were short and he could continue to sift through his office paperwork. I knew my time was up when he started to gather items to leave the room. Sadly, this pattern never changed, even after years of serving together.

Fortunately, the next congregation I served offered a very different team ministry opportunity. This next team included the pastor, assistant pastor, day school staff, custodians, secretaries, music director and me. Each weekday morning a short time was scheduled for scripture reading and prayer. Everyone was included and often everyone attended. This simple daily routine helped set the spiritual focus of our days, built our sense of community, and established our feeling of togetherness. This also strengthened lines of communication since we could talk with each other before or after our short devotional times. Consistently scheduled staff meetings and special reasons to gather (birthdays, holidays, etc.) also kept this team connected professionally and personally.

At the next congregation I served, the ministry team was similar to the first. The pastor was slightly more open to periodic planning and sharing ideas around mutual program areas like confirmation or adult education. He was supportive of me and of my work, but he was not particularly interested in building our team for more strategic or collaborative purposes.

Fortunately, I had discovered another team ministry "option" while serving at my first congregation. The youth leaders there would gather once a month for Friday night meals and program planning time. Here I found an environment of support, encouragement, feedback, and mentoring; this was possible as I was a part of a group of like-minded individuals. I felt valued as a team member and as an intern–this was crucial to developing my understanding of the meaning of 'team.' As a result, at each subsequent congregation I served, I would invite volunteer leaders who served in the areas connected to my job responsibilities to join a ministry team with me. These ministry teams–children's ministry, youth ministry, adult ministry–provided the setting for all of us to grow together as a team and in our ministry efforts.

From each of these experiences I learned a number of things about team ministry. I realized I could be proactive in building a team. I learned a team was not limited to just a pastor and a DCE. I learned how different teams could function and provide a number of personal and professional resources I could not gain as an individual. I realized that even when a team did not fit my ideal image of a team, there was still opportunity for me to give and gain support.

KNOW YOUR TEAM
AND KNOW YOUR TEAM QUALITIES

As you prepare to join a congregation as one of its servant leaders, you should consider what you will bring to that ministry team. Knowing yourself will help you know how you interact with others and what type of teammate you will be. Each person on your team will not only bring what they can do to the group, but their preferred approaches and responses. In other words, each person reacts to situations in his or her unique way. If you know what you bring to the team this will help you function better as a member of a team. As you get to know your teammates this will help you understand them and help the team see how it can function most productively.

Are you an introvert or an extrovert? Are you task oriented or people oriented? Are you time driven or priority driven? Do you want to complete a task and move on to the next thing? Do you like to spend time getting to know those you are working with and what they are thinking about the process? You may tend to be a gatekeeper, making it possible for others to share their ideas or perceptions. Maybe one of your favorite functions in a team is to help the group keep its priorities and values in mind as they consider solutions by serving as the group's standard setter. Knowledge and understanding of self is crucial.

There are a number of personal and leadership surveys that can provide a glimpse into individual preferences. For instance, knowing the Myers-Briggs profile of each member of a team can help each members understand some tendencies of other team members. No doubt you have taken these types of profiles and can use the results you have discovered to consider them in the context of real team situations. Assessments used by team members can be used to broaden understanding of members, not limit or categorize the talents of others.

Emotional intelligence (EI) would be another area to investigate for yourself and with your team. According to a number of researchers in this field, including Shankman and Allen (2008), emotional intelligence is the knowledge and management of self as well as the knowledge and management of relationships. Emotional intelligence means understanding how one's reactions impact self and others. It is the ability to manage one's personal reactions as well as manage reactions within relationships. Personal competence includes self-awareness and self-management, capabilities that determine how we manage ourselves. Social competence includes social awareness and relationship management, capabilities that determine how we manage our relationships. Taking an EI survey can indicate areas of strength to build on and limitation areas that may need to be addressed.

Your team members could read *StrengthsFinder* 2.0 by Tom Rath or a similar resource on personal strengths and aptitudes. This book and online assessment is based on years of research conducted by Gallup on individual strengths. Individuals who complete the online assessment receive a personalized strengths

summary and planning guide to apply those strengths in personal and professional activities. Your ministry team could read this book, use the online inventory results to track their individual strengths, then share their discoveries with
the team. Knowing the strengths (and limitations) of each member can help the
team better understand and effectively support each other.

FINAL THOUGHTS

Do you try to do Jesus's work by yourself or do you seek to work with
others to accomplish His mission? If you tend to do the latter, you are utilizing
the power of teams. Jesus modeled leadership for His followers. As part of this
leadership He utilized a ministry team approach to make sure His disciples–His
team–knew how to work together so His message continued on earth. Christ
knew the value in building a team and then releasing the team into the world.
Church workers have the challenge and opportunity to serve as members of
Christ's team with others who have been called as His followers. The ministry
journey can be long and the challenges too great to tackle alone. Remember, if
you want to travel far, travel together. A team can provide the support needed
for the ministry journey ahead.

CHAPTER 15

WELLNESS AND BALANCE IN MINISTRY

Bruce M. Hartung

Balance: "The stability resulting from the equalization of opposing forces <keeping his emotional balance when under stress>."[33]

Compartmentalize: "To separate into isolated compartments or categories."[34]

"The first law of health demands that we conform to God's law of regularity and that we cultivate regular habits of living. Modern conditions of life often make this difficult, and therefore so much more the determination in this respect is required. But it is worth the effort. We should rather seek to prevent illness than to cure it; rather to preserve health rather than to restore it. While illness is a result of sin and can therefore not altogether be escaped, yet much sickness is the result of neglecting the rules of health; hence it may to a large extent be avoided" (Fritz, p. 21).

"We get sick when we forget how to be well. Anonymous" (Rediger, p. 1).

---

[33] *Lagenscheidt's New College Merriam – Webster English Thesaurus* (New York: Langenscheidt), 1998, p. 64.
[34] *Langenscheidt's New College Merriam – Webster English Dictionary* (New York: Langenscheidt), 1998, p, 234.

Bruce Hartung, Ph.D., serves as Dean of Ministerial Formation at Concordia Seminary in St. Louis, Missouri.

SHERI

Sheri began her DCE ministry with enthusiasm and verve. A bright student with almost a 4.0 GPA in high school and a 3.6 GPA in college, she prided herself on intellectual curiosity and growth as well as on her compassion for and service with young people. A DCE ministry had been part of her picture of herself since late high school when she had a particularly effective and inspiring DCE join the parish staff where she and her family were members.

Now, six years into her DCE ministry, Sheri began to sense some loss of the enthusiasm that was such a part of her very being. An especial concern for her was that everything that she valued seemed to be going well: her personal devotions were regular, her support systems were active and helpful, her work was effective, challenging, and creative, consistent and positive feedback came her way from both adults and the youth with whom she worked, her most recent annual health examination was positive, she was in a very good dating relationship, and she loved the parish and the members of the staff. So, what was the problem? Perhaps, she thought, it was time to move on. Or, what was wrong with her, she wondered, that she was not feeling energized and fulfilled with everything going so well?

Sheri's response to her discontent was fairly natural – or, at least, common: a) change jobs and/or locations or b) identify pathology of some kind in her. While both are possible responses, neither should be a first response. Job and/or location change creates upheaval that could be unnecessary; pathologizing oneself creates a generally destructive attitude toward oneself, especially when there is little actual evidence for the specific cause of the difficulty.

Seeking out some counseling help, Sheri's counselor eventually asked what kinds of things Sheri had done previously in which she found fulfillment and which gave her energy. Sheri discovered that there was an area of her life very much out-of-balance and for which she simply thought there was not enough time. Beside, how important is reading anyway?

The absence of two things in her intellectual life put this area out-of-balance for her: keeping up-to-date on the latest in latency and teen-age development and sitting back and being absorbed in a science fiction novel. Her intellectual curiosity and growth was not being well-served. As a result, she made time for reading and began to feel more intellectually fulfilled. She cut back on one set of duties, in consultation with the church staff, to make time for this move toward balance.

The issue was not a personal pathology in Sheri, nor was it a problematic work situation. Rather, the issue for her was balance. She had taken some things that were very important to her, placed them into a compartment because there was no time to do them, she thought, essentially ignored and tried to forget them, and over time began to feel the effects of being out-of-balance. Sheri rediscovered a very important core reality of life: balance is crucial for health and leaving aside important components needed for balance has negative results.

JON

Jon always was big. Large-boned and 6'2" he prided himself on his athletic prowess, being a football and baseball player in high school and a football player in college. He brought these athletic gifts into his DCE ministry. Additionally he did very well in school with a GPA in both high school and college at about a 3.2. Jon's father – his adult hero really – always encouraged both intellectual and physical fitness. Jon followed suit. And, he had learned to put his relationship to Christ as a most important defining ingredient of his life.

Into his 11th year of DCE ministry and married with three children, Jon is now feeling both pressed and sluggish. Life is very busy; family life is packed; fast-food is common; quick meals on the fly are a fixture; evening meetings are regular; sexual relationships with his wife are less than adequate for both of them; financial concerns are significant. With this list of stressors and their results Jon increasingly feels "stressed" and worn down. Jon has always recognized the necessity for balance in his life, but things seem "way too out of control" in his words. His sense is that he has no real capacity to put order and balance in his "out of control" life. He is too busy meeting the multiple demands placed upon him. Jon has gained 65 pounds over the last 7 years, 35 of them within the last three years.

Knowing that the accumulating stressors in his life were closing in on him and that he was turning to food to at least calm some of the stress, Jon sought out a spiritual director to help him sort out what was happening to him and what, if anything might be done. He was surprised by one of the first questions asked by the spiritual director following Jon's telling of his story:

"How do you see God involved in all this?"

"God?" said Jon, "I'm out of touch with Him, too, so I've never really thought of that question. Obviously I have no immediate answer."

Jon's multiple conversations over the next months with his spiritual director clarified that, while the center of his life and health – his redeemed relationship with God through Christ begun at his baptism and his new relationship with others in the Body of Christ – was certainly present it was not very center to him. Thus, he had lost his center point, his internal gyroscope, and was no longer fixing his eyes on Christ. Slowly Jon's centeredness in Christ returned, under the guidance of his spiritual director, and so did, in a beginning way, Jon's capacity to manage the stressors in his life. Much more needed to be done, of course.

A vital issue for Jon was the core of his life and the spiritual hardiness that surrounds all of who we are. Jon's life was out-of-balance because he had lost his core gravity that held all aspects of his life together. It was not that the core (in our baptism we are made a child of God through Christ and placed also in new and healthy relationships with others in the Body of Christ) had moved away from Jon. Increasingly he had moved away from it. As a result, his life was in a flurry. This affects everything. In re-discovering this reality, Jon could begin to have a core place to stand that is firm enough to begin to manage the multiple stressors that he faced.

FIGURE 15.1

Wholeness Wheel

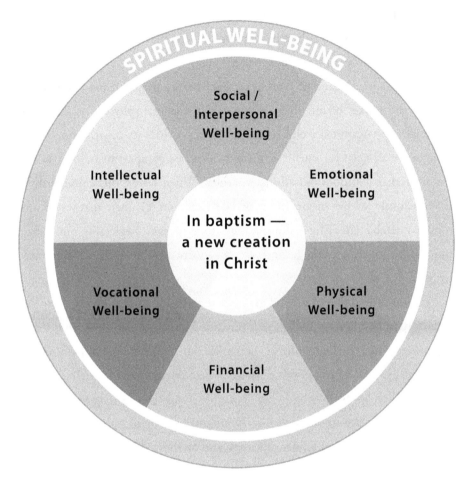

BALANCE

In order for a wheel to run in an effective and healthy way it needs a center, the balance of its spokes, and an exterior that holds the spokes together.

The center is, indeed, our baptism. As we rise every day and make the sign of the cross we are reminded of our baptism and the redemptive work of Christ. We are also reminded that we are placed into the community of followers of Christ, His Body. Our baptism is not just a 'me-and-God' happening; it is a happening in the community that binds us to others. This is why we return to our baptism again and again, and look to the community for care, support, and accountability. This moving way from the core of our lives was a source – perhaps the source – of Jon's difficulties in standing on a foundation that could help him manage the disorder of the stressors of his life.

As a baptized child of God living in the community of the baptized, we look at the spokes of our lives: emotional, intellectual, physical, social/interpersonal and vocational well-being. Each area provides its contribution to the balance we all need for our lives. Each area can be compartmentalized so that we pretend that it does not affect the others. When we do this consciously or unconsciously, we live in something of a delusion and it is there that we become most vulnerable either by overusing our strong areas or neglecting our weaker ones. This forgetting of the balance was the source of some of the concern faced by Sheri.

Surrounding the wheel and giving it the outside surface on which to run is faith-hardiness, a term borrowed from Gary Harbaugh (2000). Rather than a person's spiritual life being one of the spokes on the Wholeness Wheel, as is so with many secular wheels of this type, this wheel clearly shows the inclusive need for that which holds the wheel – all of our life – together. As long as we walk in this creation we are strengthened by Word and Sacrament as that is celebrated and lived in the Body of Christ. Both Jon and Sheri lived in the Body of Christ; both sought help from others in that Body.

FOLLOWING UP ON WELLNESS AND BALANCE

There are several things that one can do to help balance or re-balance one's life. Here are several suggestions.

1. Remember your Baptism! Every morning arise with the sign of the cross, centering your awakening in your being a child of God in Christ and a member of His Body. Every evening go to bed with the sign of the cross, centering your sleeping on your being a child of God in Christ and a

member of His Body. Seek regular spiritual direction or conversation that regularly gives you an opportunity to speak of your life and how your life is centered on God in Christ.

2. Review the spokes in the Wholeness Wheel. In what areas are you strong? What areas are you overusing? What areas are more vulnerable? Review the whole wheel for balance. In your review begin, in conversation with a trusted peer, colleague, or spouse, to plan intentionally for more balance. For instance, if "physical" is weak, partner with someone and join a local YMCA or YWCA for regular exercise; if "intellectual" is weak consider picking up a continuing education course in an area of interest at a local community college; if "social/interpersonal" is weak consider joining a book club, a social club, or other focused interest group; if "vocational" is weak consider exploration of this with a counselor or spiritual director. There are many more things to "consider." They will emerge in conversation with others, who, with you, are members of the Body of Christ.

3. Review the whole idea of faith-hardiness. You may even wish to take the "Faith-Hardiness Inventory" found in Gary Harbaugh's book *The Confident Christian*. In what areas are you seeing yourself faith-hardy? In what areas are you seeing yourself not so faith-hardy? Discuss your review with a trusted peer, colleague, your spouse, a counselor or a spiritual director.

4. Inform persons in your support systems of what you are attempting to do. Ask them both for their prayers for you and also that they hold you accountable for what you are aspiring to do.

5. Intentionally in your spiritual disciplines participate in the Eucharist often, study the Scriptures by yourself and in groups, and be in prayer by yourself and in groups. This both reminds you of your core – your Baptism – and also strengthens the outside surface – faith-hardiness – that holds our lives together.

MARTHA

Martha liked the ideas contained in this article as she read it diligently (and twice). Especially captivating was the "Wholeness Wheel" (Figure 15.1). She went away for half a day on a mini retreat by herself. Taking a copy of the "Wholeness Wheel" along with her, she examined the spokes, made a "fearless inventory" (as our brothers and sisters in Alcoholics Anonymous would say), and determined to make necessary changes in her life. She was excited and energized by this wholistic way of thinking about herself. She fervently prayed for help from God to make the changes to which she aspired happen.

Several months later she was in tears. Her resolve had evaporated; her energy was diminished; she was discouraged. Down on herself because she saw herself failing in her resolution, she berated herself for her lack of resolve, her failed energy, and her discouragement.

In desperation Martha consulted an experienced DCE colleague in a different parish. After an extended conversation, her colleague looked at her and said: "You've been doing this alone apart from supporting people who can help you. The balance of the very wheel you studied is off-kilter because the community that Christ gave you is not being used. Coming to talk over what is happening is a first step at connecting and using that community."

Relieved that her colleague had helped her make some sense out of what had happened, Martha realized that while she was working hard at the issues raised in this article she was doing so alone. With her colleague she began to create strategies and tactics to involve others. She found people who agreed to pray for her and what she wanted to achieve; she found people who would hold her accountable; she found people who would join her in healthier behaviors; she found people who would applaud her when she met her goals.

"And over all these put on love, that is, the bond of perfection. And let the peace of Christ control your hearts, the peace into which you were called in one body. Let the word of Christ dwell in you richly, as in all wisdom you teach and admonish one another, singing psalms, hymns, and spiritual songs with gratitude in your hearts to God. And whatever you do, in word or in deed, do everything in the name of the Lord Jesus, giving thanks to God the Father through him" (Col. 3:14-17).

CHAPTER 16

The DCE Career Path

Williʌm O. Karpenko II

This chapter will surface a lot of numbers, a lot of charts, plenty of findings, and ample conclusions. Beneath all of the data are the perceptions, hopes, and dreams of flesh and blood people who have spent a portion or all of their professional life serving Jesus Christ and His people, whether inside or outside of the Church, as a trained Director of Christian Education (DCE).

The material in this chapter is from the largest study ever conducted on DCEs in the Lutheran Church-Missouri Synod (LC-MS). This information is intended to:

- Deepen attraction to and affection for DCE ministry.

- Develop a deeper historical grasp of DCE ministry within the LCMS.

- Strengthen the capacity to address some of the questions and myths about DCEs that circulate even today among both congregational members and professional church workers.

- Encourage DCEs to shape, with courage and joy, their own your place within DCE ministry.

- Enhance the desire of DCEs to follow Jesus as they serve others in His Name.

William Karpenko II, Ph.D., has served as DCE Program Director at Concordia University, Nebraska and Concordia University, St. Paul. He currently serves as Administrative Executive of KINDLE.

The material included in this chapter has been extracted primarily from two documents. The first is a 340-page study completed in May 2009 and the second is a 24-page report based on this study that was completed in November 2009. Both documents can be located at http://dcecareerpath.wordpress.com.

THE EARLY YEARS

Directors of Christian Education (DCEs) have served congregations of The Lutheran Church–Missouri Synod (LC–MS) since the early 1900s. Trained as synodical teachers, these individuals assumed DCE-type positions when the school they were serving went out of existence or their particular interest and gifts matched a vital need in another area of the congregation's ministry, particularly music, Sunday school, and confirmation.

It was not until the summer of 1959, at its convention in San Francisco, that the LC–MS officially encouraged its congregations to consider calling a DCE. One year later, Neal Rabe, a graduate of Concordia College in River Forest, Illinois, accepted a call to Grace Lutheran Church in Tulsa, Oklahoma, to become the first DCE called through the synodical placement system. Two years later another synodical convention resolution formally recommended that Concordia College in River Forest, Illinois, and Concordia College in Seward, Nebraska, begin to train DCEs. Seven years later, Concordia College in St. Paul, Minnesota, joined the effort but chose not to have their DCE graduates also trained as classroom teachers.

Once these three colleges began to market their new programs and place their graduates into DCE positions, young people around the synod began to experience first-hand the winsome and talented people doing DCE ministry. There was an upsurge of interest in this new profession and a host of questions related to it came from the parents of perspective students, from congregations evaluating whether or not to call a DCE, and from college administrators and faculty who were facing demands for curriculum updates and additional faculty. Most of these questions involved DCEs serving in congregations, many of whom had large parochial schools.

Some of these questions soon morphed into inaccurate and potentially detrimental myths about this new ministry. For example, A relatively innocuous questions such as "Are most DCEs in their 20s?" became a myth that most DCEs are indeed in their 20s.

BRIEF HISTORY OF THE DCE CAREER PATH PROJECT

After various failed individual attempts to begin a study of the career paths of DCEs, those attending the 2007 DCE Summit in St. Louis urged that this project be undertaken by a team of veteran DCEs. Dr. Jack Giles, Mission Facilitator for the Northern Illinois District of the LC–MS, was asked to serve as convener. Dr. William Karpenko was identified as the project's lead researcher. He and Giles were joined on the project team by four other DCEs: Dr. Debra Arfsten, Dr. Steve Christopher, Professor Ben Freudenburg, and Bob McKinney. Once sufficient monies had been gathered, a three-phase project was conceptualized. The purpose of the project was to determine the predominant career paths for DCEs in the LC–MS.

METHODOLOGY

The initial phase of this project, which this chapter addresses, used a Zoomerang survey to gather career path information on all certified DCEs for whom email addresses had been obtained. In total, 1,183 of the 1,753 certified DCEs were sent the survey.

There were 802 DCEs who participated in this study. They had been certified[35] through one of the six Concordia universities that are located in Austin, Texas; River Forest, Illinois; Irvine, California; Portland, Oregon; Seward, Nebraska; and St. Paul, Minnesota.[36] The careers of these 802 DCEs spanned anywhere from only a few months to as long as 39 years.

---

[35] Unless otherwise noted, the term "certified" will be assumed when describing DCEs in this study.
[36] Eight of the 146 individuals certified through the program at Concordia University in Seward, Nebraska, during the 1984-87 field experience process were graduates of the Youth Leadership Training Program (YLTP) at Valparaiso University.)

This study was a self-reported survey of 162 items. All respondents completed the same initial 20 questions which were used to determine which one of eight status categories best fit their current career status: congregational DCEs (49%), non-congregational DCEs (7%), pastors (9%), teachers/principals (7%), other commissioned ministers (3%), those who were on candidate status (5%), those no longer in church work (15%), and those who had retired (5%). As the survey continued, each DCE was then asked to respond to another 2,023 items intended to better define that specific status category.

This study is built around the question "Did you serve as a congregational DCE, and, if so, how long?" The answer to this question determined the DCE's (a) career path pattern; (b) global career path type; and (c) specific career path type. Some of the DCEs' career paths were more expansive or complicated than the 16 career patterns, 7 global career types, and 165 specific career types identified in the study and did not fit as neatly into these devised categories as one might like.

Four kinds of information were gathered: personal demographics, career path demographics, experiences and practices that impacted DCEs, and DCEs' individual perspectives on various career path issues.

The data generated from the survey was organized into 12 major sections:

1. Professional Settings
2. Demographic Profile
3. Career Path Profile
4. Career Path Patterns
5. Global Career Path Type
6. Specific Career Path Type
7. Professional and Personal Experiences
8. Key Sustaining Practices
9. Career Expectations
10. Career Ladder
11. Reasons for Leaving the DCE Ministry
12. Types of Well-Being Needed for a Lifelong Career

Three final sections summarize the study by providing the reader information to address the DCE myths, some general and specific conclusions emerging from the study, and a wrap-up statement regarding Phase I of the DCE Career Path Project.

When reading a number of tables in this chapter, four terms were used to group the statistical results of the survey questions:

1. "Predominant macro" represents 10% or more of the 769 DCE career paths
2. "Predominant micro" represents 5% to 9% of the 769 DCE career paths
3. "Macro" represents 10% or more of each of the eight status categories
4. "Micro" represents 5% to 9% of each of the eight status categories

The surveys were completed between February and August 2008, which means that the responses were gathered before the full force of the economic recession hit in October 2008. Since congregations usually feel a national financial crunch a year or so later, many issues discussed today among practicing DCEs (e.g., the loss of DCE positions, encouraged early retirements, and limited placement options for new graduates) were not in play to the same extent in 2008.

PROFESSIONAL SETTINGS

When examining the career paths of the 769 DCEs who completed this set of questions, 1,253 employment settings were identified, many of which were similar in nature. Three-quarters of the most frequently cited employment settings fell into just three locations: LC–MS congregations (56%), business and industry (11%), or an LC–MS elementary school (10%). The remaining 23% were spread over 21 other employment settings in which DCEs served (see Table 16.1).

TABLE 16.1

Professional Settings in which DCEs Served

Setting	Responses	Percentage
LC–MS Congregation	702	56%
Business/Industry	141	11%
LC–MS K-8 School	129	10%
LC–MS College/University	34	3%
Public K-8 School	34	3%
LC–MS Camp	27	2%
LC–MS District/National	26	2%
LC–MS Secondary School	22	2%
LC–MS Overseas Missions	21	2%
Congregation	18	1%
Social Services Agency	18	1%
Public Service	16	1%
Para-Church Office	14	1%
LC–MS Social Services	13	1%
Public/Private College/Univ.	8	1%
LC–MS Early Childhood Center	7	1%
LC–MS Special Settings (CPH)	6	<1%
Campus Ministry Center	6	<1%
Military Base Chapel	4	<1%
College/University	3	<1%
LCMS Seminary	1	<1%
Preschool Center	1	<1%
Retreat Center	1	<1%
Regional/National Office	1	<1%

It should be noted that the maximum number of employment settings that could be reflected on the survey during each DCE's career path was three even if, in select cases, his or her career spanned five or six different settings.

As is evident from the professional settings, not all DCEs serve in a congregational setting. In fact, some respondents in the survey were not employed. In order to group them appropriately, the following eight status categories were used in the study:

1. Congregational DCE
2. Non-congregational DCE
3. Pastor
4. Teacher/Principal
5. Other Commissioned Minister
6. Candidate Status
7. No longer on the synod roster
8. Retired

In the 11 sections to follow, the eight status categories will be used to describe the differences between the various kinds of settings in which DCEs found themselves.

DEMOGRAPHIC PROFILE

A number of general demographic details were gathered from those DCEs who completed the survey. Their answers revealed that those DCEs who responded were most likely to be:

- Caucasian (98%)
- 30 years or older (81%)
- In their first marriage (77%)
- Still serving in a rostered ministry of the LC–MS (74%)
- Certified as an undergraduate (69%)
- Male (61%)

On the opposite end of the spectrum, the survey revealed that those DCEs who responded were less likely to have:

- Completed a graduate degree (38%)
- Been certified as a classroom teacher (37%)
- Had a full-time career before becoming a DCE (20%)
- Been certified before 1980 (16%)

There are also several additional "hidden nuggets" within this demographic picture of DCEs who responded to the survey:

- Eight percent (67) were 60 or older and 25 of them were still serving.

- Fifteen percent (117) were never married.

- All but three percent (25) served in the public ministry of the synod.

- All but nine percent (67) served in the DCE ministry of the Synod.

- While the majority had completed a "traditional" undergraduate DCE training program, twenty-nine percent had graduated from one of three other paths: A one-time field certification process (90/11%), a post-bachelors certification program (90/11%), or a DCE colloquy program (57/7%).

- Those who had obtained graduate degrees had done so in one of the following areas of study: Master of Divinity, Family Life Ministry, Theology, Counseling, Educational Administration, and Parish Education.

- Those who had worked full-time before becoming a DCE had been involved in the following careers: public school teacher, retail salesman, insurance salesman, social services position, Lutheran school teacher, and a unspecified business career.

When the demographics were looked at through the lens of the eight status categories, the only category in which women were in the majority (56%) was among those who had left the synod roster. The category of "retired" had the highest percentage (91%) of male respondents which is understandable since the earliest DCEs were mostly men.

Among 20-29 year-old DCEs, 28% were serving as congregational DCEs and 22% were no longer on the synod roster. These two status categories had the highest percentage of responses among the 20-29 year-olds.

DCEs currently serving in congregations were the most likely to have never been married (21%). Those on CRM status (14%) and those no longer on the synod roster (11%) were the most likely to be divorced.

The highest percentage of LC–MS teacher-trained DCEs was retired DCEs (86%) while the lowest was congregational DCEs (24%) and those no longer on the roster of the synod (29%). Female DCEs who were currently not serving as congregational DCEs were more likely to be on candidate status or not on the roster of the LC–MS. On the other hand, male DCEs not serving as congregational DCEs appeared to have more roster-related options, i.e., pastoral ministry or non-congregational opportunities like university and district positions.

Length of service as a congregational DCE was highest among non-congregational and retired DCEs who had 20 or more years of service (26% and 34% respectively).

CAREER PATH PROFILE

Each survey participant was invited to describe their career path. There were 769 DCEs (96%) who provided a description and from these descriptions, a number of interesting demographics emerged:

- The average age of 486 DCEs (63%) was 49 years.

- Two-thirds (66%) of DCEs began their church work career as a congregational DCE.

- When describing their career path, sixty-four percent of the DCEs indicated that they had experienced a major personal or professional crisis. Examples of crises included burnout, staff conflict, congregational budget issues, and vocational re-consideration.

- The impact of these crises resulted in eighty percent of these DCEs leaving their congregational setting either for a new parish, another kind of public ministry or a non-church-related position.

- Five percent of DCEs were still serving the initial congregation in which they were placed.

- Five percent of the DCEs were married to one another.

- Nineteen percent of the DCEs remained at, or returned to, their DCE intern site.

TABLE 16.2

Career Path Demographics by the Eight Status Categories

Demographic	Congregational DCE	Non-congregational DCE	Pastor	Teacher / Principal	Other Commissioned	Candidate Status	Not on Roster	Retired	Totals
Total Number	381	51	69	51	24	41	111	41	769
Submitted Career Path	98%	91%	99%	91%	100%	98%	90%	98%	96%
Average Age	39.9	48.1	51.6	48.3	47.0	45.0	43.3	70.5	49.21
Career Phases	4.2	4.6	6.4	5.3	5.0	5.4	4.2	7.1	5.28
Career Prior to DCE	18%	32%	33%	18%	17%	21%	15%	33%	23.37%
Launched as DCE	93%	84%	65%	53%	54%	76%	69%	29%	66.00%
Stepped Out	19%	30%	100%	100%	33%	100%	100%	39%	65.12%
Returned as DCE	96%	27%	0%	8%	21%	14%	4%	0%	21.25%
Working Female DCE with Family	31%	14%		39%	38%	69%	6%	0%	28.14%
Major Crisis	61%	51%	57%	75%	63%	78%	61%	67%	64.13%
Left Setting	53%	87%	85%	61%	80%	96%	98%	78%	79.75%
Still Serving Initial Congregation	37%	0%	0%	2%	4%	0%	0%	0%	5.38%
Lifelong Congregational DCE	61%	0%	0%	0%	0%	0%	0%	0%	7.63%
Years as Congregational DCE 20 +	23%	26%	10%	4%	17%	10%	4%	34%	16.00%
Years as Congregational DCE 30 +	7%	2%	0%	0%	0%	0%	1%	7%	2.13%
Married to DCE	3%	6%	2%	14%	2%	5%	6%	0%	4.75%
Stayed after interning	36%	19%	17%	28%	21%	20%	10%	0%	18.88%

When looking at the career path profile through the prism of the eight status categories, as might be expected, congregational DCEs reflected the highest percentage (93%) of DCEs who began their career in a parish while retired DCEs had the lowest percentage (27%). Sixty-one percent of the congregational DCEs in this study had spent their entire church work career in a parish setting.

The highest percentage of female DCEs, who had continued working in a professional congregational capacity while raising a family, were individuals on candidate status (69%) and those serving as congregational DCEs (31%). The highest percentage of DCEs (14%) who were married to another DCE were serving as a LC–MS teacher or principal.

A majority of DCEs in all eight of the status categories indicated that they had experienced some kind of crisis during their career as a congregational DCE. The highest percentage of DCEs who experienced a crisis as a congregational DCE was those on candidate status (78%) while non-congregational DCEs had the lowest percentage (51%). Just over one-third of congregational DCEs (36%) remained at or returned to their intern site.

Table 16.2 summarizes the data related to the career path demographics of DCEs cross-referenced by the eight status categories identified earlier.

CAREER PATH PATTERNS

On the basis of the 769 career paths that were submitted by DCEs, sixteen career path patterns were created. Each pattern attempted to address how a DCE began his or her professional career, whether it was in a church-related or non-church-related ministry, and was the position as a congregational DCE or some other kind of church worker.

- Among DCEs in this study, there were two predominant macro career path patterns: Congregational DCE only (31%) and Congregational DCE and one or more other church-related positions (16%).

- The two predominant macro and seven predominant micro career paths (5-9% of the 769 DCEs) reflected 89% of the DCEs in this study.

- The career path pattern that reflected the least number of DCEs was one or more other non-church-related positions (5/1%).

- Male DCEs reflected two predominant career path patterns: Congregational DCE only (18%) and Congregational DCE and one or more other church-related positions (11%), and female DCEs reflected one of the two predominant career path patterns: Congregational DCE only (13%).

- Overall, DCEs began their careers in three major ways: congregational DCE (57%), one or more other church-related positions (21%), or one or more non-church-related positions (16%).

- Male and female DCEs began their career in much the same ways: congregational DCE (male: 55%, female: 58%), one or more other church-related positions (male: 23%, female: 14%), or one or more non-church-related positions (male: 16%, female: 17%).

When looking at career path patterns through the prism of the eight status categories, the congregational DCE was the only status category that evidenced a predominant macro career path pattern (30%) and a micro career path pattern of having served in one or more non-church-work-related position and congregational DCE (7%).

Among the 16 career path patterns, three were reflected in all eight of the DCE status categories:

- Congregational DCE and one or more other church-related positions

- One or more other church-related positions, congregational DCE, and one or more other church-related positions

- One or more other non-church-related positions, congregational DCEs, and one or more other church-related positions

Within each of the eight status categories, Table 16.3 outlines the career path patterns that emerged among the highest percentage of DCEs:

TABLE16.3

Career Path Patterns by Status Category

Status Category	Career Path Pattern
Congregational DCE	Congregational DCE only (61%)
Non-congregational DCE	Congregational DCE and one or more other church-related positions (37%)
Pastor	Congregational DCE and one or more other church-related positions (39%)
Teacher/principal	Congregational DCE and one or more other church-related positions (35%)
Other Commissioned Minister	Congregational DCE and one or more other church-related positions (42%)
Candidate status	Career path interlude (37%)
Not on roster	Congregational DCE and one or more non-church-related positions (22%)
Retired	Congregational DCE and one or more other church-related positions (39%)

DCEs no longer on the roster of synod had the most diffuse set of career path patterns (14) while DCEs who became pastors had the most similar (4 paths = 91% of the pastoral patterns). Substantially more than any other status categories, congregational DCEs appeared to come into DCE ministry from a non-church-related position (18% vs. 4% for those other commissioned ministers).

Table 16.4 summarizes the number and percentages of DCEs whose career was captured by one of the 16 patterns.

TABLE 16.4

Summary of Career Path Patterns (n = 769)

Career Path Pattern	Raw Data	Percentage
Congregational DCE only	236	31%
Congregational DCE and one or more other church-related position	122	16%
Congregational DCE and one or more other non-church-related positions	36	5%
Congregational DCE and one or more church and non-church-related position	36	5%
One or more other church-related position	38	5%
One or more other non-church-related position	5	1%
One or more church and non-church-related position	14	2%
One or more non-church and church-related position	10	1%
One or more other church-related position and congregational DCE	29	4%
One or more other church-related position, congregational DCE, and one or more other church-related position	62	8%
One or more other church-related position, congregational DCE, and one or more other non-church-related position	17	2%
One or more other non-church-related positions and congregational DCE	52	7%
One or more other non-church-related position, congregational DCE, and one or more other non-church-related position	6	1%
One or more other non-church-related position, congregational DCE, and one or more other church-related position	48	6%
Other career path	10	1%
Career path interlude	48	6%

GLOBAL CAREER PATH TYPE

The 769 DCE career paths were also organized by types: global and specific. The global types were also built upon three questions from the survey, the starting point being, "Did this certified DCE serve as a congregational DCE?" If so, "Is this the only position s/he has served in?" If not, "What other settings did s/he serve in?" On the basis of these questions, a DCE's career path was clustered under one of the seven global types. The seven global types included the following:

- Congregational DCE only
- DCE and other congregational/school ministries
- DCE and other LC–MS ministries
- DCE and non-LC–MS ministries
- DCE and non-church profession
- DCE and interlude for personal/family priorities
- Never served as a congregational DCE

There were four predominant macro global DCE career path types (10% or more of the 769 career paths) which accounted for 82% of all DCEs who participated in this study:

- Congregational DCE only (31%)
- DCE and other congregational/school ministries (20%)
- DCE and non-church profession (18%)
- DCE and other LC–MS ministries (13%)

Those DCEs whose global career path type reflected service in a non-LC–MS ministry had the lowest percentage (4%). The strongest predominant macro global type for both male and female DCEs was among those who had served only as congregational DCEs (28% for males and 35% for females).

The greatest percentage differences between male and female DCEs occurred where the DCE had served in other congregational/school ministries (26% for men versus 11% for women) and if there had been an interlude for family/personal/professional concerns (3% for men versus 12% for women).

Chart 16.5 provides a summary of the global career path types.

CHART 16.5
Summary of Global Career Path Types (n=769)

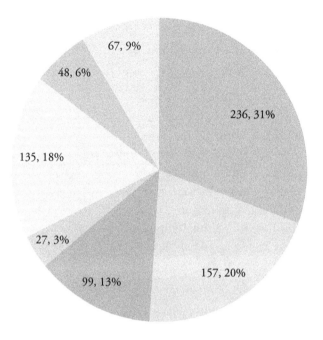

- Congregational DCE only (236, 31%)
- DCE and other congregational/school ministries (157, 20%)
- DCE and other LC–MS ministries (99, 13%)
- DCE and non-LC–MS ministries (27, 3%)
- DCE and non-church profession (135, 18%)
- DCE and interlude for family/personal/professional concerns (48, 6%)
- Never served as a congregational DCE (67, 9%)

When looking at global career path types through the lens of the 8 status categories, serving as a congregational DCE was the only predominant macro global career path type among the eight status categories.

Within each of the eight status categories, Table16.6 outlines the global career path types that emerged with the highest percentage of DCEs.

TABLE 16.6

Global Career Path Types with the Highest Percentage of DCEs by Status Category

Status Category	Global Career Path Type
Congregational DCE	Congregational DCE only (61%)
Non-congregational DCE	DCE and other LC–MS ministries (84%)
Pastor	DCE and other congregational/school ministries (80%)
Teacher/principal	DCE and other congregational/school ministries (55%)
Other Commissioned Minister	DCE and other congregational/school ministries (67%)
Candidate status	DCE and interlude for family/personal/professional concerns (37%)
Not on roster	DCE and non-church profession (46%)
Retired	DCE and other congregational/school ministries (44%)

Table 16.7 summarizes the seven global career path types by status category that emerged with the highest percentage of DCEs.

TABLE 16.7

Status Category with the Highest Percentage of DCEs by Global Career Path Type

Global Career Path Type	Status Category
Congregational DCE only	Congregational DCE (61%)
DCE and other congregational/school ministries	Pastor (80%)
DCE and other LC–MS ministries	Non-congregational DCEs (84%)
DCE and non-LC–MS ministries	Not on the roster (16%)
DCE and non-church profession:	Not on the roster (46%)
DCE and interlude for family/personal/professional concerns	Candidate status (37%)
Never served as congregational DCE	Teacher/Principal (29%)

In all eight of the status categories, it was possible to capture two-thirds of respondents in just two of the global career path types. DCEs on candidate status or who were serving as a congregational DCE had the most diffuse set of global career path types (6 of the 7) while non-congregational DCEs and pastors had the most similar global career path types (they were all captured in three types).

The greatest percentage differences among the seven status categories between male and female DCEs (pastors were excluded given that they were all male) within the global career path types are identified in Table 16.8.

TABLE 16.8

Gender Difference Among Status Categories
by Global Career Path Types

Status Category	Global Career Path Type
Retired DCE (40% more males)	DCE and other congregational/school ministries
Non-congregational DCEs (33% more males)	DCE and other LC–MS ministries
Other commissioned ministers (25% more males)	DCE and other congregational/school ministries
Candidate status (22% more males)	DCE and non-church profession
No longer on roster (10% more males)	Non-church profession
Congregational DCE (9% more males)	Congregational DCE only
Teacher/Principal (8% more males)	DCE and other LC–MS ministries

SPECIFIC CAREER PATH TYPE

The same 769 DCEs' career paths formed the data base from which 165 specific career path types were identified. Each of these specific types was housed in one of the seven global types. Given the varying career paths of 769 DCEs, some served in only one kind of professional role (i.e., congregational DCE), others in two roles (i.e., congregational DCE and a business/industry position), and others yet in three roles (i.e., LC–MS K-8 teacher, congregational DCE, and district/national executive). For purposes of manageability this study did not extend specific career path types beyond three roles.

Among the 165 specific career path types, 90 (55%) were represented only one DCE. There were two predominant macro specific DCE career path types (10% or more of the 769 career paths):

• Just launching as congregational DCE: 1 to 3 years (10%)
• Short-term congregational DCE: 4 to 12 years (10%)

Among the 769 DCEs, the five most prevalent specific career path types were:

• Short-term congregational DCE: 4-12 years of service (77/10%)
• Just launching as a congregational DCE: 1-3 years of service (73/10%)
• DCE and business/industry position (63/8%)
• Mid-term congregational DCE: 13-25 years of service (52/7%)
• Long-term congregational DCE: 26+ years of service (34/4%)

There were five other specific career path types that combined to describe at least twenty-two percent of the careers of other DCEs:

• Never served-other LC–MS church-related work (34/4%)
• DCE and pastor (24/3%)
• DCE and K-8 teacher (22/3%)
• DCE and family interlude (22/3%)
• DCE and non-rostered congregational position (13/2%)

Among the 769 DCEs, 40% of the specific career path types (298) involved only one kind of setting (i.e., short-term congregational DCE), 35% involved two settings (i.e., DCE and K-8 teacher), and 25% involved three settings. The largest number of specific career path types (48) was clustered within the global career path type of DCE and other congregational/school ministries while the lowest number was in Congregational DCE only (4).

Among the seven global career path types, the specific career path types that emerged with the highest percentage of DCEs are identified in Table 16.9.

TABLE 16.9
Specific Career Path Types with the Highest Percentage of DCEs by Global Career Path Type

Global Career Path Type	Specific Career Path Type
Congregational DCE only	Short-term congregational DCE (20%)
DCE and other congregational/ school ministries	DCE and pastor (35%)
DCE and other LC–MS ministries	DCE and LC–MS university staff/educator (14%)
DCE and non-LC–MS ministries	DCE and Christian writer (3%)
DCE and non-church profession:	DCE and business/industry position (15%)
DCE and interlude for family/per- sonal/professional concerns	DCE and family interlude (10%)
Never served as congregational DCE	Never served – other LC–MS church-related work (13%)

When looking at the Global Career Path Type in the light of the eight status categories, three of the four predominant macro and micro specific career path types were located in the "Congregational DCE" status category. Among the 165 specific career path types reported by the survey respondents, none were reflected in all eight of the status categories. Six status categories did reflect those who had never sereved as a congregational DCE but were involved in other LC–MS church-related work.

Within each of the eight status categories, Table 16.10 identifies the specific career path types that emerged among the highest percentage of DCEs.

TABLE 16.10

Specific Career Path Types with the Highest Precentage of DCEs by Status Category

Status Category	Specific Career Path Type
Congregational DCE	Short-term congregational DCE (20%)
Non-congregational DCE	DCE and LC–MS university staff/educator (14%)
Pastor	DCE and pastor (35%)
Teacher/principal	DCE and K-8 teacher (14%)
Other Commissioned Minister	DCE and family life director (17%)
Candidate status	DCE and business/industry position (15%)
Not on roster	DCE and business/industry position (15%)
Retired	DCE and K-8 teacher/principal (20%)

PROFESSIONAL AND PERSONAL EXPERIENCES

DCEs in this study were asked to identify the level of impact that 29 professional and 13 personal experiences had upon their ministry. There were 792 DCEs who responded to the questions relating to professional experience and 789 who responded to the questions relating to personal experience.

The five most impactful professional experiences that were noted by at least a majority of the DCEs in this survey included the following:

- Team/staff relationships - positive (68%)
- Senior pastor relationships - positive (67%)
- Accepting a new position (66%)
- Program or experience I created and/or led (58%)
- Daily devotional life (55%)

It should also be noted that at least one-third of the DCEs indicated that the mirror opposite – negative team/staff relationship and negative senior pastor relationships – also impacted them (33% and 38% respectively).

TABLE 16.11

Major Impact of Professional Experiences on DCEs
by the Eight Status Categories

Identify those professional experiences that had a major impact on your ministry. Includes Important & Extremely Important	Congregational DCE	Non-congregational DCE	Pastor	Teacher / Principal	Other Commissioned	Candidate Status	Not on Roster	Retired	Totals
Number of responses	389	51	70	55	23	42	121	41	792
1. Absence of call opportunities	8%	6%	11%	11%	9%	57%	20%	12%	13%
2. Accepting a new position	66%	69%	70%	82%	70%	61%	48%	81%	66%
3. Accountability group	28%	50%	27%	16%	22%	37%	15%	52%	28%
4. Building construction project	20%	20%	26%	20%	31%	22%	11%	32%	20%
5. Change in job focus	43%	64%	60%	60%	78%	39%	39%	73%	49%
6. Conflict in the congregation / school	47%	42%	43%	54%	26%	54%	40%	37%	45%
7. Daily devotional life	58%	59%	63%	47%	39%	50%	46%	53%	55%
8. Declining a call	13%	21%	18%	18%	4%	12%	10%	12%	14%
9. Engaging a coach or mentor	29%	32%	19%	14%	26%	18%	20%	27%	25%
10. Formal continuing education experiences	49%	50%	53%	44%	65%	43%	32%	74%	48%
11. Graduate education	29%	63%	68%	45%	47%	39%	31%	56%	39%
12. Job salary & benefits	33%	39%	33%	38%	26%	32%	29%	30%	33%
13. Loss of valued colleague or mentor	21%	29%	18%	13%	13%	9%	14%	27%	19%
14. Pastoral vacancy	34%	33%	32%	27%	14%	19%	21%	36%	30%
15. Position eliminated due to budget cuts	6%	12%	16%	22%	8%	25%	11%	24%	11%
16. Position hindered by budget cuts	12%	12%	14%	24%	13%	22%	10%	18%	13%
17. Professional leadership beyond church	42%	71%	21%	31%	43%	36%	33%	68%	41%
18. Program or experience created and led	60%	62%	46%	49%	61%	62%	54%	78%	58%
19. Pursuit of other career aspirations	16%	38%	37%	34%	30%	36%	56%	18%	28%
20. Reached maximum influence	18%	28%	27%	25%	30%	22%	22%	30%	21%
21. Sabbatical	3%	12%	6%	2%	4%	2%	2%	10%	4%
22. Senior pastor relationships - negative	40%	30%	36%	46%	26%	49%	32%	29%	38%
23. Senior pastor relationships – positive	74%	70%	53%	53%	74%	68%	49%	83%	67%
24. Impacted by emerging technology	28%	40%	22%	24%	22%	39%	12%	27%	26%
25. Impacted by a book/author/film	29%	38%	19%	6%	22%	24%	12%	27%	24%
26. Synodical policy or direction	5%	18%	18%	6%	8%	20%	12%	15%	10%
27. Team / staff relationships - negative	36%	32%	30%	30%	28%	43%	28%	29%	33%
28. Team / staff relationships - positive	73%	75%	63%	66%	82%	64%	51%	81%	68%
29. Unclear position expectations	31%	29%	26%	27%	8%	51%	30%	17%	30%
30. Other	16%	24%	22%	24%	14%	16%	31%	39%	21%

The following five professional experiences did not appear to have a major impact on DCEs in this study:

- Sabbatical (4%)
- Synodical policy or direction (10%)
- Position eliminated due to budget cuts (11%)
- Position hindered by budget cuts (13%)
- Absence of a call (13%)

Somewhat surprisingly, the five professional experiences that had only moderate impact were:

- Loss of valued colleague or mentor (19%)
- Impacted by emerging technology (26%)
- Pastoral vacancy (30%)
- Unclear position expectations (30%)
- Job salary & benefits (33%)

Table 16.11 compares the professional experiences of the DCEs across the eight employment status categories. The percentages of the far right column were derived from the total number of 792. The other percentages were derived from the total career path number in that status category column.

The three most impactful personal experiences, perhaps not unexpectedly, were marriage (56%), birth of a child (46%), and support of parents and spouse (45%). There were three personal experiences that did not appear to have a major impact on the DCEs in this study:

- Divorce or separated from spouse (4%)
- Inadequate living arrangements (5%)
- Special needs child (5%)

When looking at the DCEs' professional experiences through the scope of the eight status categories, the experience that was in the top three for all eight status categories was "Team/staff relationships-positive." Within each of the eight status categories, Table 16.12 identifies the professional experiences that impacted the highest percentage of DCEs.

TABLE 16.12

Professional Experiences Impacting the Highest Percentage of DCEs by Status Category

Status Category	Professional Experience
Congregational DCE	Senior pastor relationships – positive (74%)
Non-congregational DCE	Team/staff relationships – positive (75%)
Pastor	Accepting a new position (70%)
Teacher/principal	Accepting a new position (82%)
Other Commissioned Minister	Team/staff relationships – positive (82%)
Candidate status	Senior pastor relationships – positive (68%)
Not on roster	Pursuit of other career aspirations (56%)
Retired	Senior pastor relationships – positive (83%)

Table 16.13 outlines the 10 most impactful professional DCE experiences relative to the eight employment status categories.

TABLE 16.13

Top 10 Professional Experiences Impacting the Highest Percentage of DCEs by Status Category

Professional Experience	Status Category
Senior pastor relationships – positive	Retired (83%)
Accepting a new position	Teacher/principal (82%)
Staff/team relationships – positive	Other Commissioned Ministers (82%)
Change in job focus	Other Commissioned Ministers (78%)
Program or experience I created or led	Retired (78%)
Formal continuing education experiences	Retired (74%)
Professional leadership beyond the church	Non-congregational DCE (71%)
Graduate Education	Pastors (68%)
Daily devotional life	Pastors (63%)
Absence of call opportunities	Candidate status (57%)

Those DCEs who were still on candidate status (CRM) appeared to be the most heavily impacted by negative professional experiences. For example, the following had the highest percentage among the eight status categories:

- Absence of call opportunities (57%)
- Conflict in the congregation/school (54%)
- Unclear position expectations (51%)
- Senior pastor relationships – negative (49%)
- Team/staff relationships – negative (43%)

Conversely, the most positive appeared to be those DCEs who had retired.

Among the eight employment status categories, the professional experience that appeared to have the least impact was whether one had taken a sabbatical. It ranked first or second highest in all eight employment categories.

In addition to a sabbatical, the professional experiences which had the least impactful among the highest percentage of DCEs are shown in Table 16.14.

TABLE 16.14
The Professional Experiences with the Least Impact on DCEs by Status Category

Status Category	Professional Experience
Congregational DCE	Position eliminated due to budget cuts (90%)
Non-congregational DCE	Position eliminated due to budget cuts (89%)
Pastor	Position eliminated due to budget cuts (82%)
Teacher/principal	Synodical policy or direction (74%)
Other Commissioned Minister	Synodical policy or direction (87%)
Candidate status	Position eliminated due to budget cuts (74%)
Not on roster	Position eliminated due to budget cuts (78%)
Retired	Absence of call opportunities (76%)

Among the 13 personal experiences, the one that had the greatest impact for all eight status categories, except for teacher/principal, was marriage.

Among the three most impactful personal experiences, the status categories that emerged with the highest percentage of DCEs: "Marriage" (non-congregational DCE with 65%), "birth of a child" (teacher/principal with 65%), and "support from parents/spouse" (retired with 58%).

Among the eight status categories, the personal experiences that appeared to have the least impact were "divorce or separated from spouse" and "special needs child" (first or second highest percentage of least impact in all eight categories).

KEY SUSTAINING PRACTICES

There were 20 practices or behaviors that at least 10% of some 712 DCEs indicated had strengthened their capacity to be DCE. These various practices represented a distillation of the hundreds of offerings that the 712 DCEs made, some of whom suggested 6-8 different behaviors. It should also be noted that this list of 20 behaviors was created out of the suggested behaviors of 362 congregational DCEs rather than all of the 712 DCEs.

Among the 20 practices or behaviors, five appeared to have the greatest capacity to strengthen a person's ability to be a DCE. Those who were pastors, teachers/principals and other commissioned ministers were asked which practices strengthened their capacity for ministry. The five strengthening activities were:

- Maintaining a consistent devotional and prayer life (45%)
- Engaging in regular, open, collaborative communication with co-workers (32%)
- Forging ties with local and/or regional DCEs for networking, sharing, supporting, and/or learning (30%)
- Stretching self through continuing education and professional conferences (29%)
- Engaging in consistent individual and/or small group Bible study (24%)

DCEs indicated that practices focused on relationships were important in their ministry. For example:

- Engaging in regular, open, collaborative communication with co-workers (32%)

- Forging ties with local and/or regional DCEs for networking, sharing, supporting, and/or learning (30%)

- Seeking out coaches/mentors/counselors/accountability (22%)

- Nurturing yet honest relationship with spouse and family (22%)

- Building relationships with parishioners based on listening, trust, and affirmation (20%)

Similarly, another cluster of key practices among DCEs focused on the importance of continued growth and learning as experienced in "stretching self through continuing education and professional conferences" (29%), "engaging in consistent individual and/or small group Bible study" (24%), and "continuing to read books, journals, reports, and resource materials" (14%).

Another cluster of responses highlighted the importance of personal practices designed to strengthen the individual's capacity to be a DCE:

- Maintaining a consistent devotional and prayer life (45%)

- Taking time for exercise/day off/vacation/personal steward (19%)

- Taking time to reflect upon, question, and learn from good & bad experiences (16%)

- Participating regularly in worship, holy communion, and/or confession and absolution (16%)

An additional cluster of practices that strengthened one's capacity to be a DCE lifted up the significance of modeling the Christ life by "growing in compassion, perseverance, flexibility, patience, humility, transparency, wisdom, faithfulness, and integrity" (14%), "living as a servant leader who loves, forgives, and affirms the gifts of self & others" (13%), and "discerning God's will and following it" (11%).

A final cluster of behaviors that strengthened a person's capacity to be a DCE focused on equipping others by "affirming and being affirmed by staff and laity" (16%), "developing servant leaders through equipping, empowering, and supporting" (13%), and "bringing a teaming sentiment to my work relationships" (11%).

When looking at the key sustaining practices in light of the eight employment status categories, among the 20 practices that strengthened a person's capacity to be a DCE, the one that was in the top three for all eight status categories was "maintaining a consistent devotional and prayer life." Table 16.15 identifies the key practice among each of the status categories.

TABLE 16.15

Key Practices that Strengthened the Highest Percentage of DCEs by Status Category

Status Category	Key Practice
Congregational DCE	Maintaining a consistent devotional and prayer life (41%)
Non-congregational DCE	Maintaining a consistent devotional and prayer life (62%)
Pastor	Maintaining a consistent devotional and prayer life (61%)
Teacher/principal	Maintaining a consistent devotional and prayer life (64%)
Other Commission Minister	Engaging in regular, open, collaborative communication with co-workers (41%)
Candidate status	Engaging in regular, open, collaborative communication with co-workers (42%)
Not on roster	Engaging in regular, open, collaborative communication with co-workers (40%)
Retired	Maintaining a consistent devotional and prayer life (37%)

While congregational DCEs naturally indicated all 20 of these behaviors to be strengthening, those DCEs who had become pastors only identified 10 behaviors. Also somewhat surprising, pastors had very modest or non-existent responses to the importance of staff relationships and affirming/equipping laity.

Although noted by congregational DCEs, non-congregational DCEs, and retirees, it appeared that DCEs were somewhat isolated from fellowshipping, serving, and learning from church workers both outside their own parish and outside of the LC–MS.

LONGEVITY AS A CONGREGATIONAL DCE

The survey responses indicated that a majority of DCEs (58%) expected to remain in a DCE position for their entire professional career. Not surprisingly, retired DCEs expected to stay in DCE ministry for their entire professional career, given that many of them became DCEs later in life. Ironically, two thirds of those on candidate status also expected to remain in DCE ministry their entire career. Those with the least expectation (40%) were teacher/principals.

Among the eight status categories, Chart 16.16 indicates the responses of those who expect to stay in a DCE position for their entire professional career.

CHART 16.16

DCEs who Expect to Remain in a DCE Position for their Entire Career by Status Category (n=779)

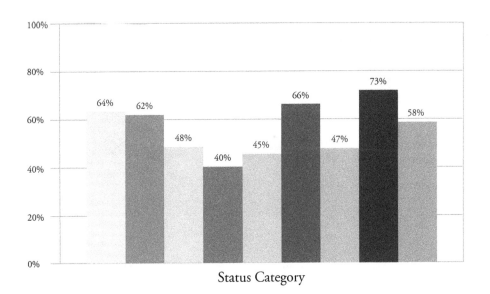

Status Category

Congregational DCE (64%)
▪ Non-congregational DCE (62%)
Pastor (48%)
▪ Teacher / Principal (40%)
▫ Other Commissioned (45%)

▪ Candidate Status (66%)
▫ Not on Roster (47%)
▪ Retired (73%)
▫ Average (58%)

CAREER LADDER

Even though the concept of a career ladder was open to individual interpretation, sixty-one percent of the DCEs in this study indicated there was no
such ladder. DCEs who were still on candidate status (CRM) were the only ones
to affirm the existence of a DCE career ladder but only by the narrowest of percent (51%). Teachers/principals were the least likely to perceive there was such a
career ladder (26%).

Chart 16.17 identifies the respondent's answers by the eight employment
status categories to the perception of the existance of a career ladder for DCEs.

CHART 16.17

DCEs Perceiving that There Is No Career Ladder by Status Category

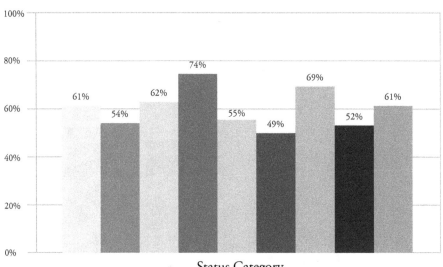

Congregational DCE (61%)   ■ Candidate Status (49%)
■ Non-congregational DCE (54%) ■ Not on Roster (69%)
Pastor (62%)   ■ Retired (52%)
■ Teacher / Principal (74%)   ■ Average (61%)
Other Commissioned (55%)

REASONS FOR LEAVING THE DCE MINISTRY

The most prevalent reasons for leaving DCE ministry were as follows:

- Felt called to another ministry of the church (i.e. pastor, teacher/principal, OCM) (77%)
- Felt my gifts could best be used outside the church's ministry (27%)
- Experienced staff conflict (23%)
- Felt drained by the demands of the position (20%)
- Desire to pursue graduate studies (20%)

When reviewing the reasons DCEs cited for leaving DCE ministry, family-related reasons did not play a major role. Only 10% of the respondents indicated that they left in order to become a full-time parent.

Of the five status categories for DCEs who were no longer practicing as a DCE, the top three reasons they left the profession are indicated in Table 16.18.

TABLE 16.18

Top Three Reasons for Leaving the DCE Ministry by Status Category

Status Category	Reason for Leaving
Pastor	Called to be a pastor; desire to pursue graduate studies; and staff conflict
Teacher/principal	Called to classroom ministry; drained by demands; and staff conflict
Other Commissioned Minister	Called to another ministry of church; drained by demands; and graduate studies
Candidate Status	Staff conflict; felt lonely and isolated; and left to become full-time parent
Not on roster	Staff conflict; drained by demands; and desire to pursue graduate studies

Of those DCEs who were no longer on the synod roster, sixty-three percent indicated that they would consider returning to the DCE ministry at some future point.

TYPES OF WELL-BEING NEEDED FOR A LIFELONG CAREER

When DCEs were asked how important a sense of well-being or health was in five areas of their life in order to pursue a lifelong career as a DCE, there was an overwhelming affirmation of the importance of spiritual health (97%) and emotional health (92%). The least important were physical health (68%) and financial health (58%).

All of the status categories, except retirees, indicated that spiritual health was most important to a lifelong career as a DCE followed by emotional health. Retired DCEs reversed the order citing emotional health as the most important.

CAREER MYTHS

A number of the more common questions raised about DCEs in the 1970s and 1980s had morphed into inaccurate, and sometimes detrimental, myths. By 2008 when this study was undertaken, there were approximately 615 DCEs serving congregations of the LC–MS and a growing number of DCEs had congregation-based careers of 30 years or more. There was finally enough history to address the myths with some certainty.

Directly addressing these myths should be very helpful.

- Prospective students and their parents could get honest answers about the promise/pain of DCE ministry.

- Professors would have current, accurate career information to help shape the identity of their students.

- Congregational staff colleagues and lay leaders would have up-to-date data regarding DCE career paths.

- DCEs who wanted understandable "big picture" information about their profession would have it in order to address their own and other's opinions, misperceptions, and questions.

- DCEs and their families could more fully understand the kind of promise their career might have when confronting calls and other decisions.

Table 16.19 identifies seven DCE career myths and indicates how the survey responses shed light on each one.

TABLE 16.19

DCE Career Myths Addressed by the Survey Responses

Myth 1: Male DCEs will become pastors	
Myth:	Male DCEs are "pastor wannabe's" and eventually head to the seminary.
Survey question:	Don't all male DCEs end up becoming pastors?
Survey response:	Seventy-five of the 491 males in the survey were pastors (15%)

Myth 2: Female DCEs leave the profession quickly	
Myth:	Very few women serve beyond 3-5 years.
Survey question:	Is DCE ministry in a congregation a viable long-term career for women?
Survey response:	Out of 291 female DCEs, three were still serving in congregational ministry after 30 years; 17 others after 20 years; and another 84 after 10 years.

Myth 3: DCE family life	
Myth:	Once a female DCE gets married and has a family, she leaves paid congregational ministry.
Survey question:	Are there any female DCEs who still serve while raising a young family?
Survey response:	Thirty-one percent (52) of the 170 female congregational DCEs in this survey had raised or were raising a young family while serving a parish.

Myth 4: DCEs have to be young	
Myth:	DCE ministry is a young person's career.
Survey question:	Are there any congregational DCEs who are in their 50s and 60s?
Survey response:	Forty-three percent of congregational DCEs were 40 years or older; Twenty-one percent were 50 years or older.

TABLE 16.19 (Continued)

DCE Career Myths Addressed by the Survey Responses

Myth 5: Lack of DCE Career Ladder	
Myth:	All "good" DCEs leave the parish and go on to "bigger and better things."
Survey question:	Is there a career ladder in DCE ministry?
Survey response:	Most DCEs (61%) believed that there was not a career ladder although some indicated that they held such a view when they were younger.

Myth 6: Reasons for Leaving DCE Ministry	
Myth:	DCEs leave congregational ministry because of "push themes," such as staff conflict, incompetence, congregational pressure or burnout.
Survey question:	Why do DCE leave congregational ministry?
Survey response:	Most DCEs left because of "pull themes" like feeling called to another ministry or desiring to pursue graduate study.

Myth 7: Career Longevity	
Myth:	A few make it as far as 20 years but that's about it.
Survey question:	Has any certified DCE spent his or her entire career in congregational ministry?
Survey response:	Over 135 DCEs (16%) had served for 20 years or more. Fifty-five of that number had spent their entire career in congregational ministry. One reached 40 years in the summer of 2009 and a handful of other DCEs will potentially get there in two years.

IN SUMMARY

The first phase of the DCE Career Path Project provided a mosaic of large groups of DCEs that reflected various pictures of DCE ministry. Eight different groupings (status categories) of DCEs, with distinctive career paths, emerged from the survey. These 800 DCEs also clustered into 16 different career path patterns, seven global career types, and 165 specific career types. In addition, the report brought to light a host of generalizable perceptions regarding various aspects of a DCE's career path.

Given all of this information, what general conclusions might be drawn? Among the many, these 24 deserve special reflection:

1. There appeared to have been five waves of DCEs in the past 50 years: early pioneers who were not certified as DCEs (1950-1960s), those who were field certified in the middle or late stages of their career (1970s-1980s), the first generation of undergraduate training program graduates (1975-1985), the second generation of undergraduates (1986-1996), and the third generation which included an increasing number who were being certified through non-traditional means (1997-2007).

2. Given the LC–MS's approach to defining those who were on its roster of public ministers, it was insightful to use these same eight classifications to describe the career paths of DCEs, i.e., DCEs who became pastors or who were on candidate status for rostered ministry, etc.

3. DCEs' career paths appeared to be reducible to seven global types.

4. While there was substantial variation in the specific career path types of DCEs, there was less variation in the settings in which they served.

5. Those who trained to be a DCE followed through on that intention to serve a congregation, and if not, they usually pursued another ministry to the LC–MS.

6. Congregational DCE ministry was a lifelong career for a small but growing number of DCEs.

7. Once a DCE left congregational ministry for another rostered ministry, that ministry, rather than DCE ministry, became his/her professional identity except for non-congregational DCEs.

8. The senior pastor had a major professional impact, for positive or negative, on DCEs, as did team/staff relationships.

9. When DCEs experienced a major crisis, it seemed to have had a major impact on their career path, usually resulting in a move to another parish or shifting out of congregational ministry.

10. The majority of crises among DCEs tended to take place in the first decade of their service.

11. Individuals used a variety of non-traditional avenues to become certified as a DCE.

12. A small but growing number of DCEs retired while serving as a congregational DCE.

13. There was a difference between the career path of male and female DCEs, particularly as it related to career length, continuous service, and pursuit of an ongoing church work career so that the longer a male DCE stayed in congregational ministry the fewer female peers he had.

14. A critical factor in the growing number of married female DCEs who continued serving a congregation while raising a family was the parish's flexibility regarding full and part-time service.

15. The vast majority of DCEs had not experienced either a loss of their position due to budget constraints or a cutback in their program budget.

16. There appeared to be a gross undervaluing of the importance of one's physical and financial well-being among DCEs when describing the capacity to pursue a long-term career in DCE Ministry.

17. The DCE internship was a significant factor in how and where a number of congregational DCEs began their career path.

18. A pastoral vacancy did not appear to have a major professional impact on a DCE.

19. A hunger for additional study, whether in a graduate, certificate, or other continuing education program, had a major impact on a DCE's career path, often launching them into a new ministry emphasis, i.e. pastor, family life director, etc.

20. DCE certification provided numerous DCEs with a "gateway" to explore and/or transition into various other church-work-related professions.

21. Very few DCEs chose to pursue religious education service in the military.

22. DCEs whose career path included "DCE and LC–MS district/national executive" appeared to remain in a ministry of the synod rather than leaving roster status of the LC–MS.

23. When a DCE chooses to leave congregational ministry, a higher percentage of male DCEs than females tended to remain in professional church-related roles because they had more ministry alternatives.

24. Once certified as a DCE, there was a strong desire to do the work of a DCE even to the point of volunteering when there was no position available or one had retired.

When looking at the findings in light of the eight status categories a number of additional specific conclusions can be made. For example, the absence of a call appeared to have little professional impact upon DCEs except for those on candidate status. Those DCEs whose future rested in school ministry tended either to transition out of congregational DCE ministry in their twenties or not serve in a DCE congregational position at all.

There seem to be three primary paths by which DCEs entered the pastoral ministry: the first is going straight to the seminary after obtaining a bachelor degree; the second is "tuning up" by serving as a congregational DCE for a period of time; and third, migrating to the seminary after moving from non-church-work, to a non-certified DCE position, to a certified DCE position, and finally to the pastoral office.

A notable number of the DCEs who were not on the roster of the synod were "early transitionals" – that is, they never served as a congregational DCE, transitioned into marriage and raising a family after several years as a congregational DCE, entered another kind of full-time church-work, or struck out into non-church-related positions.

Even though two-thirds of those DCEs no longer on synod's roster indicated an openness to consider returning to DCE ministry at some future point in their professional career, there appeared to be no data to suggest that they were doing so, particularly if they were female. A substantial portion of those DCEs, who were on candidate status, expressed the most disappointment, pain, and unsettledness related to their life as a DCE even as they expressed appreciation for their training as a DCE and their hope to return to that ministry.

CONCLUSION

As the next 50 years of DCE ministry unfold, thousands of certified and uncertified Directors of Christian Education will continue to follow their Lord and Savior Jesus Christ into a host of ministry settings. Among them will be the 600 plus DCEs whose current ministry focus will be the equipping of children, youth, parents, and other lay leaders for sensitive, relevant and timely service in the name of Jesus. May the Holy Spirit, who calls, enlightens and keeps us all in the one true faith, continue to edify and guide those full-time Ministers of the Gospel we salute as Directors of Christian Education. To God alone be the glory!

CHAPTER 17

Ministry in the Emerging Culture

KEVIN BORCHERS | GARY SCHULTZ | RICK STENGL

Historically, Directors of Christian Education (DCE) have been called upon by their congregations to develop programs that teach the unchanging truth of Scripture in a culturally relevant way – a task that is increasingly becoming a greater challenge due to cultural shifts in the way people think about and relate to institutionalized religion. The *American Religious Identity Survey 2008* reported that the number of people who identify themselves as being affiliated with mainline churches and denominations, like the Lutheran Church–Missouri Synod, experienced steep declines from 2001 to 2008. On the other hand, the number of people responding who identified themselves as non-denominational increased during those same years. The report also shows that the decline in affiliation with Christian churches is not due so much to challenges coming from other religions as much as it from our culture's rejection of all forms of organized religion (Kosmin & Keysar, 2008).

Kevin Borchers serves as Assistant Director of the DCE Program at Concordia University Chicago.

Gary Schultz serves as Senior Pastor of Trinity Lutheran Church, Wausau, Wisconsin.

Rick Stengl serves in the area of Youth and Children's Ministry at Trinity Lutheran Church, Wausau, Wisconsin.

As we look to the future of DCE ministry, it would appear that the decline in participation and rejection of the institutionalized church is not due to individuals' rejection of theology and religious teaching, though this might be the case with some. Instead, it seems as though this rejection of organized religion is a cultural response to ways in which religious groups' attempt to engage the people in our changing yet emerging culture. Doing things the way they have always been done is no longer effective. It begs the question: "What can and needs to be changed without compromising the Biblical truth we proclaim and teach?" It is a question of the methodology and approach by which we engage people, not of the substance we carry.

Postmodernism began in the 1950s in the world of architectural design – a shift we can still see today in the differences between church structures and facilities built prior to World War II and those built since. By the late 1970s and early 80s, the shifting culture had infiltrated the arts and literature. Such cultural changes and the way in which people related to organized religion were visible to church leaders and congregations back in the 60s and 70s, but little was done to develop new strategies to engage the people of this emerging culture. Instead, many within the church attempted to paint a picture showing the emerging culture as a growing evil.

It was not until the 1990s that the church began seeking to understand the cultural paradigm shifts that had occurred. Not until then did we begin to make efforts to review and compare our held values, rooted in the Modern Era, to the new postmodern culture. With such comparisons and with open dialogue, churches began to understand that the emerging culture preferred personal experience over reason, subjectivity over objectivity, spirituality over religion and visual images over spoken and/or printed words.

These new preferences continue to challenge the way our church attempts to share the central message to our Lutheran theology – that our salvation is a free gift from God that is received by faith in Christ Jesus. It is not the result of anything we personally do or any conscious decision we make (see Eph. 2:8-10). It is not this message but the way in which it is communicated that continues to challenge many church leaders, pastors, DCEs and congregational members.

If we insist on doing things "the way they have always been done, even though we can see that they are no longer effective, then we can expect to see a continued decline in participation in our churches. On the other hand, if we are willing to submit ourselves to a ministry audit that evaluates the methods by which we seek to communicate the Gospel message to the people in the emerging culture, and if we are willing to change our approach to the way we try to engage people, then we might begin to see a slowing and eventual turning around from the decline in affiliation we are currently experiencing.

Gibbs and Bolger quoted one pastor as saying, "Church, as we have inherited it, is no longer working for the vast groups of people...the term *emerging church* is nothing more than a way of expressing that we need new forms of church that relate to the emerging culture" (2005, p. 41). Arnold and Hall may have said it best: "New approaches are needed in new times: old wineskins will not hold the new wine. Those involved in nurturing faith development need to come to grips with the fact that the paradigm has shifted, and that the shift brings wonderful new opportunities for nurturing faith" (2009, p. 240). This may sound threatening to some church workers, leaders and congregational members, but this is not suggesting changes in the way we do ministry simply for the sake of change. On the contrary, methodological changes that do not compromise the Biblical message are needed so that the Gospel message may continue to be spread and shared with all cultures throughout the world.

The apostle Paul mentions the adaptations he made in his own ministry style in order to share the message of Christ. He wrote, "I have become all things to all men so that by all possible means I might save some. I do all this for the sake of the Gospel, that I may share in its blessings" (see 1 Cor. 9:19-23). In these verses, Paul gives some important principles for ministry: 1) build unconditional relationships; 2) avoid a know-it-all attitude; and 3) be incarnational.

BUILD UNCONDITIONAL RELATIONSHIPS

It is very important that relationships be established before the topic of religion even comes up. The mindset of the emerging culture is more often than not suspicious of anything religious and often rejects anything having to do with organized religion. Therefore it is highly important that emerging DCEs focus and concentrate on building strong relationships without ulterior motives. DCE Joel Dietrich writes, "Too often we build relationships in order to share the Gospel... The problem is we are constantly looking for our opportunity to bring up Jesus, attempting to steer conversations towards the church... The postmodern mind will see right through this. Teenagers [and other postmoderns] do not need another phony relationship. They desire friends for friends' sake" (2007, p. 2).

Emerging DCEs must be relational – deeply connected to God in a personal relationship, and personally and genuinely connected to other people. Jesus said it best: "'Love the Lord your God with all your heart and with all your soul and with all your mind and with all your strength'" and "'Love your neighbor as yourself'" (Mk. 12:30-31). It is not only about church workers being in relationships with people, but we must also be very intentional in our equipping of other people to build personal relationships with others. Paul writes, "Consequently, you are no longer foreigners and aliens, but fellow citizens with God's people and members of God's household, built on the foundation of the apostles and prophets, with Christ Jesus himself as the chief cornerstone" (Eph. 2:19-20). God's household is not a building but a group of people who share community (i.e. *"common unity"*) in the Triune God. It is no accident that God created us for community with himself and with one another. His three-in-one nature demonstrates that God is in community with himself and that he desires community with us.

One of the best ways community is built among the people of a church is through small group ministry. The type of relationship building that can happen in a small group provides the type of life-on-life, personal relationship desired by postmodern individuals. The relationships formed in the group can, and we pray will, provide the connection by which we can engage individuals. For this reason, small group ministry needs to be a big part of our efforts to reach out and to engage the emerging culture.

Your church's small groups may or may not intentionally study the Bible. Some might be support groups. Others might gather in a local coffee shop or restaurant to discuss a book or some other topic of cultural interest. Whatever the case, we need to focus on connecting people with each other. Then, according to God's timing and his Spirit's work, he will begin to develop and nurture relationships with those from within the culture who are touched by God's grace through the lives of God's people.

Besides the relationships that can be fostered in small groups, we must be intentional about exploring every opportunity in and through which relationships between people across the lifespan can be developed. Adults and teens have been able to develop strong relational bonds through serving together. Through intergenerational programming, older adults have been able to develop healthy relationships with younger children through community events like vacation Bible schools. The opportunities for building relationships are limited only by our imaginations.

AVOID A KNOW-IT-ALL ATTITUDE

Postmodern culture tends to be suspicious of organized religion of any kind, not just Christianity. This suspicion often leads to personal rejection of institutionalized religion and a desire for a personal spiritual experience. Once again it is the personal and the experiential nature to which postmoderns are naturally attracted. It is not the modernistic methodology of an "expert talking head" who will engage them in a winsome way.

Something we should consider is whether our passion to proclaim God's truth comes across to the postmoderns, who view all truth to be subjective rather than absolute, as arrogance. Could it be that our methodology presents a message that is unintentional? Just by virtue of our presentation are we perceived as having an "I'm right and you're wrong, so there's nothing to discuss" attitude?

Such an attitude or demeanor does great harm to the efforts to engage individuals from the culture with the transforming love of God in Christ.

Postmoderns view truth subjectively, many believing there is nothing that is absolutely true for all people. Truth in a postmodern world is simply a personal preference. So for us to present ourselves as having the One answer they need, even though we Christians confess this to be true, can be an immediate hindrance or threat to any possibility we have in engaging the people. Postmoderns value personal choice. They are savvy consumers, and they exercise their rights to choose and their consumer mentality in all areas of life.

Since congregations are the people, this consumer mentality has increasingly affected the way each congregation chooses to do ministry and conduct business. Some churches have adopted a mentality that they must compete with culture in an adversarial way. Other congregations do their best to attract people by developing programs and events that attempt to replicate parts of the outside world that vie for the attention of our children, young adults and families. Both efforts may experience some success, but that is not why Jesus' Church exists. God has called us to share the love we have received from him and the life-changing message of forgiveness and eternal life through faith in Christ through our words and actions.

BE INCARNATIONAL

We need to let other people see Jesus in our actions, attitudes and the way we interact with other people. More importantly, we are called to have lives in which Christ is seen by others. Jesus said, "You are the light of the world…let your light shine before men, that they may see your good deeds and praise your Father in heaven" (Matt. 5:14-16).

Jesus became one of us (without the sin). He set aside his heavenly glory to become a human being with flesh, bone, emotion and all that makes a person. He was sent into the world where he spoke the language of the people and followed the customs of their culture. This is the model we need to emulate.

Rather than being limited to just talking about what Jesus did, we need to live it out in our own lives and in our ministries. Our Lord humbled himself to become a servant, and he taught his disciples to serve by washing their feet, among other things. So, too, if we want those whom we disciple to serve, then we ourselves must serve. If we want them to be students of the Bible, then we ourselves must be students of that same Holy Word. Pastor John C. Maxwell writes, "If I don't live it, I won't teach it. I won't try to export what I don't possess. As leaders, we teach what we know, but we reproduce what we are" (2006, p. 41-52). Postmoderns are looking for community with real people. They desire genuine relationships and quickly recognize people who do not walk their talk. If emerging DCEs hope to achieve any success in reaching people in the emerging culture, then we cannot afford to put up a good front.

Congregations, pastors, DCEs and others need to do away with the old idea that if we build it (facilities, programs, etc.) they will come. That kind of thinking is attractional, and with postmoderns it will not work. The preconceived notions that many postmoderns have about the church and about Christians, in general, need to be dispelled by a missional church and missional Christians. Being missional means that you are willing to enter into a culture and engage it on its terms and turf. It is only in this personal and corporate engaging of the culture that we have any hope of being relational and relevant, for it is in the culture that we touch peoples' lives, meet their needs, answer their questions and face the challenges they throw at us.

Being missional, participating in God's mission as it is set forth by Jesus' Great Commission (see Matt. 28:19-20), is the opposite of being attractional. Being missional means getting out of our church offices and the walls of our church buildings in order to get out on the street to meet people where they are. Any number of pastors, DCEs and others from congregations who are experiencing any success in engaging the postmodern culture are developing relationships and engaging in open discussions with people in places like a local coffee shop or restaurant. The point is they are not expecting people to come to them. These effective ministers are going to the place where they can meet people. In some cases, depending upon the local culture, they are being invited into the homes of people they meet, once they have developed a level of trust.

These same pastors also recognize that they are not in competition with the other Christian congregation down the street. They don't fall into the trap of having to compare themselves with other pastors or DCEs in a numbers game. It is only after we ourselves have been transformed by God so that we become missional in our thinking and practice that God will begin to free us from our need to compete.

Being missional implies that we see ourselves as missionaries to the postmodern culture. As such, it is very important for us to learn the language, customs and practices of the local culture. Missionaries, however, are also very intentional about investing in the lives of individual members of the culture. These missionaries recognize that their efforts to train up indigenous missionaries who reach out to their own people will eventually yield a greater harvest than what the foreign missionary can ever hope to accomplish on his or her own. In the same way, we DCEs must take seriously the task of equipping and training others to be missionaries who make disciples in their own homes, schools and work places, communities and globally. The methods by which we do that, however, must be culturally relevant yet Biblically sound.

Change does not come easy to people, and changing the teaching style that has been traditionally held by the church will be a challenge. Emerging DCEs who minister in a postmodern culture, however, need to make such a transition. The lecture-based, one-way communication used to share God's story and to explain it needs to be replaced with styles that incorporate more interaction, dialogue and open discussion, visual images, sound and experiences that engage all five senses. This is not to say that we should simply add a slideshow that includes a fill-in-the-blank outline that simply follows along with our teaching. Instead, we must seek to discover ways bridge the gap from people simply being passive, inactive audiences to active participants.

In some emerging churches, entire teaching messages or sermons are being replaced by audio-visual experiences and/or experiential opportunities in which God's story intersects with personal and community stories. As stated earlier, postmoderns are more interested in experience than they are reason and plausible explanation. The message must remain unchanged, but the delivery method could be changed in order to meet the needs of the people in that place and at that time. The declines many churches are experiencing, mention before, seem to suggest that it must change.

For a church to be considered an emerging church, it must be attempting to effectively engage the postmodern culture. The emerging church does not teach postmodernism, which is a bcultural worldview. Instead, it seeks to reach and to minister to those individuals who embrace postmodern thinking. The pastors and other leaders of emerging churches are not attempting to transform people with a modernistic mindset into postmoderns, but rather they are challenging these moderns to reevaluate beliefs, assumptions, and practices to determine their validity (Zorgdrager, 2008). Most notably this has to happen in the means the church uses to accomplish its mission.

What the church must ultimately do is define what it means to be a healthy church that can effectively continue to proclaim the Gospel message of God's love for us in Christ Jesus. The church in Martin Luther's day was in need of radical changes – we call it the Reformation – so that the people in that time and place could be touched by the life-changing Gospel message and be spiritually fed and nurtured. Is a similar overhaul of the way we do ministry needed today? If changes or repairs are needed, then each DCE also needs to ask what he or she needs to do or change in order to move forward in ministry in the emerging culture.

References

Ablaze! Origins, theology, structure, impact. (2005). *Issues in Christian Education, 39*(2): 1-28.

Allen, R. (1956). *Missionary methods: St.Paul's our ours?* Chicago, IL: Moody Press.

Althaus, P. (1966). *The theology of Martin Luther.* Philadelphia, PA: Fortress Press.

Arches, J. (1991). Social structure, burnout, and job satisfaction. *Social Work, 36*(3), 202-206.

Arfsten, D. J., & Seifert, V. (2006, Winter). Celebrating as women in DCE ministry. *Shaping the Future, 3*(4), 34-36.

Arnold, S. & Hall, K. (2009). Christian faith formation for the 21st century: A renewing way. *Lutheran Education Journal, 142*(4), 237-245.

Babbie, E. (1990). *Survey research methods* (2nd ed.). Belmont, CA: Wadsworth.

Bachman, J. (2007). *First use of the law in congregational life.* Irvine, CA: Concordia University-Irvine.

Barrett, D. B. & Johnson, T. M. (Eds.). (2003). *World Christian trends, AD 30-2000: Interpreting the annual Christian megacensus.* Pasadena, CA: William Carey Library.

Barrett, D. B. (1987). *Cosmos, chaos and gospel: A chronology of world evangelization from creation to new creation.* Birmingham, AL: New Hope.

Barry, A. L. (2000). *Issues in our synod: The growing shortage of pastors and teachers.* Retrieved from http://www.lcms.org/president/statements/shortage.asp

Beal, W. (Ed.). (1976). *The work of the minister of education.* Nashville, TN: Convention Press.

Best, E. (1960, July). Spiritual sacrifice: General priesthood in the New Testament, *Interpretation, 14*(3), 273-299.

Blanchard, K. & Hodges, P. (2003). *The servant leader: Transforming your heart, head, hands & habits.* Nashville, TN: Thomas Nelson.

Blanke, M. (1995). DCE: Generalist or specialist? *Lutheran Education, 130*(4), 195-199.

Board for Congregational Services. (2003). *Certified DCEs serving congregations.* St. Louis, MO: Lutheran Church–Missouri Synod.

Bobbitt, S. A., Leich, M. C., Whitener, S. D. & Lynch, H. F. (1994). *Characteristics of stayers, movers, and leavers: Results from the teacher follow-up survey.* (Publication No. 94-337). Washington, DC: National Center for Education Statistics.

Bobek, B. (2002). Teacher resiliency: A key to career longevity. *Clearing House, 75*(4), 202-208.

Bouma, J. (2007). Toward a postmodern youth ministry: An examination of postmodern youth culture in conversation with the emerging church. *Precipice Magazine.* Retrieved from http://www.precipicemagazine.com/postmodern-youth-ministry.html

Brantsch, R. (2001, February). *LEA-TEAM survey of synodically certified DCEs.* Survey results presented at the DCE Summit meeting, Austin, TX.

Breckenridge, J. & Breckenridge, L. (1995). *What color is your God? Multicultural education in the church: Examining Christ and culture in light of the changing face of the church.* Grand Rapids, MI: Baker Books.

Brons, M. (Ed.). (2002). *Concordia University St. Paul DCE colloquy.* Retrieved from http://wwtest.csp.edu/cvm/colloquy/dcecolloquy.html.

Caroselli, M. (2000). *Leadership skills for managers.* New York, NY: McGraw-Hill.

Carter, R. (2002). The ministry of every Christian: Theological perspectives. *Issues in Christian Education, 36*(2), 12-16.

Choy, S. P., Bobbit, S. A., Henke, R. R., Medrich, E. A., Horn, L. J. & Lieberman, J. (1993). *America's teachers: Profile of a profession* (Publication No. 93-025). Washington, DC: National Center for Education Statistics.

Commission on Ministerial Growth and Support. (2000). *Teacher 2000: A survey of teachers in the Lutheran school system.* St. Louis, MO: Lutheran Church–Missouri Synod.

Commission on Theology and Church Relations. (1981). *The ministry: Offices, procedures and nomenclature.* Retrieved from http://www.lcms.org/ctcr/docs/ctcr-01.html

Concordia University System (2002). *Directors of Christian education who have been certified by a synodical school of the LC–MS: 2002.* St. Louis, MO: Author.

Concordia University System. (2003). *Directors of Christian education who have been certified by a synodical school of the LC–MS: 2003.* St. Louis, MO: Author.

Concordia University System. (2008). *Directors of Christian education who have been certified by a synodical school of the LC–MS: 2008.* St. Louis, MO: Author.

Creswell, J. W. (2002). *Educational research: Planning, conducting, and evaluating quantitative and qualitative research.* Upper Saddle River, NJ: Merrill Prentice Hall.

CUEnet. (2003). *Concordia online teacher colloquy program.* Retrieved January 10, 2003, from http://www.cuenet.edu/colloquy

Cullen, W. (2001). [Director of Christian Education District Survey for 2001]. Unpublished raw data.

Culture. (2000). In *American heritage dictionary of the English language online* (4th ed.). Retrieved from http://dictionary.reference.com/browse/culture

Davison, T. (1978). *A determination and comparison of perceptions of selected leader behaviors of directors of Christian education held by selected Lutheran parish personnel.* (Doctoral dissertation, Northern Illinois University). Dissertation Abstracts International, 39, 08A, 4728.

DCE Summit Minutes. (1999). Available from DCE Summit Secretary.

DELTO. (2003). *Distance education leading towards ordination: What is DELTO?* Retrieved from http://higher-ed.lcms.org/408-pastoral-delto.asp

Dietrich, J. (2007, February). Emerging youth ministry. *Youth Supports, 8*(2), 1-2. Retrieved from http://www.nowlcms.org/Resources/Educ/Youth/ys0702.pdf

Dillman, D. A. (2000). *Mail and internet surveys: The tailored design method* (2nd ed.). New York: John Riley & Sons.

Dittes, J. E. (1987). *When work goes sour.* Philadelphia, PA: Westminster Press.

Durkin, E. & Montague, J. D. (1995, February 11). Surveying U.S. nuns. *America Press, 172*(4), 11.

Ebensteiner, P. G. (1977). *A comparative study of the professional status and office of Christian education directors within the Lutheran Church.* Unpublished thesis, Seattle Pacific University, Seattle, WA.

Elias, J. L. (2002). *A history of Christian education: Protestant, Catholic, Orthodox perspectives.* Malabar, FL: Krieger.

Elmshauser, J. M. (2001, February). *DCE ministry competency survey.* Survey results presented at the DCE Summit meeting, Austin, TX.

Emler, D. G. (1989). *Revisioning the DRE.* Birmingham, AL: Religious Education Press.

Ewen, R. (1966). A theory of human motivation. *Psychological Review, 50*(4), 370-396.

Ferguson, D. B. (2000). NSTA teacher survey lists teachers' dissatisfactions. *Curriculum Administrator, 36*(7), 18.

Festinger, L. (1957). *A theory of cognitive dissonance.* Evanston, IL: Row, Peterson.

Feuerherd, J. (2002, September 20). Job satisfaction high among Catholic clergy. *National Catholic Reporter, 38*(40), 13.

First graduates of the Concordia online teacher colloquy program. (2001, Spring). *Concordia Chronicle*, p. 3.

Freyholtz, J. F. (1972). The DCE as educator. *Lutheran Education, 107*, 239-246.

Fritz, J. H. C. (1932). *Pastoral theology.* St. Louis, MO: Concordia Publishing House.

Furnish, D. J. (1968). *An historical analysis of the work of the director of Christian education.* (Doctoral dissertation, Northwestern University). Dissertation Abstracts International (UMI No. 6901833).

Furnish, D. J. (1976). *DRE/DCE—The history of a profession.* Nashville, TN: Christian Educators Fellowship.

Furnish, D. J. (1984). The profession of director of minister of Christian education in Protestant churches. In M.J. Taylor (Ed.), *Changing patterns of religious education* (pp. 193-204). Nashville, TN: Abingdon Press.

Gall, M. D., Borg, W. R. & Gall, J. P. (1996). *Educational research: An introduction.* New York, NY: Long Publishers.

Gangel, K. O. & Benson, W. B. (1983). *Christian education: Its history and philosophy.* Chicago, IL: Moody Press.

Gerrish, B. A. (1965, December). Priesthood and ministry in the theology of Luther. *Church History, 34*(4), 404-422.

Gibbs, E. & Bolger, R. K. (2005). *Emerging churches: Creating Christian community in postmodern cultures.* Grand Rapids, MI: Baker Academic.

Giles, J. L. (1983). *A study of directors of Christian education in the Lutheran Church–Missouri Synod and their perceived roles in parish education administration* (Doctoral dissertation, Northern Illinois University). Dissertation Abstracts International, 44 12A, 3555.

Glennon, F. (1999). Assessment for the right reason: The ethics of outcome assessment. *Teaching Theology and Religion, 2*(1), 14-25.

Griffin, D. (1981). *The director of Christian education: Information bulletin* #14081. St. Louis, MO: Board for Parish Services of the Lutheran Church–Missouri Synod.

Griffin, D. E. (1995). The birth of a profession. *Concordia Historical Institute Quarterly, 68*(3), 133-145.

Harbaugh, G. L. (2000). *The confident Christian.* Minneapolis, MN: Augsburg Fortress Press.

Harris, M. (1976). *The D.R.E. book: Questions and strategies for parish personnel.* New York, NY: Paulist Press.

Harrison, R. K. (1980). *Leviticus: An introduction and commentary.* Downers Grove, IL: Inter-Varsity Press.

Herman, E. (1921). *Creative prayer.* London: James Clarke & Co.

Herzberg, F., Mausner, B., & Snyderman, B. (1959). *The motivation to work.* New York, NY: John Wiley & Sons, Inc.

Hesselgrave, D. J. (1991). *Communicating Christ cross-culturally: An introduction to missionary communication.* Grand Rapids, MI: Zondervan.

Howse, W. L. (n.d.). *The minister of education.* Nashville, TN: Convention Press.

Huba, M. E., & Freed, J. E. (2000). *Learner-centered assessment on college campuses: Shifting the focus from teaching to learning.* Needham Heights, MA: Allyn & Bacon.

Hugick, L., & Leonard, J. (1991). Job dissatisfaction grows; "moonlighting" on the rise. *Gallup Poll News Service, 56,* 1-11.

Isenhower, J. Jr. (2002). Committee oks revisions to LC–MS DELTO program. *LCMSNews, 72.* Retrieved from http://www.lcms.org/news/2002_072.html

Janzow, F. S. (1978). *Luther's large catechism: A contemporary translation with study questions.* St. Louis, MO: Concordia Publishing House.

Janzow, W. T. (2002). The ministry of every Christian: A needed perspective. *Issues in Christian Education, 36*(2), 6-11.

Jayaratne, S. & Chess, W. A. (1985). Factors associated with job satisfaction and turnover among child welfare workers. In J. Laird & A. Hartman (Eds.), *A handbook of child welfare* (pp. 760-766). New York, NY: Free Press.

Johnstone, P., & Mandryk, J. (2001). *Operation world: When we pray God works.* Waynesboro, GA: Paternoster.

Joosten, J. (1996). *People and land in the holiness code: An exegetical study of the ideational framework of the law in Leviticus 17-26.* Leiden, NY: Brill.

Karpenko, W. O. II. (1975, Spring). 1974 DCE Call Trends, *DCE Bulletin.*

Karpenko, W. O. II. (1978). *The relationship of FIRO compatibility theory and Mitchell's multiple staff principles for pastor-director of Christian education teams serving congregations of the Lutheran Church–Missouri Synod* (Doctoral dissertation, University of Nebraska). Dissertation Abstracts International, 39, 11A, 6466.

Karpenko, W. O. II. (1980, Fall). Women and men in DCE ministry: A comparative study. Part I: A demographic profile. *DCE Bulletin.*

Karpenko, W. O. II. (1986). *A brief summary of the pertinent findings from phase I and II of the DCE curricular development and validation project involving directors of Christian education (DCEs) of the Lutheran Church – Missouri Synod.* Unpublished manuscript, Concordia College, Seward, NE.

Karpenko, W. O. II. (1990). *A brief summary of the pertinent findings from phase III of the DCE curricular development and validation project involving directors of Christian education (DCEs) of the Lutheran Church – Missouri Synod.* Unpublished manuscript, Concordia College, Seward, NE.

Karpenko, W. O. II. (1992). *Findings and interpretive comments based upon a Survey of district presidents' and district education executives' perceptions regarding staff relationships within congregations and schools of the district they serve.* St. Louis, MO: LCMS Team Ministry Project.

Karpenko, W. O. II. (1997). [The identification of the roles and sub-roles in which most directors of Christian education (DCE) engage]. Unpublished raw data.

Karpenko, W. O. II. (1997). *Influences of being a female DCE upon one's ministry.* Unpublished manuscript, Concordia University. Chicago, IL.

Kay, W. K. (2000, January). Job satisfaction of British Pentecostal ministers. *Asian Journal of Pentecostal Studies, 3*(1), 83-97.

Keyne, L. K. (1992, April). Fourteen steps of professionalism. *DCE Directions,* 11-15.

Keyne, L. K. (1995). *Who do you say I am? The professional identity of the director of Christian education in the Lutheran Church–Missouri Synod* (Doctoral dissertation). University of Southern California, Los Angeles, CA.

Kieschnick, G. B. (2009, June 26). *LCMS director of Christian education 50th anniversary proclamation.* St. Louis, MO: The Lutheran Church–Missouri Synod.

Klaas, A. C. & Klaas, C. D. (1999). *Clergy shortage study.* Retrieved from http://higher-ed.lcms.org/pdf/clergy-shortage-study.pdf

Kleinig, J. W. (2003). *Leviticus.* St. Louis, MO: Concordia Publishing House.

Knohl, I. (1995). *The sanctuary of silence: The priestly Torah and the holiness school.* Minneapolis, MN: Fortress Press.

Koehler, E. W. A. (1952). *A summary of Christian doctrine.* (Rev. 2nd ed.). St. Louis, MO: Concordia Publishing House.

Kolb, R. (1993). *The Christian faith: A Lutheran exposition.* St. Louis, MO: Concordia Publishing House.

Kosmin, B. A. & Keysar, A. (2009, March). *American religious identification survey (ARIS 2008) summary report.* Retrieved from http://www.americanreligionsurvey-aris.org/reports/ARIS_Report_2008.pdf

Kottack, C. P. (1994). *Cultural anthropology.* New York: McGraw Hill.

Kraft, V. R. (1957). *The director of Christian education in the local church.* Chicago: Moody Press.

Kristof, A. L. (1996). Person-organization fit: An integrative review of its conceptualizations, measurement, and implications. *Personnel Psychology, 49*(1), 1-49.

LaSor, W. S., Hubbard, D. A., & Bush, F. W. (1996). *Old Testament survey.* Grand Rapids, MI: Eerdmans Publishing.

Lawson, M. S., & Choun, R. J., Jr. (1992). *Directing Christian education: The changing role of the Christian education specialist.* Chicago, IL: Moody Press.

LCMS World Mission. (2010). *Introduction to LCMS world mission. 2010 synod convention report.* St. Louis, MO: Author.

Lee, J. M. (1992). Teaching the faith. *DCE Directions, 2*, 6-10.

Lines, T. A. (1992). *Functional images of the religious educator.* Birmingham, AL: Religious Education Press.

Lingenfelter, J. E. & Sherwood, G. (2003). *Teaching cross-culturally: An incarnational model for learning and teaching.* Grand Rapids, MI: Baker Books.

Linville, P. W. (1987). Self-complexity as a cognitive buffer against stress-related illness and depression. *Journal of Personality and Social Psychology, 52*(4), 663-676.

Luke, W. H. (1932). *Concordia Sunday School Teacher's Quarterly, 17*, 58-69.

Luther, M. (1955). *Luther's works.* St. Louis, MO: Concordia Publishing House.

Luther, M. (1959). *The large catechism.* Philadelphia, PA: Fortress Press.

The Lutheran Annual 2002 of the Lutheran Church–Missouri Synod. (2001). St. Louis, MO: Concordia Publishing House.

The Lutheran Annual 2009 of the Lutheran Church–Missouri Synod. (2009). St. Louis, MO: Concordia Publishing House.

Lutheran Church–Canada. (1987). *Operating agreement between Lutheran Church–Canada and Lutheran Church–Missouri Synod.* Winnipeg, MB: Author.

Lutheran Church–Canada. (1988). *Convention proceedings.* Winnipeg, MB: Author.

Lutheran Church–Canada. (1990). *Convention proceedings.* Winnipeg, MB: Author.

The Lutheran Church–Missouri Synod. (1998). *Handbook of the Lutheran Church–Missouri Synod: 1998 edition.* St. Louis, MO: Author.

Lutheran Education Association. (2002). *Ethical guidelines for directors of Christian education.* River Forest, IL: Author.

MacDonald, G. (2003). *Ordering your private world.* Nashville, TN: Thomas Nelson.

Majovski, L. F. 1982. *The role of psychological assessment in ministerial selection.* (Doctoral dissertation, Fuller Theological Seminary). Retrieved from ProQuest Digital Dissertations database. (Publication No. AAT 8223416).

Maslach, C., & Pines, A. (1988). Burn-out: The loss of human caring. In A. Pines & C. Maslach (Eds.), *Experiencing social psychology: Readings and projects* (2nd ed., pp. 246-252). New York, NY: Random House.

Maslow, A. (1943). A theory of human motivation. *Psychological Review, 50*(4), 370-396.

Masten, A. S., Best, K. M., & Garmezy, N. (1990). Resilience and development: Contributions from the study of children who overcame adversity. *Development and Psychopathology, 2*(4), 425-444.

Maxwell, J. C. (2006). Reflections on model the way. In J. M. Kouzes and B. Z. Posner (Eds.), *Christian reflections on the leadership challenge* (pp. 41-52). San Francisco: Jossey-Bass.

McCain, P. T. (Ed.). (2005). *Concordia: The Lutheran confessions.* St. Louis, MO: Concordia Publishing House.

Minatrea, M. (2004). *Shaped by God's heart: The passion and practices of missional churches.* San Francisco, CA: Jossey-Bass.

Moore, D. W. & Newport, F. (1995). People throughout the world largely satisfied with personal lives. *The Gallup Poll Monthly, 357,* 2-7.

Moreira, H., Fox, K. R., & Sparks, A. C. (2002). Job motivation profiles of physical educators: Theoretical background and instrument development. *British Educational Research Journal, 28*(6), 845-861.

Mueller, S. P. (Ed.). (2005). *Called to believe, teach, and confess: An introduction to doctrinal theology* (Vols. 1-3). Eugene, OR: Wipf & Stock Publishers.

Mundinger, C. S. (1947). *The government in the Missouri Synod: The genesis of decentralized government in the Missouri Synod.* St. Louis, MO: Concordia Publishing House.

Noordtzy, A. (1982). *The book of Leviticus.* Grand Rapids, MI: Zondervan.

Olson, L. (2000). Finding and keeping competent teachers. *Education Week, 19*(18), 12-18.

Palola, E. G. & Larson, W. R. (1965). Some dimensions of job satisfaction among hospital personnel. *Sociology and Social Research, 49,* 201-213.

Pamperin, B. F. (1987). Creative school social workers and job satisfaction. *Social Work in Education, 10*(1), 60-71.

Pazmino, R. W. (1997). *Foundational issues in Christian education: An introduction in evangelical perspective.* Grand Rapids, MI: Baker Books.

Perie, M. & Baker, D. P. (1997). *Job satisfaction among America's teachers: Effects of workplace conditions, background characteristics, and teacher compensation.* (NCES Publication No 97-471). Washington, D.C: National Center for Education Statistics.

Peterson, E. H. (1989). *The contemplative pastor.* Grand Rapids, MI: Eerdmans.

Peterson, E. H. (2005). *Christ plays in ten thousand places.* Grand Rapids, MI: Eerdmans.

Pew Forum on Religion and Public Life. U.S. Religious Landscape Survey. (2008). *Religious beliefs and practices, diverse and politically relevant: Detailed data tables.* Retrieved from http://religions.pewforum.org/pdf/table-ethnicity-by-denomination.pdf

Porter, L. W. (1963). Job attitudes in management: Perceived deficiencies in need fulfillment as a function of size of company. *Journal of Applied Psychology, 47*(6), 386-397.

Pragman, J. H. (1983). *Traditions of ministry: A history of the doctrine of the ministry in Lutheran theology.* St. Louis, MO: Concordia Publishing House.

Preus, H. A. (1979, March). Luther on the universal priesthood and the office of the ministry. *Concordia Theological Journal, 5*(2), 55-62.

Proceedings of the forty-fifth regular convention. (1962). St. Louis: Concordia Publishing House.

Proceedings of the forty-fourth regular convention. (1959). St. Louis: Concordia Publishing House.

Proceedings of the thirty-seventh regular convention. (1938). St. Louis: Concordia Publishing House.

Proceedings of the thirty-sixth regular convention. (1935). St. Louis: Concordia Publishing House.

Rath, T. (2007). *StrengthsFinder 2.0.* New York, NY: Gallup Press.

Ratzinger, J. C. (2004). *Introduction to Christianity.* (J. R. Foster, Trans.). San Francisco, CA: Ignatius Press.

Rediger, G. L. (2000). *Fit to be a pastor: A call to physical, mental and spiritual fitness.* Louisville, KY: Westminster John Knox Press.

Reed, J. E. & Prevost, R. (1993). *A history of Christian education.* Nashville, TN: Broadman & Holman.

Schaeffer, R. B. (1972). *The role of the director of Christian education in parish ministry.* (Thesis), Concordia Theological Seminary, Springfield, IL.

Schmidt, S. A. (1972). *Powerless pedagogues: An interpretive essay on the history of the Lutheran teacher in the Missouri synod.* River Forest, IL: Lutheran Education Association.

Schoepp, P. & Warren, T. (2009). Directors of Christian education: Telling the family history. *Lutheran Education, 142*(4), 224-236.

Schoepp, P. W. (2003). *Lay practitioners of parish-based Christian education ministry with the Lutheran Church–Missouri Synod (LC–MS): A survey of demographics, ministry roles, and certification interest* (Doctoral dissertation, University of Nebraska - Lincoln). Available from Dissertation Abstracts International database. (UMI No. 3092591)

Schroeder, T. W. (1975, April). A history of directors of Christian education in the Lutheran Church–Missouri Synod. *Director of Christian Education Bulletin, 9*(2), 4-16.

Scott, W. R. (1998). *Organizations: Rational, natural, and open systems* (4th ed.). Upper Saddle River, NJ: Prentice Hall.

Shankman, M. L. & Allen, S. (2008). *Emotionally intelligent leadership: A guide for college students.* San Francisco, CA: Jossey-Bass.

Spector, P. E. (1997). *Job satisfaction: Application, assessment, causes, and consequences.* Thousand Oaks, CA: Sage Publications.

Stolle, V. (2003). *The church comes from all nations: Luther texts on mission.* (Schulz & Thies, Trans.). St. Louis, MO: Concordia Publishing House.

Stubblefield, J. M. (1993). *The effective minister of education: The role of the minister of education.* Nashville, TN: Broadman & Holman Publishers.

Sweet, L. I. (1999) *Soul tsunami.* Grand Rapids, MI: Zondervan Publishing.

Tidwell, C. A. (1982). *Educational ministry of a church: An introduction to educational administration.* Nashville, TN: Broadman Press.

Tracy, E. M., Bean, N., Gwatkin, S., & Hill, B. (1992). Family preservation workers: Sources of job satisfaction and job stress. *Research on Social Work Practice, 2*(4), 465-478.

Unsworth, T. (1998, February 6). He visited 450 parishes, finds morale at low ebb. *National Catholic Reporter, 34*(14), 15.

Veith, G. E. (1999). *The spirituality of the cross: The way of the first evangelicals.* St. Louis, MO: Concordia Publishing House.

Veith, G. E. (2002). *God @ work: Your Christian vocation in all of life.* Wheaton, IL: Crossway Books.

Vinokur-Kaplan, D. (1990). Job satisfaction among social workers in public and voluntary welfare agencies. *Child Welfare, 70*(1), 81-91.

Walther, C. F. W. (1964). *Year of grace.* (D. E. Heck, Trans.). La Valle, WI: Donald E. Heck.

Walther, C. F. W. (1987). *Church and ministry: Witnesses of the Evangelical Lutheran Church on the question of the church and the ministry.* St. Louis, MO: Concordia Publishing House.

Warren, T. P. (2008). *Back to the future. Revisiting key questions in director of Christian education preparation: Identification of a baseline of program outcomes* (Doctoral dissertation, Capella University). Available from Dissertation Abstracts International database. (UMI No. 3310717)

Wilkes, C. G. (1998). *Jesus on leadership: Discovering the secrets of servant leadership from the life of Christ.* Wheaton, IL: Tyndale House.

Willis, B. (2003). *Distance education at a glance.* Retrieved from http://www.uiweb.uidaho.edu/ eo/distglan

Wingren, G. (1957). *Luther on vocation.* Philadelphia, PA: Muhlenberg Press.

Wolfmueller, B. (2006). *A simple way to pray (…for Master Peter the barber).* Aurora, CO: Hope Lutheran Church. Retrieved from http://www.hope-aurora.org/docs/ASimpleWaytoPray. pdf

Zorgdrager, R. (2008, November 15). *The Gospel and our culture network: Ecclesiology of the emerging church.* Retrieved from http://www.gocn.org/resources/articles/ecclesiology-emerging-church

CPSIA information can be obtained
at www.ICGtesting.com
Printed in the USA
FFHW021017161218
49868457-54452FF